COMMUNITIES AND THEIR UNIVERSITIES
The Challenge of Lifelong Learning

COMMUNITIES AND THEIR UNIVERSITIES

The Challenge of Lifelong Learning

edited by
JANE ELLIOTT, HYWEL FRANCIS,
ROB HUMPHREYS, DAVID ISTANCE

Lawrence & Wishart
LONDON

Lawrence & Wishart Limited
99 Wallis Road
London E9 5LN

First published 1996
Copyright © Lawrence & Wishart, 1996
Individual essays © the authors

ISBN 0-85315-850-9

Photoset in North Wales by
Derek Doyle & Associates, Mold, Clwyd.
Printed and bound in Great Britain

CONTENTS

CONTENTS

II. Equality, Development and Communities

ACKNOWLEDGEMENTS

This book has arisen largely out of papers presented to the Annual Conference of the Universities Association for Continuing Education, which was held in April 1995 at the University of Wales Swansea. We would like to thank Professor Dick Taylor, the UACE Secretary, and Dr David Watson, the UACE Chair, for all the help that they gave in supporting colleagues at Swansea in arranging the Conference. We also wish to record our thanks to Judith James and Sioned-Mair Richards who were mainly responsible for Conference arrangements, Sheila Carter for dealing with the financial matters and Chris Nutt for the secretarial and technical work, first on the Conference and subsequently on this book. We owe a particular debt to Chris for her speed, efficiency and patience.

Communities and their Universities: The Challenge of Life Long Learning is published to coincide with the 75th Anniversary of the University of Wales Swansea, and we are especially indebted to our Vice-Chancellor, Professor Robin Williams, for the wide-ranging discussion he has initiated on the interface between our own university and the wider community. An important aspect of this developing policy has been the success of the Community University of the Valleys. We are also indebted to the former Principal of University of Wales Aberystwyth, Professor Kenneth O. Morgan, for giving his permission to publish the inaugural lecture for the launch of the Community University in October 1993; he gave this lecture in his capacity as Vice-Chancellor of the University of Wales during its centenary year.

Finally we would like to thank Sally Davison of Lawrence and Wishart for her support in publishing this book.

NOTES ON CONTRIBUTORS

Peter Alheit is Professor of Non-institutional Adult Education and Director of the Institute for Applied Biographical and Lifeworld Research at the University of Bremen. He is a founding member of the European Society for Research of the Education of Adults (ESREA), and Academic Co-ordinator of the largest ERASMUS-ICP in Adult Education in Europe.

John A. Andrews is Chief Executive, Further and Higher Education Funding Councils for Wales, responsible for funding further and higher education institutions in Wales, and related activities. He was Professor and Head of Department of Law University of Wales Aberystwyth until 1992 and Vice-Principal 1985–88.

Brenda Bell is Associate Director of the Center for Literacy Studies at the University of Tennessee, and Co-ordinator of the Southern Literacy Communications Consortium, one of the regional technology networking and expansion projects of the National Institute for Literacy.

Roseanne Benn is currently Access Co-ordinator at the University of Exeter, responsible for the programme of Certificate Courses run throughout Devon and Cornwall by the Department of Continuing and Adult Education.

Jeff Braham is a Senior Lecturer in Educational Development at Coventry University. He is Manager of the University's four year Community Education development project, funded by HEFCE under its Widened Provision initiative.

Jane Elliott is a Lecturer in Women's Studies in the Department of Adult Continuing Education, University of Wales Swansea. She is responsible for Women's Studies programmes offered at foundation, certificate and masters level.

NOTES ON CONTRIBUTORS

Roger Fieldhouse is Director of Continuing Education and Professor of Adult Education, University of Exeter.

Hywel Francis is the Professor of Adult Continuing Education at University of Wales Swansea and is a founder of The Valleys' Initiative for Adult Education and the Community University of the Valleys.

William S. Griffith is Professor of Adult Education at the University of British Columbia and serves as a referee for the *Adult Education Quarterly*, *Canadian Association for University Continuing Education*, and *Adult Basic Education*.

Barry J. Hake is Senior Lecturer in Adult Continuing Education at the Centre for Adult Education, Leiden University, Netherlands, with special interests in comparative and historical research. He is Secretary of the European Society for Research on the Education of Adults (ESREA).

Dennis Hardy is Pro Vice-Chancellor and Dean of Humanities at Middlesex University, with responsibility for community liaison; he has written books on various aspects of planning and community history.

Rob Humphreys is Lecturer in Cultural Studies in the Department of Adult Continuing Education at the University of Wales Swansea, and is Co-ordinator of the Community University of the Valleys.

David Istance is a lecturer in the Department of Adult Continuing Education, University of Wales Swansea, where he has been since 1994. For fifteen years he worked in education and training policy research at the OECD, Paris.

John Mohan is Reader in Geography at the University of Portsmouth. His contribution to this volume draws on work carried out during the tenure of a Harkness Fellowship (at the University of Pennsylvania in 1992-3) studying relationships between universities and their communities in the USA.

Kenneth O. Morgan was Vice-Chancellor of the University of Wales, Aberystwyth 1989–95 and is Honorary Fellow of the University of

Wales Swansea. The most recent of his books is *Modern Wales: Politics, Places and People*.

Steve Morris is Lecturer in Welsh (language) in the Department of Adult Continuing Education, University of Wales Swansea. He has responsibilities in the Department's Welsh for Adults programme and the Certificate of Higher Education in Welsh.

Mairead Owen is Lecturer in Women's Studies at Liverpool John Moores University.

Davinder Panesar is a member of the Council of Sikh Gurdwaras in Coventry and the Ethnic Minority Development Association. He is the former manager of the Indian Community Centre and is active in developing innovative partnerships between the community and education providers at all levels.

Alan Parton is the Director of the Educational Development Unit at Coventry University. He represents Coventry University on the Council of UACE and is a member of the Executive of the Association for Education and Training.

Marion Price is Head of Sociology at Liverpool John Moores University.

Hans G. Schuetze is a Professor of Higher Education at the Center for Policy Studies in Education at the University of British Columbia in Vancouver, Canada.

Peadar Shanahan is Senior Lecturer in the School of Social and Community Sciences in the University of Ulster, Magee College, Derry, Northern Ireland. He is involved in adult education, local community development, and in the Diploma and PhD Networks, *Studies in European Adult Education, Societal Change and Culture*.

Mary Stuart has worked in community education in both the UK and South Africa since 1976. She is currently Assistant Director responsible for Student Experience and Educational Equality in the Centre for Continuing Education at the University of Sussex.

Shirley Walters is Professor of Adult and Continuing Education at the University of the Western Cape and founding director of the Centre for Adult and Continuing Education (CACE). She is chairperson of the Western Cape Provincial Education and Training Forum, a provincial forum representing major education and training stakeholders.

Kevin Ward is Assistant Director (Academic) at the University of Leeds, Department of Adult Continuing Education. He has developed a range of action-research programmes with socially and educationally disadvantaged adults over the past twenty years and has been responsible for university-community links.

INTRODUCTION

Jane Elliott, Hywel Francis, Rob Humphreys, David Istance

COMMUNITIES, UNIVERSITIES AND LIFELONG LEARNING

This book has been written in a new era of uncertainty and opportunity for higher education. The optimism associated with the 1960s to the late 1980s (the exact periods depending on the country in question) is no more, but a growing realisation that the relationships between universities and wider society are being, and should be, re-defined, is becoming increasingly evident. And these shifts of emphasis are linked to a growing focus on the concept of lifelong learning, which now has a resonance in political, as well as educational, discourse: 1996 has been designated as the Year of Lifelong Learning by the European Union.

The present uncertainty emanates in part from the familiar pressures of financial restriction, but just as significantly from questions about the universities' role in wider society. The insecurity such uncertainty brings has generated a healthy debate about the future and revolves around the question of the contribution that the university can and should make to the community. That debate has addressed definitions of 'appropriate' communities, including the tensions between a focus on those sections of society which have historically been socially excluded from the academy, and the aim to strengthen ties with the 'business' community. Whichever way the debate will be resolved, one thing is certain: universities will need to transform themselves from elitist institutions to ones significantly contributing to the creation of a more just and equitable society. Whether all can or wish to do so, is the great unanswered question.

What is certain amid this uncertainty is that increasing numbers of influential voices are scrutinising the role of the universities to arrive at a general conclusion: they must become more responsive to the social and economic needs of the wider society (some contributors to this book point, however, to conflicts between the social and economic agendas). That responsiveness must ensure that universities are, to borrow from contemporary jargon, in the mainstream rather than at the margins of societal change; and it is here that, as well as uncertainty, there are new opportunities, and grounds for optimism. In addressing these issues, the adult continuing education community is in a pivotal position. On the one hand, it represents that part of the university sector to the fore in recognising the key links between universities and their surrounding communities, and from which the arguments have been strongly voiced for re-defining the boundaries between the mainstream and the marginal. On the other, it is a field that is itself frequently marginalised, despite the value of its approaches and practices in informing the move to greater responsiveness.

Given the distinct position of adult continuing education, especially valuable perspectives on these general debates about contemporary universities are found in this book, as the chapters are based primarily on papers delivered at the 1995 annual conference of the Universities Association of Continuing Education (UACE). Its title is deliberately provocative. Rather than the conventional formulation 'universities and their communities', the reversal of the order makes clear that communities, however defined, should have clear and growing expectations of their universities. Universities should be more active in translating their 'community' missions into practice. In this, the adult continuing education world has a potentially invaluable part to play, within a broad framework of lifelong learning. In so doing, it must negotiate a tangled set of pressures and considerations.

CONTRADICTORY DEFINITIONS AND AGENDAS

The relationships between communities and 'their' universities are contemporary, but elusive. Even to grasp what is a 'community' or a 'university', still less to delineate their inter-relationships, is especially elusive in the 1990s. Higher education and its institutions are undergoing rapid and far-reaching changes on an international scale, and this has given rise to a renewed and vigorous debate about the very nature and purpose of universities.[1] The difficulty in defining the concept of community is well known and well documented, but it remains an especially powerful political and cultural idea, with highly normative connotations.[2] Representations of 'community' can be imagined in a number of different ways, and can signify and encompass very different kinds of social formation. Competing definitions of a single community can be, and are, constructed, and such definitions are re-made through time and across space. To add to this already complicated brew, the relationships between universities and communities – however expressed or defined – are increasingly subject to flights of rhetoric, certainly from a university side of the equation now obliged (in Britain at least) to produce 'mission statements' and therein strike an acceptable assembly of notes for public consumption.[3] 'Of course', the modern university professes to be in tune, indeed arm-in-arm, with all manner of 'communities'. But questions remain about how much in practice has changed, and how far change is in the directions trumpeted by mission statements. A further question is whether change has gone too far or not far enough. Authors in this volume arrive at very different answers to these questions.

The pressure for such strategic changes comes, in part, from deep-seated shifts in the economy and social structure of industrialised nations in the late twentieth century. Lengthy discussion of these developments is not possible here, but economic restructuring has led to the decline of many older industries, with a consequent decline in the prospects for communities within regions based upon those industries (for example the decline in employment and prosperity in those communities based upon coal and steel in South Wales).[4] There have been changes in the nature of industrial production (for example the growth of the 'flexible firm') and a growth in so-called 'knowledge industries'. But such changes will also act on, and be acted upon by, the political and cultural spheres. New pressures are exerted on social communities through increasing individualism, employment precariousness, a growing cultural diversity, and what might be described as 'identity politics'. Widespread social and cultural changes have led to new forms of community that are not based on locality.[5] These do not necessarily replace older and more local ties and loyalties; rather, they overlay and interact with them. Changes such as these are taking place at a global level, but their impact will vary between different nation states and economies, and, indeed, between regions within such states and economies. Major political and cultural realignments have had a radical impact on the situation in South Africa and Northern Ireland, as discussed in this book.

Universities, and higher education more generally, are inevitably being shaped by, and influence, such developments. Universities are to some extent well-placed to intervene in and to shape future economic and social patterns, as they are knowledge-based institutions, and are often at the cutting edge of communications technologies. Along with pressures to become more flexible and adaptive, and less hierarchical, the same technologies are also creating the potential for the very institutional shape of higher education to be altered. It has been argued that the same trends which are operating in multi-national companies, and to some extent in other large public organisations, will also reshape institutions of higher education.[6] But universities are also faced with other demanding challenges in the late twentieth century, which interact with these changes. These include huge increases in student numbers without a *pro rata* increase in financial resources, and a far more diverse student body in terms of age and social background. There are also shifts in the nature of the funding regimes for higher education, with funding often being more conditional than has previously been the case. In the European Union, the European state is a significant factor in the funding of higher education, as well as the nation state. These and other developments have meant that questions about the exact nature of universities in the next century remain open. It may well be true to say that a discourse of 'crisis' in contemporary higher education owes more to professional status and practices being under challenge, than to any threat to the actual existence of universities, students or academics, but the fact that the future shape of higher education and its institutions is still in the process of being moulded, helps to explain the potency of the questions and the extent of the debate.[7]

While the pressures for change are diverse, education is increasingly understood, nationally and internationally, as a lifelong process. 1996 has been designated the European Year of Lifelong Learning. Practitioners in the field of continuing education are therefore well placed to contribute to the changes which are taking place in higher education. As Duke has expressed it, 'Continuing education is at the cutting edge as universities become more fully "learning organisations".'[8] In turn, from the students' perspective, higher education becomes a 'kind of education', rather than a physical location or institution. It will be a lifelong experience, and 'will be offered in many forms and locations, by a variety of agencies'.[9]

Rhetoric must, however, be disentangled from reality. The

university adult continuing education community warmly embraces such symbolic recognition of lifelong learning as the European Year of Lifelong Learning, as being supportive of their enterprise. But this does not mean that official recognition of the principle is matched by its systematic implementation in practice, or that those who currently benefit from lifelong patterns of learning are the 'disadvantaged' communities and individuals addressed in several of the chapters in this collection. Whatever the individual examples of practice that seek to break the mould, adult learning, and the institutional arrangements to promote it, remain predominantly reflective of the structured inequalities of the society and economy in which they operate. Again, a constructive scepticism about the rosier claims of new beginnings is urged.

The adult continuing education community is at the fulcrum of many of these relationships and conflicting pressures. In Britain and elsewhere, it has traditionally represented the section of the university institution that has taken its responsibilities to the community, at least that defined in local terms, most seriously. In the British case, however, this has often meant that in the old universities, which have most often followed this institutional pattern, extra-mural – or continuing education – departments, have tended to be out on a limb from the rest of the institution. The new universities (the former polytechnics) have by contrast had a more local and regional role in an institutional sense. One of the key questions for British higher education in the years ahead will be whether the two patterns merge to a greater or lesser extent.

Sections of the adult continuing education world can claim to have been in the vanguard of developing innovative structures and practice in higher education; in Duke's words, 'CE departments are "transmural". They build bridges and face both in and out'.[10] Potentially, therefore, they might be regarded as being at the heart of changing university environments defined increasingly through an emphasis on lifelong learning and of strengthened ties with regions and localities. But the mood in British adult continuing education university departments – where they have survived recent funding upheavals – is far from buoyant or secure. They are confronted with uncomfortable questions of how they will fare in the future, whatever the resolution of the question, 'will the mainstream be marginalised and the marginal mainstreamed, or will traditional relationships prevail?' That discomfort comes through in the paradoxical mix of enthusiasm, caution, and, at times, beleagurement, in much of this book.

These are the questions and issues that we sought to debate at the Swansea conference in 1995. We invited international participation: higher education, and universities, are subject to profound pressures for change throughout much of the world. Across countries in Europe and North America, the dual effects of increasing student numbers and constraints on public expenditure have not only seen an increased emphasis on cost-effectiveness; they have led to a transformation in the nature of the student body in higher education, and to its institutional structures. In South Africa, higher education is central to the post-apartheid struggles for equality and development. Within Britain, the university sector has expanded markedly over recent years, bringing in new groups of student, including growing proportions of older adults, with a richer mix of work and life experiences. This has undoubtedly had some impact on traditional university practices, and on the continued development of new modes of delivery of course provision: it is still not clear how radical an impact this has in fact been.

The pressures making for change are not all positive. Professor Andrews' up-beat assessment of an out-moded 'European monastic university' tradition in its final throes stands alongside the experience of severe difficulties which have also emerged, such as graduate unemployment, declining student living standards, and the creation of new 'second-class' university departments and institutions. The relative decline in the value of student financial support has forced many prospective students to reconsider their choice of university in favour of more local enrolment. (This has led to a renewed local and regional focus for many higher education institutions, a welcome, if unexpected outcome.) Pressure on university funding has placed an increasing premium on diversification and income generation. Whilst this has promoted the search for new students, and professional and research clienteles – in effect, new communities – it can also skew the perception of which of these they can 'afford' to serve. Moreover, a number of the contributors point to the tension which exists between improving the research output of individual academics, and of the institution as a whole, and efforts to extend the institution's role within its region and local community. A theme which recurs throughout the book is that, although the dismantling of 'ivory towers' is to be greatly welcomed, the building of meaningful partnerships with communities, particularly if they are communities which have been hitherto under-represented in higher education, requires patience and commitment. It will not be achieved quickly or simply, and is relatively labour intensive.

These complex developments provide the context for the 'macro' considerations of university and adult education developments in general, and the second part looks at 'micro' evaluations of innovations and developments on the ground. A strong sense of history runs through these contributions, which are nevertheless about supremely contemporary questions. Many of the authors share a strong sense of social responsibility in a university world where hard (and hard-nosed) dictates have become the norms of professional life – a retrograde step for some, a welcome shake-up of comfortable, elitist institutions for others.

CHANGING UNIVERSITIES: GLOBAL PERSPECTIVES

This section of the book addresses the 'macro' issues affecting university and adult education. The authors share a concern for the nature of the relationships between universities and their communities in a period of wider social and economic change. Several authors address the ever-changing nature of communities and the problematic nature of the notion of 'community' itself; there are diverse references as to what constitutes a community – including territorial, cultural and economic definitions. For this reason alone, the relationships of communities with universities is a correspondingly diverse and complex one.

Kenneth O. Morgan, in this published version of the Inaugural Lecture of the Community University of the Valleys, which he gave in his capacity as Chancellor of the University of Wales, raises questions about the rootedness of his institution in the wider community. In a specifically Welsh context, the concept of 'community' could be interpreted simultaneously as the national community of Wales and also simply 'the people' through the unofficial motto of the University 'Brifysgol Y Werin' – 'The People's University'. He describes the institution as a creature and creation of the emerging Welsh middle class in the latter part of the nineteenth century. It was, to a large extent, separate from the aspirations of the expanding and turbulent coalfield society of the South Wales valleys where autonomous working-class educational traditions emerged around the Workers'

Educational Association, Marxist classes and the Workmen's Institutes and their libraries. The chapter concludes, however, by suggesting that these two distinct traditions are synthesised by University of Wales Swansea's initiative in the 1990s in creating the Community University of the Valleys.

Some of the historical themes discussed by Morgan are raised by Dennis Hardy in the more general context of British higher education. Focusing especially on communities defined in a territorial sense, Hardy points out that relationships between universities and 'their' communities have been paradoxical. Universities have often appeared to be isolated and apart from these communities, but at the same time, whether by design or otherwise, universities have made, and continue to make, a significant contribution to the local economy and local employment. In the 1990s, we are witnessing a 'renegotiation of traditional relationships with the community', due in part to the redesignation of the polytechnics as universities, and to the Higher Education Funding Councils' requirement that each university should produce a mission statement. He shows how all this can have potential benefits and costs. Benefits derive especially from opening up access to higher education. Potential problems, however, can arise in part from the differing ideological motivations of those who wish to see universities playing a larger role in their local and regional communities. A programme of widening access might be seen as a response to unacceptably high unemployment figures for school leavers. However, a widening of access and increase in student numbers without matching additional resources has implications in terms of quality of provision and student experience. The greatest danger, perhaps, is that of raising false hopes and expectations of what a university might achieve, in terms of links with communities.

Roseanne Benn and Roger Fieldhouse examine the 'university continuing education community' in the context of five notions of community: the social, geographical, distance, 'role' and professional communities. They show how ideas about the university adult education community have changed during the twentieth century, the emphasis now being on 'improved work prospects', 'wealth creation' and 'individual development', rather than the early twentieth century commitment to 'social purpose' and 'social collective sub-sets'. This does not imply that the targeting of non-traditional students is no longer acceptable, but that the philosophical imperatives which shape the provision have changed. Sometimes contradictory changes have influenced all the identified categories of community; geographical communities can be, on the one hand, undermined by the increased opportunities facilitated by new technologies, but, on the other, remain important because local, mature students are forming a greater proportion of undergraduate students. While adult continuing education continues to be subject to new right priorities, a critical understanding of ideas of community, both historically and in the present, can offer adult educators real choices.

Peter Alheit examines possibilities for change in the German university sector after unification in a context of both reform and conformity. His focus on the nature of the German university as an elite institution and the need to broaden student participation parallels a concern of several of the contributors to this book. He begins with an historical account of the roots of the modern university in the Enlightenment and shows how a tradition of conformity emerged, though in modern times with a progressive potential. Throughout the nineteenth century, the university remained an elite institution with little concern for the social problems existing in the wider community, not unlike the Welsh university as described by Morgan. By the early twentieth century, the spirit of reform emerged with an attempt by some progressive professors to broaden the social base of student participation, yet the German university remained largely unchanged. In examining the post-unification era, Alheit remains 'cautiously optimistic' in terms of the potential for reform and the widening of participation amongst working-class students and women, while noting the contradictory tendencies, such as the phenomena of well-qualified students being unable to find appropriate employment. In charting the considerable changes within the German university, he proposes: 'We have made enough changes to the world. The point now is to interpret it.'

Barry Hake acknowledges the problematic nature of defining the 'community' or 'communities' with which universities inter-relate. He clarifies the 'varied, if not contradictory understandings' of communities by conceptualising them as a series of 'publics' with which universities enter into closer or weaker ties. These may be individually defined – particular categories of actual or potential student – or they may be 'collective publics' (organisations, socio-geographic communities, associations, political bodies, broader interests and movements). He is critical of the system within which he has worked over many years – that of the Netherlands – and especially the 'traditional' universities. These universities have in general failed to broaden their enterprise to the 'service' (as opposed to their conventional 'teaching' and 'research') functions; more specifically, they have neglected such elements as continuing professional education, especially that geared to the non-traditional student. Far from the optimistic picture that some would paint of re-vamped and reforming institutions, outward-looking and socially responsible, Hake describes the Dutch 'traditional' university as among the most stubbornly traditional in Europe, with the trend, if anything, to retrenchment.

Hans Schuetze shares the view that the university, whether in Europe or North America, remains largely traditional and inflexible in the face of its 'industrial community', though North American universities have tended, he maintains, to regard these 'service' roles as more central to their purpose than many of their European counterparts. In contrast with other contributors, such as Griffith, who lament the dominance of economic goals, Schuetze's thesis is that universities are insufficiently effective in meeting the demands of industry, especially when these come from the small and medium-sized firms that are now such an important aspect of development and employment. As with other contributors, a significant part of the problem is seen to reside in the continued dominance of established academic hierarchies and arrangements. Relationships between universities and their industrial community should not, however, focus exclusively on the university side of the equation: the relationships are, in fact, complex and interactive. Schuetze argues that 'technology transfer' has too often been seen as a uni-directional flow of knowledge from the university lab to the workbench in the firm, disregarding the co-operative nature of most knowledge creation and development. The innovation process is about learning and is an organisational and social process as much as it is about technologies. Comprehensive perspectives are needed, therefore, to move beyond narrow understandings of the nature of the industry/university interface, innovation, and the full role of higher education.

William Griffith shows how the shift in university adult education practice and priorities away from an explicit social and community responsibility fits the North American experience. He argues that economic forces have become increasingly important in shaping the universities' educational agenda. There has been a shift from a social focus to the greater individualism implied by the economic priority, and a change in the target student population, under financial pressures, towards the affluent individuals and professional groups who can pay the high fees. Evidence from diverse studies in both Canada and the United States reinforces this characterisation of the trends, charting the increasing neglect of community development and social activism, and the pre-eminence of vocational preparation and the marketing of their programmes. The way forward, Griffith maintains, is to promote the broad vision of what adult continuing education can achieve in recognition that the university's contribution to society will not often be best met from a single-minded concentration on the goals of economic growth. This is unlikely to occur unless the adult education community itself fully grasps 'the grand vision, the great tradition'.

John Mohan also focuses on higher education in the USA. He addresses the social contribution of American universities to 'their' local communities and uses this as a backdrop for consideration of existing parallel relationships and possible new developments in Britain. Urban decay and social deprivation in American inner cities have led to the re-thinking by universities of ideas of social purpose and policies for local economic and social regeneration. Some American universities have sought to make a contribution in these fields through specific programmes of urban and community development. He argues that partnerships which depend too heavily on the institution itself are unlikely to succeed and that the aim should be to 'build the capacity of the community to solve its own problems.' This theme of equality in partnerships is a common one to several contributors. Mohan suggests that as British universities seek to increase their local and regional activities, there are lessons to be learned from the successes and failures of the American experience. Echoing Hardy's call for 'community liaison', Mohan suggests that an 'academically-related public service' may be needed, 'in which research and teaching activities are focused on the needs of an immediate geographical community'. This would benefit the institutions and the community. An inhibiting factor could well lie, in Britain at least, in the increasing emphasis on research funding priorities, which university and community links.

These shifts in British higher education policy are explored by John Andrews. Writing from the perspective of a prominent policy-maker in further and higher education, he uses an ecclesiastical metaphor to explore the history, culture and traditions of European universities. They were at one time, he says, dominated by a 'monastic aspect', essentially male institutions which were 'residential and introspective'. Whilst this tradition was partly reshaped with the development of civic universities, higher education still retains elements of an elitist, selective culture, which has enormous influence in determining the professional structure of contemporary British society. In that society, however, higher education has become a mass system, with a target participation rate of 30 per cent. This, Andrews argues, has several far-reaching consequences. Demands on public expenditure will necessarily require universities to play a role in economic and social development, as tax-payers seek a return on their investment. The range of subjects taught in higher education institutions will widen, in particular to include those which are vocationally orientated. Investment in research will become more focused on economically beneficial outcomes. Education as a whole will be a lifelong experience in the future, and it is here that the continuing education field will have a key role to play in shaping higher education provision. Andrews concludes by calling for universities to be responsible to the 'community without', rather than solely to the 'community within'. 'The challenge', he argues, 'is that universities should play a central role in revitalising our communities and our economy'.

Questions about the relationship between higher education, the state, and communities are posed in a particularly acute form in post-apartheid South Africa. Shirley Walters addresses these issues, and explores the tensions which exist between the competing claims of equality and development. The chapter is written at a time when 'historically black universities' and 'historically white universities' are entering a new political, cultural, and educational paradigm; issues of access, resourcing, democratic governance, and relationships with communities – whether defined locally or nationally – are being debated and fundamentally re-defined. Walters explores how the case for continuing education has had to be fought for, particularly in the context of national debates about the future of higher education provision. She also shows how discourses of education are being re-shaped in the post-apartheid political and cultural context. When in opposition, the forces for change concentrated on issues of democracy and equality in education; now, the government, universities and communities are faced with problems of prioritising finite resources, in a context of education and labour market demands. These issues have a resonance for adult education in Europe and North America, informed historically by normative ideas about promoting equality, yet reconciling these with others such as training for labour market needs. As public expenditure becomes tighter, these tensions become more universal, for adult education and for universities in general.

EQUALITY, DEVELOPMENT AND COMMUNITIES

In this section, the authors examine the 'micro' issues emerging from a wide range of local university and community initiatives. This diversity includes cross-border initiatives in Northern and Southern Ireland, Welsh language provision, ethnic minority community programmes, and industrial partnerships.

Peadar Shanahan places the active involvement of university adult education in community development and 'cross-border' initiatives in the North and South of Ireland in the larger context of European Union (EU) policies. He documents the Europeanisation of Irish universities especially in relation to inter-regionalism, training and development, and policies for the integration of the 'excluded'. While his themes are broad and far-reaching, the focus is on very concrete, specific developments in cross-border co-operation between university adult education in four campuses. He charts the difficulties and frustrations that they have encountered and outlines the complicated, and often contradictory, role of state intervention in adult education in Ireland.

Stephen Morris explores the way in which universities can participate in one particular aspect of cultural development. The University of Wales, as he sees it, has a responsibility, indeed a duty, to restore the Welsh language within rural and industrial communities throughout Wales. This has, indeed, been a long-standing defining feature of university continuing education in Wales. Morris details the considerable successes which have been achieved amongst adults, paralleling other European initiatives such as in the Basque country and Catalunya. The Welsh language community is given added legitimacy through its university's recognition of the importance of lifelong learning in achieving greater cultural distinctiveness.

Mairead Owen and Marion Price discuss the role of Women's Studies within the higher education community, examining key issues in the context of their own Women's Studies programmes in a new university in Britain. While Women's Studies programmes have flourished since the 1970s, this achievement exists alongside a sense of unease. Feminist interventions in higher education are not without their contradictions, being 'both in and against the mainstream'. A democratic view, of teachers and students steeped in notions of equality, contradicts traditional academic approaches to teaching and learning. This contradictory position of Women's Studies, as a radical innovation within traditional academic institutions, in many ways mirrors the position of university adult education in general.

Mary Stuart focuses on the needs of the many communities in a particular locale in the South of England. She challenges traditional notions of community and, like Benn and Fieldhouse, stresses that communities are not static. These ideas are explored through two particular partnership initiatives developed in the Sussex area directed at community change, where 'communities' represent a range of interests. She argues that adult education community initiatives should not be divorced from the wider social changes which have reshaped our society and communities over the past fifteen years, while community educators need to recognise the internal diversity which precludes the simple identification of a 'cultural group'. Many communities in Britain are marginalised from mainstream 'British' society, so that the emphasis on 'education for citizenship' may not be relevant or empowering for them. She concludes that university continuing education must 'recognise that the polarisation of our society now requires us to be partial in our choice of partnerships'.

The opportunities and problems arising from the relationship between universities and communities defined in a cultural sense are explored by Alan Parton, Jeff Braham, and Davinder Panesar, in a case study of a developing partnership between Coventry University and the Sikh community in that city. Coventry University is a 'new' British university – a former polytechnic which has always had a locally orientated mission. The authors argue that 'a paradigm shift' is required in educational provision, 'so that institutions serve the needs of communities, in all their cultural, economic and educational diversity'. In their university, work with communities has been spearheaded by an Educational Development Unit, in contrast with the 'old' university sector in Britain, in which similar initiatives have generally been located in departments for adult education. In its work with the Sikh community, the Educational Development Unit has created a community-based network, a relationship founded on a culture of discussion, negotiation, and collaboration. The aim has been to create a 'responsive university-based infrastructure'. The work is at a relatively early stage, but is already promising. The partnership is, at one and the same time, creating educational opportunities for the Sikh community; re-making the university curriculum; and re-shaping to some degree the material and physical environment of the institution as some of the provision is offered in local community centres, schools and colleges. Coventry University is becoming a more decentralised institution as a result of its engagement with the Sikh community.

Kevin Ward argues that the concept of community is perceived by many in universities as being very specifically and narrowly 'the business community'. He questions the validity of many university 'missions' which carry the rhetoric of commitment to the wider community, and examines the extent to which this has been translated into practical action. In particular, he focuses on the relationship between social exclusion and economic regeneration. Looking at a case study in Leeds, he concludes that one crucial way forward is through partnerships between such bodies as Training and Enterprise Councils (TECs) and universities.

Certain of the issues explored by Ward are developed by Brenda Bell in a different local context. In outlining the work of the Centre for Literacy Studies at the University of Tennessee, she describes how a particular higher education institution has reached out to socially excluded groups such as rural communities and women's groups. The strategy is very much informed by the radical educational approaches of the Tennessee's Highlander Research and Educational Centre and Paulo Freire's literacy campaigns in South America. Literacy is seen as a key to opening the doors of economic, community and cultural development, as well as participatory democracy. Bell, moreover, highlights the importance of harnessing new technological developments and distance learning in building new university/community relationships.

The final contribution to this collection, by Hywel Francis and Rob Humphreys, addresses the Community University of the Valleys (CUV), an initiative in community-based higher education in the South Wales coalfield. This is a region which, in recent years, has experienced substantial economic and social decline and fundamental cultural changes, particularly in the area of gender relations. Writing within an historical context, Francis and Humphreys show how the CUV may superficially appear to be a continuation of what is a very rich tradition of adult education in the region. It represents, however, a sharp break with that tradition, as the nature of the partnership with community organisations is very different from that which existed in the past. They chart how the CUV was a response to the crisis facing communities in the coalfield following the collapse and virtual disappearance of the coal industry in the mid-to-late 1980s. In this new 'post-coal' context, the notion of 'community' is to some extent being redefined. The CUV was developed in partnership with a local training organisation, which was established and is run by women. It also emerged in the context of a rapidly changing set of funding regimes for higher education in Wales, in which the European dimension is of importance. Educational equality, and economic and social regeneration, are central aspects of the CUV project, though not always without tensions existing between them.

The CUV is analysed as a response to rapid social change in communities in the South Wales coalfield, and at the same time as an attempt to influence that change. But it also contributes to a re-making of the relationship between the university in Swansea and its surrounding communities, and in turn it shows signs of beginning to re-shape the institution itself. It was thus natural that the UK university adult continuing education body should come to Swansea in 1995 to debate the theme 'Communities and their Universities'.

NOTES

1. See, *inter alia*, M. Allen, *The Goals of Universities*, Open University Press, Milton Keynes 1988; W. Birch, *The Challenge to Higher Education*, Open University Press, Milton Keynes 1988; M. Reeves, *The Crisis in Higher Education*, Open University Press, Milton Keynes 1988; C. Ball & H. Eggins (eds), *Higher Education into the 1990s*, Open University Press, Milton Keynes 1989; R. Barnett, *The Idea of Higher Education*, Open University Press, Milton Keynes 1990; J. Wyatt (ed), *Commitment to Higher Education*, Open University Press, Milton Keynes 1990; T. Schuller (ed), *The Future of Higher Education*, Open University Press, Milton Keynes 1991; C. Duke, *The Learning University*, Open University Press, Milton Keynes 1992; A. H. Halsey, *The Decline of Donnish Dominion*, Oxford University Press, Oxford 1992; T. Tapper and B. Salter, *Oxford, Cambridge and the Changing Idea of the University*, Open University Press, Milton Keynes 1992; J. Goddard *et al*, *Universities and Communities*, CVCP, London 1994; B. Salter and T. Tapper, *The State and Higher Education*, Woburn Press, Ilford 1994; P. Ainley, *Degrees of Difference: Higher Education in the 1990s*, Lawrence & Wishart, London 1994; P. Scott, *The Meanings of Mass Higher Education*, Open University Press, Milton Keynes 1995; T. Schuller (ed), *The*

Changing University, Open University Press, Milton Keynes 1995; F. Coffield (ed), *Higher Education in a Learning Society*, University of Durham, 1995.

2. The literature on the concept of 'community' is extensive, but see, *inter alia*, M. Stacey, 'The Myth of Community Studies', *British Journal of Sociology*, 20, 2, 1969, pp 34–47; D. Clark, 'The Concept of Community: a re-examination', *The Sociological Review*, 21, 3, pp 63–82, 1973; R. Williams, *Keywords*, Fontana, London 1985, pp 75–76; H. Butcher, 'Introduction: Some Examples and Definitions', in H. Butcher *et al* (eds), *Community and Public Policy*, Pluto Press, London 1993, pp 3–21; G. Day and J. Murdoch, 'Locality and Community: coming to terms with place', *The Sociological Review*, 1993, pp 82–111; M. Mayo, *Communities and Caring*, Macmillan, London 1994, pp 48–68.

3. See G. Peeke, *Mission and Change*, Open University Press, Milton Keynes 1994; J. Goddard *et al, op.cit.*, and C. Duke, *The Learning University*, *op.cit.*, pp 28–44.

4. Again, the literature is vast. For useful introductions to these developments, see S. Lash and J. Urry, *The End of Organised Capitalism*, Polity Press, Cambridge 1987, and D. Harvey, *The Condition of Postmodernity*, Blackwell, Oxford 1989.

5. See J. Rutherford (ed), *Identity: Community, Culture, Difference*, Lawrence & Wishart, London 1990; S. Lash and J. Friedman (eds), *Modernity and Identity*, Blackwell, Oxford 1992.

6. See P. Brown and R. Scase, *Higher Education and Corporate Realities*, UCL Press, London 1994, and P. Scott, *The Meanings of Mass Higher Education, op.cit.*

7 M. Tight, 'Crisis, What Crisis? Rhetoric and Reality in Higher Education', *British Journal of Educational Studies*, 42, 4, 1994, pp363–374; For attempts at future projections, see P Scott, 'The Idea of the University in the 21st Century: a British Perspective', *British Journal of Educational Studies*, 41, 1, 1994, pp4–25, and S. Sutherland *et al, Universities in the Twenty-first Century*, National Commission on Education, London 1994.

8 C. Duke, *The Learning University, op.cit.*, p4.

9 NIACE, *An Adult Higher Education: a Vision*, NIACE, Leicester 1993, p9.

10 C. Duke, *The Learning University, op.cit.*, p116.

1

Y Brifysgol a'r Werin: The People's University

Kenneth O. Morgan

It is vital, for social and cultural as well as educational reasons, that the university remains in close touch with local grass-roots initiatives within the community. 'Outreach' is an attractive word, but, like patriotism, it is not enough. The besetting sin of academics everywhere is exclusiveness, whether in an ivory tower or a plate-glass monolith. It has never been more necessary that a university such as that of Wales, created for, and to some extent by, the common people, should identify itself with the world of work and dynamic movements of social change, and perhaps of social protest, around it. I hope that this contribution will be seen as a small part in this process.

The University of Wales has always prided itself on being a people's university, *prifysgol y werin*. Its first official historians wrote in 1905 that 'the history of education is the history of the people of Wales itself'.[1] It is more than an educational institution. It is a monument to popular achievement, to aspirations of equality and of enterprise, and a unique badge of Welsh nationhood. But *which* people did this people's university specifically represent? Did the new university colleges of Aberystwyth, Bangor and Cardiff in the 1880s and 1890s identify with the emigrant farm labourers or with the sprawling proletariat of the mining valleys or with the inner city population of Cardiff or Swansea or Newport? My own grandfathers were working men in rural Wales, a blacksmith and a fisherman. How, if at all, did the national university speak to them?

Almost from its inception, in fact, the University of Wales, like its equivalents in England and (perhaps to a lesser degree) in Scotland, came to embody bourgeois aspirations – social mobility, professional advancement – as part of the onward march of 'imperial' South Wales at the turn of the century. Many working people entered the new university Colleges, but they tended to be migrants from their class, never to return. The youthful pledge of the fledgling Criccieth solicitor, David Lloyd George, spoke for them all – 'My supreme idea is to get on' – and in time he did so, all the way to Downing Street.

Of course, the new University of Wales had many meritorious features. It had a far higher proportion of working-class or poorer students than most other British universities at that time. It was socially adventurous. Cardiff pioneered the way in admitting women students in 1884, with Aberdare Hall being established as a hostel for women a year later. There were numerous women students at Bangor and Aberystwyth also, well before the federal university came into being in 1893. But compared even with the land-grant colleges of the American Mid-West, of which the University of Wisconsin was to be the proudest examplar, the university of Wales was erecting new social barriers even while demolishing old ones. Whatever the sentimental rhetoric about *y werin*, the higher education system in Wales helped to ensure that it was anything but a classless society. Unwittingly, it was adding new divisions to those already pre-existing within the capitalist system of which South Wales in the 1880-1914 period was perhaps the outstanding example in the world.

The adult education movement in Wales in the first three decades of this century was in large measure a response to this perceived gulf between the institutions of higher education and Welsh community life. It is largely a remarkable story of voluntarist action and self-help, a story recently set out with admirable clarity in Richard Lewis's monograph, *Leaders and Teachers* (University of Wales Press, Studies in Welsh History series, 1993). What emerges from this account is that there were two main strands of adult education, usually taken as being intrinsically opposed to each other in practice and ideology.

First, there was the tradition associated with the Workers' Educational Association. It was the work of high-minded middle-class people in Wales after the turn of the century – Daniel Lleufer Thomas, Sir Henry Jones, later on, Percy Watkins and Thomas Jones of Rhymney who became its first district treasurer. It arose from a powerful belief that university extension classes were not enough and that a much more regular and directed study for the workers was required. It was in this belief that Albert Mansbridge founded the

WEA in 1903, in association with Oxford figures such as R.H. Tawney and William Temple. It was in time to prove the most enduring system of adult education in Wales: indeed the great Tawney himself began a notable class in Wrexham in 1908.

By the end of the first world war, the WEA was firmly established in much of Wales, in the mining valleys above all. John Davies became a charismatic district secretary in 1919, while Silyn Roberts, the famous socialist minister-bard, created the North Wales branch in 1922. The Association's purpose was liberal and humane – Tawney saw it as the basis of a new form of social citizenship – although there was also an underlying substratum of fear lest the ill-disciplined workers break out into revolution. There was an emphasis on the training of working-class people for public service, in local government, the trade unions, the co-operative movement, the world of social and community life. It struck a powerful chord amongst the Welsh, in both rural and industrial areas, with their tradition of local, voluntarist adult education notably in the Sunday schools. It was especially appealing to members of the nonconformist chapels, amongst whom knowledge and faith were inseparably linked.

The WEA was given new vigour after the first world war with the impetus given by the Haldane commission on the University of Wales in 1918 to the entire system of extension teaching. One important outgrowth in 1927 was the formation of Coleg Harlech, mainly through the Fabian good offices of Thomas Jones, as Peter Stead (in his study of Coleg Harlech) and Ted Ellis (in his biography of T.J.) have both explained to us. The mood was now different. The original foundation of the WEA assumed an era of unending industrial prosperity and growth. Coleg Harlech, by contrast, was the product of a time of mass unemployment and industrial collapse. Men like Thomas Jones and David Davies, heir to the patrimony of Llandinam, were anxious to reconcile capital and labour and find constructive approaches in education to promote industrial reform and harmony. They were anxious to suppress Bolshevism and class war ideas which had made South Wales the 'El Dorado' of the British revolutionary left. In so doing, and through Coleg Harlech in particular, they gave the WEA tradition new life.

There was, however, a powerful alternative approach to that of the WEA. Many workers in South Wales in the Edwardian period came to feel that the essence of the WEA's liberal and humane philosophy was social conformity and acceptance of the capitalist order. Instead, some militants argued, especially within the Miners' Federation, there was need for an authentic working-class form of adult education. The links of the WEA with elitist Oxford University were condemned; its upper-class supporters were suspect. Hence there came the famous strike at Ruskin College, the founding of a workers' college at Oxford, in 1909, in which many future Welsh miners' leaders such as Noah Ablett and Ted Gill were prominent. As a result, a separate institution was created, the Central Labour College, including amongst its staff the former principal of Ruskin, Denis Hird. Based at first in north Oxford and then in Regent's Park in London, the Central Labour College was a powerful force. It was controlled by workers' representatives; it was largely financed by the South Wales Miners' Federation. Its Marxist tutorial classes in economics, sociology and political theory, especially in the Rhondda and Cynon valleys, were a crucial component of the social history of south Wales in the first quarter of this century. Curiously, only one account of its history exists, W.W. Craik's partly autobiographical little book of 1964.

The Central Labour College drew on a wider range of support, the Plebs' League and the Unofficial Reform Committee based in Tonypandy, and the industrial unionism (some called it 'syndicalism' on the French model of Sorel) of that famous pamphlet *The Miners' Next Step* (1912). It was at the centre of a massive ideological ferment, without parallel in the history of Wales, and was powerfully influenced by local Marxist leaders like Noah Ablett and Will Hay. Will Mainwaring, perhaps the chief author of the *Miners' Next Step* who received a scholarship from the Miners' Federation to study at the CLC, was an influential tutor for the College movement in the Rhondda. The College survived the war and after 1918 was to generate a new working-class elite – Jim Griffiths, Aneurin Bevan, Ness Edwards, A.J. Cook, Lewis Jones – an entire brilliant generation of socialist or communist workers' leaders to rival, and in time surpass, Tom Ellis, David Lloyd George, Llewelyn Williams and the Liberal elite of the Cymru Fydd years in the past. In the late 1920s the College merged into the wider National Council of Labour Colleges (NCLC), again with strong links with the Welsh miners and their Federation.

The importance of the Central Labour College in the stormy years 1910–30 is transparently clear. It influenced many young workers' leaders who never studied there at all, Arthur Horner being one notable example. It was above all an agency for training industrial workers, not just to serve, but to achieve the conquest of power and to transform an unjust and corrupt capitalist order. It generated many myths and a 'reds under the bed' approach encouraged by the Conservative government and the Special Branch at the time of the General Strike in 1926. During the hunger marches and 'stay-down' stoppages in the 1930s, the NCLC was again under fire, not least in the late-imperial mind of Captain Lionel Lindsay, the class warrior Chief Constable for Glamorgan – if not for Jurassic Park.

These two traditions – the WEA and the NCLC – were generally held to be very different. In some ways they undoubtedly were. Marxism was a fundamental barrier between the two. In time, the NCLC was to suffer from this, especially at the time of the Popular Front in the mid-1930s. In 1937 it was reported that the NCLC had only 142 classes in the Welsh coalfield (itself a very generous estimate), as against 265 for the WEA. The opposition of TUC giants such as Ernest Bevin was unrelenting. By the time of the outbreak of the war, the Labour Colleges were much weaker and their activities being increasingly supplanted by the WEA. In the 1960s, they were formally taken over by the TUC and their separate identity disappeared.

But it would be a mistake to draw too extreme a distinction between the two. In the 1930s, at the time of the Spanish Civil War, it was hard to differentiate between the WEA and the NCLC in south Wales. They contained many of the same people. Both of them sent volunteers to the International Brigade to fight for the Spanish Republican cause. The WEA in its turn was also revitalised by the collective endeavour kindled by the mass unemployment and suffering of the 1930s. Ideas of class and community merged; indeed they had never been very far apart. Each tradition drew strength from the tutorial method of the other. Certainly both were vital facets of the history of adult education in South Wales.

The point is underlined by the career of R.H. Tawney, a giant as scholar, ideologue and educationalist. He worked from the outset for Albert Mansbridge and the WEA. But he did so as a socialist, a prophet of social change. Education he saw as vehicle of social solidarity which would in due time bring the capitalist edifice crumbling down. He was anxious to preserve the WEA for working-class people, not to turn it into an agency for professionally ambitious middle-class people seeking an additional qualification. This was the gospel he preached from his Oxford extension class in the Potteries, with its outpost at Wrexham. He always saw education as a dynamic force, a key to social equality, not a barrier to creating a common culture.

From all these exciting developments, the University of Wales tended to keep aloof. Extension classes were formed by both Bangor (1911) and Aberystwyth (1913) before the first world war in their rural hinterlands; Cardiff, for some reason, was much slower to respond. However, there was a distinct breakthrough after the first world war, even though Cardiff's continuing apathy towards extra-mural provision continued and was widely condemned. Aberystwyth was the first to set up a fully-fledged extra-mural department in 1920. Its director was the Rev. Herbert Morgan, a Christian socialist and a Baptist who had earlier been the minister of Lloyd George's own chapel, Castle Street just behind Oxford Circus in London. He was to be followed by a sequence of notable personalities – Ben Bowen Thomas, Ifan ab Owen Edwards and then Alwyn D. Rees. Bangor soon followed on, while Swansea had extra-mural classes as an important part of its operation from its foundation in 1921. The historian Ernest Hughes was a giant in the early years of the Swansea world of adult education; another was Illtyd David, who succeeded P.S. Thomas as director in 1941. From the second world war, the university colleges of Wales were increasingly active in promoting links between university life and local community involvement. Adult education was increasingly professionalised, without losing contact with the initial humane impulse.

At the present time, we see a newer vision emerging, with some far-reaching implications, financially and culturally. Extra-mural education is being transmuted into the broader, more vocational notion of continuing education. There is a growing emphasis on the theme of access and diversity of entry patterns, on the idea of education for all. The European Community, through notable Welsh figures such as Hywel Ceri Jones, has added a powerful emphasis on lifelong learning, not least as a feature of industrial retraining.

In this whole area, the Open University, with which the Community University is linked, has been a massive pioneer, with its innovations in distance learning and its breaking down of the barriers between the educationalist and the citizen in his or her home or workplace. It is worth reflecting that the Open University was a product of the Wilson years in the 1960s, popularly abused nowadays yet in social terms a time of liberalism and humanity.

Another important feature relevant for adult education today is the dramatic impact of new technology, in which the information revolution of our time has, among many other things, minimised the physical isolation of rural settlements or remoter mining villages. As a result the very concept 'Y Brifysgol a'r Werin' has acquired a totally new significance. In Wales, we have seen the university colleges come together to collaborate in access consortia. The South West consortium, initially led by Swansea, also involves Aberystwyth and Lampeter, for instance. There remains a place for liberal and humane non-award-bearing courses of the traditional type, perhaps especially appropriate for senior citizens. But there has been official encouragement for award-bearing, grant-aided courses with specific qualifications, with an emphasis on specialist skills and vocational training. Universities are extending their part-time degree programmes in consequence, in a way appropriate for their own particular area; for instance, a growth area in the Aberystwyth region is part-time degrees in Welsh, not confined to the humanities.

Swansea's concept of a Community University marks an exciting new step forward in all this. There is the formal university dimension since it involves the development of part-time degree schemes, a growth area as we have seen. But it also bases itself on a wide range of local and voluntary bodies in the community, and seeks to raise awareness amongst them. Rather than being imposed from afar, it derives its inspiration in large measure from local needs and cultures, including the particular needs of dependent groups such as the unemployed, single parents, women in general and the disabled. It is based on the original ideas of the DOVE workshop developed during the 1984-5 miners' strike, a fascinating example of how that great industrial calamity nevertheless produced an important sense of communal reassessment and rediscovery. It has, therefore, an open-ended range of objectives, and is in all ways an exciting and imaginative development, unique in Wales. The fact that it draws on the earlier traditions that I have been describing is, I believe, a major source of strength.

As Vice-Chancellor of the University of Wales, my message is that our university must involve itself in these developments, and for a number of reasons. In its earlier years, the university stood aloof. There remains a danger of creating new barriers in our divided society, instead of 'tearing down the barriers of the mind'. It would be sad indeed if, after ending the gulf of the 'binary divide' between the universities and the polytechnics, we were to create a new kind of gulf between the world of higher education in general and that of further or community education. We need another imaginative leap beyond the horizons conceived in the innovative Robbins report of the 1960s.

It is also necessary that all public and voluntary associations act together to repair the systematic social damage created in the 1980s. The Community University is part of our response to those philistine politicians who claimed then that 'there is no such place as society'. Beyond these immediate difficulties, there is the wider role of education as an agent of cultural liberation, of spiritual enlargement. Nye Bevan wrote of how 'democracy is protected by extending its boundaries. Each freedom is made safe by adding another to it'. The Community University should operate in that spirit.

I hope that the University of Wales will assist these developments in every way feasible – through the accreditation of award-bearing courses where appropriate; through providing teachers and assisting in staff development, library, work-station facilities and all the exciting options available through information technology; through encouraging also non-award-bearing courses of a traditional kind; and more generally in proclaiming to the world a non-elitist message of fraternity and partnership. The medium and the message are one and indivisible.

The diffused, decentralised nature of the University of Wales means that this is best done locally, in the way that the Community University has been sponsored by the Adult Continuing Education Department in Swansea. But the federal university as a whole also has a valuable role, through the Academic Board and the new University Subject Panels, which includes one that covers Continuing Education and includes representatives from outside the university sector. The essential yardstick of the validation of courses in other institutions is another way in which the University as a whole can be active and as Vice-Chancellor I shall encourage it to do so.

R.H. Tawney, once commented ironically on how it always took a war for the British to undertake educational reconstruction. A new educational reform, in a time of peace, more socially integrative than the work of Fisher is 1918 or of Butler in 1944, is now possible. We have the chance to create, in the right climate of public support, a wider and more worthwhile educational transformation. In earlier years, the University of Wales stayed on the sidelines, distancing itself both from the WEA and the Central Labour College, from Mansbridge and Marx. In 1922, Sir Alfred Zimmern had condemned the fact 'that the University should mean so little to the coalfield, that it should even display, on occasion, a deliberate preference for the unlettered, if titled, capitalist over the zealous and lettered proletarian'. As late as 1944 there was an unseemly conflict between the University Extension

Board and the Welsh WEA, basically a simple territorial dispute. Let us pledge that this will never happen again. Let us make sure that our national university, in the years of its centenary, will not stand aside this time around. Let us ensure that (to quote the mildly chauvinist language of *The Miners' Next Step* back in 1912) that 'mankind has leisure and inclination to live as men and not as the beasts that perish'.

NOTE

1. For an assessment of W. Cadwaladr Davies and W. Lewis Jones' *The University of Wales*, London 1905, see my article 'The People's University in Retrospect' reprinted in *Modern Wales: Politics, Places and People*, Cardiff 1995.

2
UNIVERSITIES, COMMUNITIES AND LOCAL REGENERATION: QUESTIONING THE CASE

Dennis Hardy

The issue of a close relationship between universities and local communities is a significant item on the higher education agenda of the 1990s. While recognising the comparative nature of this issue, this chapter draws largely from British experience. Thus, one can cite as evidence of its growing importance the commissioning and findings of the report of the Committee of Vice-Chancellors and Principals (CVCP), *Universities and Communities*.[1] Not only does this report provide valuable generalisations about current practice, but it also points to the extent and diversity of local links from one university to another. One can also cite as evidence the Government's *Charter for Higher Education*, in which there is acknowledgement of the rights of members of the local community to know what facilities are open to the public and at what charge (a limited interpretation of what the public might reasonably expect of universities, yet not to be ignored).[2]

The strengthening of local links, and the fact that this issue enjoys official recognition, is generally regarded as an encouraging trend in contemporary higher education. While not dissenting from this apparent consensus, the purpose of this chapter is to look at some of the costs as well as the benefits, and to urge a note of caution. The fact is that higher education will always be vulnerable to political initiatives and trends that may seem favourable at the time, but which may later prove to be inimical to the core activity of providing a learning environment for students. It would be prudent to ensure that the costs do not outweigh the benefits.

In the rest of this chapter, there are three sections – the first examining something of the origins of the present trend of closer links between universities and their communities; the second reviewing the main arguments in favour of what is happening; and the third highlighting some of the associated costs and countervailing pressures.

TOWNS, GOWNS AND THE CORPORATE ETHOS

There have always been links between universities and their communities. That is inevitable, in that universities are by their very nature influential and usually large institutions, which are bound to have an impact on their surroundings; just as universities are, in turn, influenced in different ways by the communities in which they are located. What has changed over time is not the existence of a mutual relationship, but the way in which this is shaped.

It was certainly very different in mediaeval times, and modern Vice-Chancellors – often accused of holding too much power – might care to reflect on the omnipotence of their fifteenth-century counterparts in Bologna, where successive rectors exercised judicial rights, not only over their own students and officials, but also over 'scribes, binders and illuminators and other groups of tradesmen' who served the university.[3] In France, such was the importance of the scholar that lodgings could be compulsorily acquired, and artisans' workshops that caused nuisances such as noise or bad odours were subject to forced removal.[4]

Continuing this theme of adversarial contact, Rowland Parker sub-titles his book on the relationship of town and gown in Cambridge, 'the 700 years' war in Cambridge'.[5] He points to a succession of incidents, at times culminating in riots, and to draconian powers and legal rights instituted in favour of the university, enforced, on behalf of the Vice-Chancellor, by enrobed proctors and their constables (known as bulldogs) wearing top hats and patrolling the streets in search of misdemeanours. The arrest of lewd women, punishment (or discommoning) of traders with whom the university took issue, and restriction of passengers using the railway station were amongst the powers that led to continuing disputes between town and university authorities. Not until 1901 was the infamous Spinning House, a house of correction where the University directed transgressors, taken out of use and demolished.

Not that the history of Oxford is any more harmonious, an

essentially uneven relationship where town has served the needs of gown, more than the reverse. The colleges have traditionally looked inwards, excluding by their very architecture the rest of the town; whereas ceremonial events and student antics have for long spilt into the surrounding streets, for the town to engage in as spectator. Fiction it may be, but the decadent picture of Oxford student life between the wars that was portrayed in Evelyn Waugh's *Brideshead Revisited*, and popularised in a television series, has bequeathed images that remain hard to erase. 'Oxford was then still a city of aquatint. In her spacious and quiet streets men walked and spoke as they had done in Newman's day; her autumnal mists, her grey springtime, and the rare glory of her summer days ... '[6] Although Sebastian, clutching his teddy bear, Aloysius, in one hand, and a bottle of champagne in the other, has long gone, certain images refuse to die.

Along with ivory towers, town and gown is one of those cliché-ridden phrases that evokes a persisting sense of division and elitism; universities were not so much a part of their community as apart from it. The one was withdrawn from the everyday world of work and commerce, and those ordinary mortals who entered the hallowed precincts of a university crossed a social and cultural divide. In Willie Russell's *Educating Rita*, it was hard not to feel empathy with poor Rita, the Liverpool hairdresser, when she encountered for the first time her tutor's study, lined with books and with an air of casual disorder. 'How d'y' make a room like this? ... It's like something from a romantic film, isn't it?'[7] Rita is momentarily overawed, aware of a gulf of experience between her and her tutor, Frank, though, of course, the real moral of the tale is that it is Rita's own, working-class culture that eventually captivates the degenerate Frank.

Rita's personal discomfort on embarking into higher education, and a record elsewhere of division between universities and their communities, has to be seen alongside a history of attempts to carve for universities a distinctive role in civic life. This has been especially evident in provincial cities, where the university has for long been a key institution, and where the Vice-Chancellor remains an important figure in the local establishment. In such situations, the university has performed a dual role: one being of assurance and ceremony, a symbol of continuity and influence, with all the ritual of robes and maces on civic occasions; the other being a more active role of disseminating culture – through its museums and special collections, through public lectures and through (aptly named) extra-mural classes. Yet neither the ceremonial nor the cultural aspects of local contact were designed to bridge the gap between town and gown confronted by the likes of Rita, nor did these functions do much to assuage the prejudices of a citizenry who have continued to see it all as a case of *us* and *them*.

Rita might, in fact, have done better to have found her way to a polytechnic, as, since their inception in the 1960s, the so-called public sector was more attuned to the needs of non-standard entrants and to vocational links with local industry. Managed, as they were, as local authority institutions, it was inevitable that much of their work would be community-orientated; polytechnics were, for instance, pioneers in placement degrees, in which students spent a period working in a local organisation; and in part-time education, not as extra-mural studies but often as a means for students to obtain qualifications while in employment. The new polytechnics were cast a role as educational centres for the community at large, filling a vacuum that had never been filled by the universities.[8] Although many of these same polytechnics were lured increasingly into the kinds of activity (notably, research and less vocational courses) that characterised the 'real universities', in a little over twenty years they had the effect of breaking an historic mould, demonstrating a variety of ways in which higher education could be more closely attuned to local needs.

During the 1980s, although starting from a different ideological premise, two aspects of higher education policy reinforced this trend. One, an outcome of value-for-money priorities, questioned educational traditions which encouraged students to live away from home at the State's expense; and funding policies that allowed university buildings and equipment to be unused for a large part of the year. The other aspect of change was that which stemmed from an ideologically-driven opposition to universities as ivory towers, engaged in internally-derived priorities rather than a more functional definition of the needs of the country. For these and other reasons, the advent of a market-led system of higher education, driven more directly by the needs of the economy, was already in train.

By the start of the 1990s, although vestiges of town and gown were still in evidence, it was apparent that higher education was experiencing significant changes, one outcome of which was a renegotiation of traditional relationships with the community. The polytechnics were redesignated as universities, and, far from abandoning their community commitment, they have tended to use university status to upgrade this work in the eyes of the public.

13

Moreover, the requirement of the Higher Education Funding Councils for each university to produce a mission statement has brought to the surface the extent and ways in which different institutions see their role in relation to local communities. Change has been further encouraged by a more rigorous funding regime, that has forced universities to seek more external income, often in association with other corporations.

Thus, across the sector, new partnerships with local agencies have emerged, comprehensive in scope and designed for mutual benefit. This new-style relationship takes many forms, depending on the particular characteristics of the university and the unique cultural history of its locality. And, although the 'new' universities are more likely to see community links as a priority than the 'old',[9] few would deny the growing importance of the issue as such. To differing degrees, and in different ways, all modern universities now have an interest in strengthening local links.

THE WATCHWORD IS PARTNERSHIP

Ostensibly, closer links between universities and local communities can offer something, if not for everyone, then at least for the major players – universities, business interests, cultural groups and residents. Potential rewards are attractive, and various parties are drawn into the collaborative frame. What distinguishes this from the past is that, instead of one party or the other (usually the university) setting the terms – the prerogative of an elite – the watchword for the new order is partnership.

For the hardened observer of the politics of higher education, this brave new world of partnerships – where everyone can win, and no one can lose – sounds too good to be true. Thus, caution invites a more careful look at the process, acknowledging apparent benefits, prior to revealing some of the less obvious costs. There are, indeed, real benefits in closer community links, and these can be summarised in terms of five areas of activity: promoting access to higher education, stimulating technological change, contributing to economic regeneration, and making full use of both human skills and capital assets.

Promoting access to higher education

The question of access to higher education has become one of the crucial issues of the 1990s. To put current trends into perspective, one can note that at the start of this century – after more than a hundred years of industrialisation – no more than 1.2 per cent of the population cohort was admitted to a university; even by the eve of the Second World War this figure had only doubled to 2.4 per cent; and in 1962 it was (including teacher training) still no more than 6.5 per cent.[10] The measure of the change is that school-leavers now have a nearly sixty per cent chance of going to university, either direct from school (about thirty per cent) or later in life. What is more, while the immediate government policy objective of a one in three entry figure is close to achievement, opposition politicians and expansionist Vice-Chancellors are talking openly of higher entry targets, of forty per cent and even fifty per cent, within the next decade.

In relation to community liaison, there are three immediate implications of this trend. One is that, in order to achieve higher intakes, students will need to be attracted from schools and sixth-form colleges that have not, hitherto, sent many of their number into higher education. Even if these potential students choose not to enter their local university, experience suggests that building local links at an early stage can help to bridge what at first seems an untraversable gap. School visits by tutors, workshops for teachers, university students working in schools, and open days are all well-tried ways to increase local interest; some universities are even forging links with primary schools, as much with the intention of familiarising parents with higher education as with the young pupils.

A second implication of greater access is that, as each year a higher proportion of the population experiences higher education, then so too will more people have personal knowledge of someone 'getting to university'. Until quite recently, this experience was restricted to a broad band of middle-class families, and a limited number of working-class families, where especially bright students overcame an extra set of obstacles that was placed in their way. As Britain moves closer to a form of mass higher education, barriers are broken and more people feel comfortable with the idea of the university as a place with which to retain links after graduation, and to use as a local resource. This offers, in turn, greater opportunities for universities to become open institutions within their own community.

Finally, there are important financial implications associated with wider access. In the face of a regrettable but probably inevitable worsening of student finances, there is already a discernible trend in favour of students living at home. This will lead to more universities developing coherent local marketing policies, including access agreements and compacts with local schools and colleges. Associated with this trend, universities will also develop more attractive part-time opportunities for local students, the Liverpool model of a *City of Learning* being one that will become a norm elsewhere.[11]

Stimulating technological change

Universities have a key role in stimulating technological change. Some of this contribution will be at a national level, but there is a distinctive role, too, that can only be developed through local contacts. One area that has attracted particular attention is that of technology transfer.

Technology transfer is, quite simply, the acquisition and adoption of new technologies by firms. Significantly, the transfer originates outside the reception firms, and the flow of information is stimulated by various agencies, including universities – through such means as business innovation centres, and through the creation of networks of potential innovation partners.

It has been claimed that support for technology transfer is 'one of the main external linkage activities of the universities, and is identified in mission statements as perhaps the most important issue in terms of local interaction'.[12] Value is attached to the mainstream university activities of informal networking with industry, student placements, staff secondment and consultancy initiatives. It is recognised, however, that the headlines for technology transfer have been captured by two high-profile activities in particular, the creation of spin-off firms and science parks.

The former term refers to campus companies and to off-campus firms that have been established by academic staff and students. Examples of campus companies are those of University of Leeds Innovations Ltd and Salford University Business Services Ltd, each with multi-million pound turnovers; while some of the biggest spin-off firms in recent years have been created by universities in Newcastle and Bath. Although spin-off firms tend to be in the software and consultancy fields, a number of specialised firms have been created in biotechnology.[13] The other high-profile, technology transfer initiative, science parks, have a mixed record of achievement, but after a rapid growth in the 1980s, 'are now an accepted feature of the university industry landscape'.[14] Some of the largest parks are associated with the universities of Cambridge, Heriot-Watt and Surrey.

Contributing to economic regeneration

Universities are, in economic terms, one of Britain's few growth industries; the rapid expansion of higher education has led to a more than doubling of the participation rate between 1987 and 1995, leading to some 1.5 million students in the system.[15] Significantly, this impressive rate of growth has been achieved at the same time as British manufacturing industry has continued to decline and when jobs have been lost in the service sector as well. Thus, in London, between 1987 and 1991, university employment increased by 9.6 per cent, in contrast with a loss of jobs in the capital of 7.2 per cent.[16] Although the situation varies regionally, it is hard to overstate the importance, existing and potential, of universities as a source of local economic regeneration. For what has been seen in this recent period is not simply higher student numbers, but also an unprecedented construction programme, with the campuses of many universities reshaped to meet changing demands and (especially in the new universities) the building of new residential accommodation for students.

Often supported by European money, the scale of joint schemes involving public and private agencies can be substantial. In Sunderland, Teesside and Liverpool, for instance, universities are engaged in large-scale redevelopment schemes, in partnership with local authorities and the private sector; in Sheffield, Hallam University is a partner in a £50 million town centre expansion plan.[17]

There are methodological difficulties in demonstrating the precise extent and ways in which a university can stimulate growth in the local economy, yet various studies to date all point to a positive impact in terms of employment and local expenditure.[18] As an example, a three-part project at Middlesex University will look, in turn, at the impact of expenditure by students, staff and through university purchasing.[19] What the first findings show is that, within a 5-mile radius of the university, the 15,528 students at Middlesex in 1993/94 spent £54 million and, through this spending, generated 659 jobs. If a multiplier of 1.2 is applied, to take account of secondary spending and job generation, these figures rise to £64.8 million and 790 jobs.

Making full use of human skills

Another dimension of community liaison is that of ensuring that the skills within a university, those of students as well as staff, are available to the community. Motives for doing this range from the selling of skills with a view to raising income for the university, to a more altruistic notion of sharing.

In addition to a research and consultancy role in technology transfer, universities play a central role in business support – through membership of local chambers of commerce and other business groupings, and through partnerships in employment initiatives and in the work of Training and Enterprise Councils (TECs). Typically, Business Schools will offer a range of training and other programmes, and will engage in local projects. This pattern of skills involvement will be found in other vocational areas, too, such as health, social work, engineering and media arts.

No less important is student involvement in the community, through schools and other placements, and through course-based projects. A national scheme that promotes this kind of activity is Community Enterprise in Higher Education (CEHE). Launched ten years ago, the intention is to assist students to put their assessed skills to good use, through projects varying from conservation to social surveys. It is claimed that 'students gain a deeper knowledge of their subject through applying it to *live* problems as well as finding extra motivation from their CEHE projects. At the same time voluntary and community groups gain access to resources which would not otherwise be available or affordable.'[20]

Beyond the more instrumental motives of income generation or course requirements, there is also a wealth of activity where the primary aim is to share with neighbours some of the benefits of scholarship and the joys of learning. This is a traditional source of activity, with the older universities for long offering public lectures and extra-mural classes. In addition to evening and part-time day courses, a form of provision which attracts increasing numbers is that of weekend and summer schools. There is also ample evidence of university staff who, in spite of increasing pressures on their time, willingly and freely offer advice to voluntary groups. Even if material gain is not a motive, there are undoubtedly advantages to a university in terms of public relations and the possibility of future political support.

Making full use of capital assets

A traditional view of universities is that they represent an enormous stock of capital investment, most of which is used for less than half the year. Times are changing, as a result of higher student numbers and consequent demands on facilities, more rigorous requirements for research students to complete higher degrees on time (and, therefore, to be in attendance for longer), and because of new contracts for lecturers which break into hitherto protected blocks of time. Notwithstanding these changes, campuses are still underused in the evenings, at weekends, and during student vacations. Inevitably, in a more cost-conscious climate, with a trend towards charging for space in an internal market, universities are looking increasingly to find ways to generate income through more external use. Outdoor concerts, wedding receptions, dog shows and even car-boot sales can be found on university campuses, in addition to more conventional use of premises for conferences and summer schools.

There is also a strong cultural tradition in the use of university premises, sometimes through specialist facilities like libraries, museums and art galleries, as well as public access to theatres and arts productions. Although, as in all activities, the differences are lessening, the older universities are more likely to stress this cultural role than the new.[21]

COUNTING THE COSTS

The benefits of closer community links are considerable, but disbenefits there are too. These disbenefits need to be disentangled, lest they get in the way of a variety of otherwise attractive programmes and plans. It is suggested that the drawbacks of working with communities are threefold: the potential contradiction of embracing different ideological perspectives, the possibility of raising false hopes and expectations in the community, and the opportunity cost of alternative activities.

Different ideological perspectives

The very notion of community is ideologically charged, carrying with it connotations of conservatism at one extreme and a suggestion of communism at the other. Even in a pragmatic sense, the term can signify various commonalities of interest and it has to be recognised that a university will be dealing not with a single community but with many. A failure to recognise such complexities might well lead to subsequent difficulties in policy implementation.

Yet, however defined, there remains a shared sense that 'working with community' is a worthy activity in a democratic society; indeed, Raymond Williams asserts that 'unlike all other terms of social organization ... it seems never to be used unfavourably.'[22] A long history of altruism and charity lends support to this notion, epitomised most vividly in this context by late nineteenth-century university settlements to aid the 'urban poor'. It is, paradoxically, this very sense that working with the community is basically a good thing that allows the possibility of its misuse for other purposes. Thus, while universities are generally in favour of widening and deepening access, with an associated strengthening of local links, there is a less palatable side of this process. The fact is that widening access is partly a political response to unacceptably high unemployment figures for school-leavers, with university places offering a means to conceal this. Moreover, governments are unlikely to fund this increase in higher education without displacing some of the costs onto students and their parents, one effect of which is to encourage more local attendance.[23] The outcome is that universities, because they favour higher participation rates, are, through increasing local access opportunities, indirectly assisting the Government in cutting the level of student financial support.

There is another way, too, in which university involvement in the community serves sometimes conflicting motives. Since Margaret Thatcher came to power in 1979, successive Conservative administrations have worked to reduce the powers and authority of local government. In place of predictable annual budgets to local authorities, these bodies have been forced to engage in a complex bidding process for a myriad of project funding, often in partnership with other agencies. Not only have universities been encouraged to enter this process as partners, but they have emerged in many cases as the major player in the local arena. Indeed, in some policy areas, education being a notable example, the role of the local authority has in certain instances largely given way to a system of school trusts and college and university corporations. This kind of local power vacuum has created new opportunities for universities, but it should be recognised that there is also a sense in which this gain is at the expense of a different tradition of public service. The danger is that universities can become tainted by a process that is inimical to their own values.

Raising false hopes and expectations

A public commitment to working with the community carries costs in terms of appearing to promise more than can possibly be delivered; hence the warning that 'university links should not be regarded as a panacea for too many community ills'.[24] With some justification, the local press, community organisations and individuals will make capital of this commitment, in order to support particular causes or, when things go wrong, to quote back to the university its declared aims and intentions.

A common source of local concern is the disruptive impact of students in quiet neighbourhoods. The construction of new, off-campus halls of residence has been a mixed blessing in this context, with numerous reports of noise and unsocial behaviour, and with the local press eager to portray such confrontations in the starkest terms. Is this, it is asked, what the university means by a commitment to the community? Perhaps understandably, on these occasions the economic benefits that students bring, and longer-term benefits of engagement in higher education, are seldom acknowledged.

There is a broader sense, too, in which universities – if they are seen to be gaining more than some of their less influential partners – can alienate sections of the community. This is especially so where leadership groups are formed to determine priorities for development, or where universities become involved directly in property schemes. There is increasing evidence that the interests of residents and the voluntary sector become marginalised, with the consequent danger that universities will be caught in a political backlash. On the other hand, universities, more than local authorities and some other agencies, retain an advantage in being able to withdraw from the political fray in order to play a more traditional role of honest broker and arbiter of disputes. There is a difficult balancing act to be achieved, playing an active role as universities in local partnerships, yet not becoming so implicated that they adopt the culture of the development process itself. Critics will be quick to make capital if this line is crossed, and it will actually be in the universities' best long-term interests if such transgressions are, indeed, pointed out. The only sustainable, long-term role in the community is one that is based on enduring intellectual strengths and values, rather than short-term gain.

Opportunity costs of alternative activities

At a time of diminishing resources for higher education, there has to be a coherent case for additional activities; the opportunity cost of taking on new work can be measured by the loss of something else. The adoption of a community liaison policy is unlikely to win unqualified support amongst university colleagues, and the potential benefits have to be clearly demonstrated. This is true of any new policy, but perhaps even more so in the case of community liaison, where there lingers a sense that this type of work is less prestigious than other, more traditional, activities.

There will be unavoidable costs, but these have to be measured in the context of the mission of the institution. Thus, the way forward in terms of reconciling competing priorities is to recognise that each university will choose its own distinctive mix of activities. The idea of product differentiation is one way to express this, with some universities (mainly the former polytechnics) playing the community card to the full, and others (in support of a research-centred mission) concentrating on aspects like technology transfer. In a competitive market, each will play to its own strengths and the costs of community liaison will be carefully calculated in relation to potential benefits.

PROSPECTS

In spite of recent trends, there is some way to go before traditional relationships between universities and their communities are effectively redefined, and before new possibilities are fully embraced. One must be realistic about the costs as well as the benefits of this process. There is nothing more likely to impede progress than a messianic zeal that sees community liaison in terms of unblemished virtue; no policy can live up to that.

Yet, given a sense of realism, it is confidently anticipated that university links with the community will, within a few years, become a mainstream element of higher education. This process will be assisted if the concept of diversity is acknowledged, allowing universities to develop in different ways that are consistent with their individual missions. Thus, community liaison will take a variety of forms, and will embrace many aspects of university life, but a common element will be the development of coherent strategies as part of a corporate planning process.

As a measure of what can be achieved, comparison can be made with the two primary activities of research and teaching, where, for funding and other reasons, universities have developed strategies to optimise performance. For comparable reasons, it is not unrealistic to predict community liaison as a third dimension of corporate strategy.

NOTES

1. J. Goddard *et al*, *Universities and Communities: A Report by the Centre for Urban and Regional Studies for the Committee of Vice-Chancellors and Principals*, CVCP, London 1994.
2. Department for Education, *The Charter for Higher Education*, DFE, London 1993.
3. A. Cobban, *The Mediaeval Universities: Their development and organisation*, Methuen, London 1975, p72.
4. *Ibid*, p233.
5. Rowland Parker, *Town and Gown: The 700 years' war in Cambridge*, Patrick Stephens, Cambridge 1983.
6. Evelyn Waugh, *Brideshead Revisited*, Chapman and Hall, London 1945 (1964 edition), p29.
7. Willie Russell, *Educating Rita*, Longman, Harlow 1985 (1992 edition), p15.
8. Eric Robinson, *The New Polytechnics*, Penguin, Harmondsworth 1968, pp168–69.
9. Evidenced in Goddard *et al, op.cit.*
10. A. Smithers and P. Robinson, *Post-18 Education: Growth, change, prospect*, Council for Industry and Higher Education, London 1995, p2.
11. See, for instance, *The Business of Learning*, Liverpool City Challenge, Liverpool 1994.
12. Goddard *et al, op.cit.*, p20.
13. *Ibid.*, p26.
14. *Ibid.*, p26.
15. 'CVCP calls for 20,000 more students by year 2000', *Times Higher Education Supplement*, 1167, 17.3.95, p3.
16. Goddard *et al, op.cit.*, p14.
17. 'Culture clash finds Sheffield's town and gown in conflict', *Planning Week*, 3 (no.6), 9.2.95, p3.
18. Goddard *et al, op.cit.*, Appendix II, pp 61–71.
19. David North, *The Impact of Middlesex University on the Local Economy. Part 1: Student Expenditure*, Centre for Enterprise and Economic Development Research, Middlesex University 1994.
20. Susan Buckingham-Hatfield, 'Community enterprise in higher education: another CSV success story', *Community Enterprise in Higher Education*, Issue 6, Spring 1995, p1.
21. Goddard *et al, op.cit.*, p3.
22. Raymond Williams, *Keywords: A vocabulary of culture and society*,

Fontana, Glasgow 1976, p66.
23. David Charter, 'Now home is where HE is', *Times Higher Education Supplement*, 1186, 28.7.95, p6.
24. Goddard *et al, op.cit.*, p4.

3

NOTIONS OF COMMUNITY FOR UNIVERSITY CONTINUING EDUCATION

Roseanne Benn and Roger Fieldhouse

This chapter considers five broad concepts of community as they relate to university continuing education. These are the social, geographical, distance, 'role' and professional communities. It concentrates exclusively on the communities for university continuing education: it does not explore the many other communities associated with other forms of adult, continuing and community education. It is argued that these notions of community are not absolute or permanent concepts. They derive very largely from ideology, and they evolve and change with changes in the dominant ideology. This chapter attempts to show how these notions of community have changed over time, and are likely to change further in the future.

THE PAST

The social community

While it is debatable whether nineteenth-century university extension had a strong sense of a social community – it was widely regarded as extending higher education to 'the whole nation' – there is no doubt that the university tutorial class movement which grew up in the early years of the twentieth century in conjunction with the Workers' Educational Association (WEA) had a real commitment to the working class, although there has been plenty of argument about whether this was its ideal mission rather than reality.[1] Its old adversaries in the Labour Colleges and Plebs League, as well as many more recent detractors, would question the effectiveness of the tutorial class movement's social purpose commitment to the education of the working class.[2]

But there is a great deal of evidence that during the first half of the century it made a very considerable contribution to providing a second chance education for many working-class people. During the first three decades of the century the link between the trade unions and the tutorial class movement, championed by such people as G.D.H.Cole, ensured a degree of working-class involvement in university adult education. Between the wars this link with the trade union movement began to weaken and the proportion of students who were manual workers declined. However, in 1931–32, one-third of all classified students were manual workers. There were also 23 per cent clerical, shop and postal workers, and another 23 per cent women students engaged in 'domestic and home duties', many of whom came from working-class backgrounds.[3] University adult education particularly contributed to the effectiveness and level of activism of those working class students who were already engaged in some form of social or political activity.[4]

However, the reality did change after the second world war, by which time almost all universities had established extramural departments. These departments were anxious to reduce their dependency on the WEA by emphasising that, unlike the this body, they were not confined to providing for any one sector of society. This was enshrined in the Statement of Principles issued by the newly established Universities Council for Adult Education in 1948, which stated that the universities could not 'regard their services as available exclusively to any one organisation or section of the community'. This was back to the 'whole nation' as the universities' community. Nevertheless, despite this statement, many university extramural departments and adult educators continued to regard the 'educationally underprivileged' or the socially deprived or (more old fashionedly) the working class as their special community.[5] But as the twentieth century progressed, other social groups became increasingly identified as part of the university adult education community. As the notion of 'working class' became ideologically more problematic, and the ties with the trade union movement became ever more tenuous, the concept of the social community switched to other groups perceived as educationally disadvantaged, for example, women, older people, the unemployed or ethnic minorities.

The geographical community

From their early extension days, the universities had a very strong sense of serving identified geographical areas. Indeed, their continuing education activities have been described in terms of building definable empires.[6] With the recognition of the universities as adult education 'responsible bodies' (that is, responsible for providing university adult education in a particular geographical area) and the gradual creation of extramural departments in most universities between the wars, this geographical commitment became firmly established and caused some rivalry between universities. There were probably several reasons for this territorial empire building, the most straight forward being that, having established extramural departments and appointed directors, they saw it as their mission to expand. But particularly for the smaller universities and university colleges, which were amongst the most assertive, there was also a strong desire to make themselves better known in their regions, partly as a public relations exercise but also to support their appeals for financial endowments and local authority grants.[7] Thus the geographical community became a very real and well defined one, although some parts of these communities (e.g.those in or near university towns or centres) were better served than others. Universities have always experienced difficulties in serving their community more than twenty miles from the university. A number of universities partially overcame this problem by establishing university centres in outlying towns, or appointing resident tutors. The latter were very important in making the universities' service to the whole of their geographical community a reality, and their gradual replacement by staff tutors/lecturers in recent years has considerably undermined the reality of full extramural provision. The emergence of new universities from the 1960s onwards, with a desire to offer a service to their regions, began the fragmentation of the old territorial 'empires'.

More specifically *local* communities were identified after the creation of Community Development Projects (CDPs) in the 1970s as in Liverpool and Leeds. These continue to be important sub-communities within the universities' overall geographical communities.

The distance community

For much of the twentieth century the model for university continuing education has been the Oxbridge tutorial tradition. The aim was to extend traditional university face-to-face teaching beyond the walls. The result was a distinctive and valuable adult pedagogy which emphasised informal teaching, group discussion, and student-centred learning. Describing university tutorial classes in 1912, Albert Mansbridge declared that 'the students control the class ... It is *the* class of the students – each student is a teacher, and each teacher is a student; the humblest is not afraid to teach, and the most advanced is willing to learn.'[8] Although this may have been a somewhat idealised picture, this liberal tradition remained predominant for many years. There was a mutually beneficial co-operation between professional knowledge and expertise on the part of the educator, and life experience in all its variety on the part of the students. The class was seen as a partnership, a mutual exploration, rather than a one way transmission of a body of knowledge from the expert to the ignorant.[9] The success of this adult pedagogy meant that until very recently there has been little interest in alternative distance teaching methods, and very little linkage with adult education organisations such as the Open University (OU) which have developed distance learning expertise. Indeed, it has been argued that the notion that adults can be successfully taught at a distance, which was at the very heart of the Open University's mission, was seen as threatening to 'traditional' university adult education. Consequently 'it is not difficult to see why links between the OU and adult education were not particularly strong ... despite the number of staff, particularly in its regional offices, who had come from adult education backgrounds. University extramural departments were even more stand-offish, wishing to hold their own face-to-face traditions intact.'[10]

'Role' as community

Particular adult education communities have been identified by their 'role', for example, trade unionists (part of working-class community, as mentioned earlier); local government councillors; school governors; groups of industrial workers (for example, leather workers targeted by the Leeds Department after the second world war); and the growing number of welfare state professionals. For example, a survey carried out in 1969 found that one-third of all university social work courses were located in extramural departments.[11] In 1973 the Russell report identified 'role education' as one of the functions of university adult education, by which it meant:

> ... education of a liberal and academic nature designed to provide a relevant background of knowledge and appropriate intellectual skills for groups whose common element is their role in society. They may be occupational groups from industry or the professions – such as training and personnel officers, doctors, clergy, or social workers – or their role may be voluntary, as with magistrates or local councillors.[12]

Generally speaking, these groups were not identified as part of the universities' social community. Nor were they primarily selected as a means of economic regeneration or continuing professional development (CPD) (as is now the case). They became part of the universities' community because they were seen as just another market for university adult education. But they did merge into the professional community.

The professional community

Until quite recently, CPD formed quite an insignificant part of the universities' continuing education activity. This began to change in the 1970s and accelerated after the Department of Education and Science (DES) introduced Professional, Industrial and Commercial Updating (PICKUP) funding in 1982 to encourage colleges, polytechnics and universities to undertake more continuing vocational education for industry, business and the professions. In 1992 the new higher education funding councils introduced development funding to replace the recently terminated PICKUP scheme. With all these financial incentives, CPD has become a much more predominant part of university adult education during the past decade.

Professional training for adult educationalists also fulfilled a minor role in university adult education, with a few notable exceptions (at Edinburgh, Glasgow, Hull, Leicester, Liverpool, Manchester and Nottingham), until the growth of certificate/diploma/M.Ed. programmes in the 1970s and after.

The transformation from the past to the present and future

Over the past eighty years there has been a transformation of the notion of the 'university adult education community'. There is no longer a space for all the traditional communities. The total adult education community has gradually evolved from one predominated by people seeking social purpose or fulfilling civic responsibilities to one of individuals seeking personal development, improved work prospects and wealth creation. This evolution has speeded up very considerably in the past fifteen years, giving rise to rather different concepts of the adult education community.

PRESENT AND FUTURE NOTIONS OF THE CONTINUING EDUCATION COMMUNITY

The social community

New right ideology has given greater predominance to individual development and the need for a well educated work force to improve wealth creation.[13] The effect of this in the 1980s and 1990s has been to reduce the emphasis on social collective sub-sets, for example, the working class, the educationally disadvantaged, women or older people – whilst increasing the emphasis on social and economic function. These sub-sets will get less attention in future *unless* they are fulfilling economic/social functions. For example the 'educationally disadvantaged' will not be targeted in the cause of greater equity or more equal opportunities, but because society needs them to be better skilled workers or at least capable of financial self-sufficiency in order to reduce the national social security burden.

Access and adult literacy campaigns are good illustrations of this trend. Both began, at least in part, as social egalitarian movements but are now regarded more as means of equipping people to fulfil economic/social functions or to be more effective contributors to economic regeneration.

Government ideology drives funding which affects institutional perceptions and priorities. These factors influence practitioners. Recent research on a group of adult educators working in Access provision illustrated this effect.[14] Although there is a strong rhetoric within the Access movement that supports the more emancipatory approach, practitioners contradicted this when questioned about the prime purpose of Access. After a decade and half of New Right individualism, the notion of the social purpose of adult education seems to have been replaced by education which is primarily concerned with the bureaucratic notions of 'widening the market' where students become consumers. This, together with the current preoccupation of professional training towards student-centred, self-directed learning, leads to the inevitable conclusion that from a philosophical point of view, Access turns out to be concerned primarily with the self-development of the individual. Even if practitioners have individual ideologies that are coloured by a radical or social purpose approach to education, the dominant ideological thrust, the 'cultural capital' of a class-based society and the inherent biases found within the system restricts their practice. Commitment to collective action and a belief in a more egalitarian society are forced into the background of the mosaic by more urgent imperatives which stem from the Government's, and hence the funding bodies', vision of education for social conformity and a well trained workforce. This research was carried out with Access practitioners mainly from further and community education but arguably can be extrapolated to the wider body of adult educators.

The hegemonic forces previously described lead to the current emphasis on accreditation. It is as yet unclear what effect this will have on notions of community. Accreditation in university adult education will be predominantly at level one (Council for National Academic Awards; Credit Accumulation and Transfer Scheme) or higher. This is likely to appeal to those without previous higher level qualifications leading to a notion of community of those without tertiary education. However it may deter third age participation or return to learners intimidated by degree level assessment within a few weeks of commencing the course.

'Role' as community

There has been a fragmentation from a collective society to individual responsibility. This has been reflected in university adult education. Where previously 'role' was seen as a function of collective institutions, now much adult education services the individual. As a result, in the new ideological climate, some roles have become less important – for example, local government councillors and trade unionists – because they are not seen as fulfilling useful functions. Others have become more important, for example school governors and people engaged in counselling in many walks of life. These are the groups needed to help break the power of local authorities and support the move to individualism. The effect of this can be seen in the considerable decline in trade union education within the overall continuing education provision of the universities, while courses for school governors and counselling courses have enjoyed a considerable growth in recent years. Another area of expansion has been in the industrial community which has been transformed from just another market for university adult education to a central role for university continuing vocational education (see 'Professional' below).

The geographical community

As shown earlier, university adult and continuing education has long had a commitment to the provision of higher education to those in their geographic region but outside the university's walls, that is, adults in the community not traditional eighteen to twenty-one year old undergraduates. Recently there has been a fundamental change in the participation of adults in higher education. By 1991–92, over a third of all full-time entrants and over a half of all full and part-time undergraduates were over twenty-one.[15]. This dramatic change has given rise to a new notion of community for university adult educators, namely the body of intramural adult students. This community is still developing and changing. Some universities enthusiastically became involved in the provision of Access to Higher Education courses in the 1980s and early 1990s, though this involvement is reducing as a result of funding changes. Some run part-time degrees. There is a growing tendency for the boundaries between full and part-time provision to overlap. This, together with the accreditation of continuing education provision in line with the home university's mainstream provision, has almost obliterated the line between the continuing education student and the traditional undergraduate. This implies that the whole undergraduate body, but certainly all those who are adult, are now the community of university adult educators. As a corollary, there is a further intramural constituency, that of the university staff, through provision of higher degrees in higher education itself (see 'professional' below).

However the major commitment is still to those outside the walls, but here the future is far less clear cut than it used to be. It is frequently argued that, with the advent of new inexpensive technologies and the breaking down of political boundaries between countries, notions of strictly defined geographical communities have become less and less relevant. 'Europe' is as relevant as 'Devon' as a concept of the university's geographical community. The dwindling power of the local education authorities, which used to be the universities' regional continuing education partners further undermines the notion of the geographical community. However, as the Universities Association for Continuing Education itself argued in its response to the Department of Education on the future of higher education, as demand from adults for higher education continues to grow, a much greater proportion of higher education will be part-time and lifelong and hence the local and regional dimension will become more significant.[16]

The distance community

Up till the present, university adult education (excluding the OU) has provided little in terms of non-face-to-face distance education. This has been on the whole a principled decision located in the tradition of the tutorial system. However, with tightening economic strictures, it is becoming increasingly difficult to service distant regions (particularly rural areas). There are other factors effecting a commitment to face-to-face teaching for those not in the immediate vicinity of the institution. Emphasis on those in work hinders daytime provision, safety factors inhibit evening provision. But just as importantly, the increased emphasis on individual needs satisfaction has led to reduced reliance on group-tutorial learning with greater emphasis on individualised student-centred learning rather than socially- or institutionally-orientated learning. This implies provision at a time, place and pace to suit the individual rather than the group or institution. Again there is an intrinsic conflict between these needs and the powerful social cohesive factor of the group. However a continued emphasis on weekly group sessions is likely to result in the centralisation of provision and a loss of the notion of 'wider in the geographical sense' access. The current process of accrediting university continuing education programmes, stimulated by the new funding methodology is likely to accelerate rural deprivation and lead to a greater concentration of provision within a few major centres for two reasons. There will be the difficulty of providing adequate resources for award-bearing courses at numerous centres distant from the university and it will be impossible to provide sufficient numbers of accredited modules in small rural areas to accumulate towards a university award within a reasonable length of time.

To preserve the notion of the distant community, university adult education may need to harness the new technologies to enable learning opportunities to become more accessible. For example, video conferencing allows groups geographically spread to interact at the same time whilst computer conferencing is limited neither by time or location. This may however increase other constraints such as finance. This form of learning is usually designed for the individual learner rather than for groups but could allow concentration on specifically identified communities, for example, the unemployed, rural or housebound. Technologies could improve opportunities for lifelong learning and allow adult educators to redefine the communities that they are able to service but it needs to be noted that telephone, radio and television have had a minimal impact on the delivery of traditional higher education in Britain. Technology is not an independent force or set of objects but rather is the practical knowledge that is part of different communities' capabilities. Use of technologies will be accepted by some groups but not by all. It is not the technology but its integration in provision that determines the effect.[17] Hence knowledge and expertise in adult learning needs to underpin any developments in this area if this approach is to genuinely widen access to provision.

The professional community

It is now over ten years since the Department of Education and Science decision to switch a sizeable proportion of funding for university adult education from liberal adult education to pump-priming post-experience vocational education. In this period universities have increasingly become providers of continuing professional development, largely through the medium of short courses which provide practitioners with intermittent periods of learning. The stimulating effect of PICKUP and funding council pump-priming development grants has already been mentioned. The trend is increasingly away from short up-dating courses to accredited CPD. This has now become a major strand of university adult education provision and industry, commerce and the professions are now included centrally in the universities' notions of community.

Another area of growth in the professional community for university continuing education is that of adult education providers and tutors. Again there are several reasons for this. With the increased professionalisation of the further education sector there is a growing demand from adult educators in further and community education for appropriate and relevant further professional studies particularly if this is at Masters level or higher. In addition, the increased emphasis in university adult education on research and development has had two effects. There are now more academics researching and publishing in the field of adult education and provision at degree level or above is an appropriate outlet for this research and scholarship. It is also an efficient and effective utilisation of talents and abilities for this group to communicate their notions of community to influence the considerably wider student body of further and community educators.

THE CHOICE FOR THE FUTURE

Although there are many reasons, both social and economic, for lifelong learning, learning is always undertaken by the individual. No matter what notions we may have of community, in reality our community consists of those individuals who choose to learn with us. For adults, learning must relate not only to everyday life but must be achievable within the constraints besetting all of us, e.g. time, money, desire, capability, motivation etc. By using new technologies, we may allow other, different groups to define themselves as our community. Our task is to include these other groups who would wish to use our services and to avoid creating or adding inequalities. It is also crucial to remember that technologies may facilitate and enhance provision of education but the role of the educator is to preserve the human component because human interaction is the key to the successful education.

Continuing education is likely to continue to be driven by new right ideological forces and post-modernism away from old notions of community tied to social groups and physical boundaries, towards *functional communities* – communities defined by their function. This chapter has outlined these changes. But we would argue that a critical awareness of past and present notions of community allows us as university adult educators a real choice. We do not have to be passive and deterministic. Within funding imperatives and perhaps alien ideologies, there is still space to ensure that as a community itself, university adult educators continue to debate these notions and identify not just communities but also appropriate, effective and relevant learning strategies and delivery techniques.

NOTES

1. R. Fieldhouse, *The WEA: Aims and Achievements*, University of Syracuse, New York 1977; R. Fieldhouse, 'Conformity and Contradiction in English "Responsible Body" Adult Education 1925–50'. *Studies in the Education of Adults*, 17, 2, 1985.
2. W.W. Craik, *The Central Labour College 1909–29*, University of Syracuse, New York 1964; J.P.M. Millar, *The Labour College Movement*, NCCL Publishing Society Ltd, London 1979; B. Simon, *The Search for Enlightenment*, Lawrence & Wishart, London 1990.
3. S.G. Raybould, *The WEA: The Next Phase*, WEA, London 1949, ppxii, 5–10, 38–53, 102–3; R. Fieldhouse, 1977, *op.cit.*, pp28–30.
4. R. Fieldhouse, 'The Ideology of English Adult Education Teaching 1925–50', *Studies in Adult Education*, 15, 1983, pp11–35 (28–30).
5. R. Fieldhouse, *Optimism and Joyful Irrelevance: The Sixties Culture and its Influence on British University Adult Education and the WEA*, NIACE, Leicester 1993, pp25–40.
6. S. Marriott, *Extramural Empires: Service and Self-Interest in English University Adult Education 1873–1983*, University of Nottingham, Nottingham 1984.
7. *Ibid.*, pp97–110.
8. A. Mansbridge, *The Kingdom of the Mind*, J.M. Dent and Sons, 1944 p24.
9. R. Taylor, K. Rockhill and R. Fieldhouse, *University Adult Education in England and the USA*, Croom Helm, London 1985, pp17–8.
10. N. Sargant (forthcoming), 'The Open University' in R. Fieldhouse *et al*, *A History of British Adult Education*, NIACE, Leicester.
11. G. Cunliffe, *Analysis of Social Work Courses in Universities*, University of Bristol, Bristol 1969.
12. Department of Education and Science, *Adult Education: A Plan for Development*, London, HMSO, The 'Russell report, 1973.
13. R. Benn and R. Fieldhouse, 'Government Policies on University Expansion and Wider Access,1945–1951 and 1985–1991 compared', *Journal of Studies in Higher Education*, 18(3), 1993, pp299–314.
14. R. Benn and R. Burton, 'Access and Targeting: an Exploration of a Contradiction', *International Journal of Lifelong Education*, 14(6) 1995.
15. Department for Education, *Student numbers in Higher Education – Great Britain 1980–1990 Statistical Bulletin*, DES, London 8/1992.
16. UACE, Unpublished evidence submitted to the Department of Education review of Higher Education, 1995.
17. B. Standford, 'Using Technologies for lifelong learning: strategies for relevance in flexible and distance learning', Proceedings of the First Global Conference on Lifelong Learning, Rome 1994.

4

BETWEEN REFORM AND CONFORMITY: CHALLENGES AND OPPORTUNITIES FOR THE GERMAN UNIVERSITIES AFTER UNIFICATION

Peter Alheit

THE 'UNIVERSITY OF THE ENLIGHTENMENT'

The modern German university has its roots in the Enlightenment, which was pervaded by the notion that the liberation of human beings depends on knowledge and education. This is clearly seen when we consider, for example, the daring idea advanced on the eve of the nineteenth century by Goethe, to make the sixteenth-century University of Jena a Reformist University, and to appoint the great rebel thinkers of the age, Schiller, Hegel, Schelling and Fichte, to teach there. The subversion of this move lay in its Kantian definition of education: the capacity of all people to exploit their powers of reason and to throw off their self-imposed lack of political will, as opposed to education as the preserve of the privileged upper classes. The aim was a world in which *every* individual had the opportunity, indeed the duty, to develop freely and where individual action was constrained only by the equal right and duty of free development on the part of every *other* individual.

The fact that this idea was not mere theory, but that its protagonists were prepared to make real sacrifices to achieve it, is shown again by the Jena project of creating a 'University of the Enlightenment'. These young professors had little chance of earning a livelihood with their professorships. Hegel could not have developed his famous *Jena Realphilosophy*, an avidly debated series of lectures on the philosophy of mind and nature, dealing also with such trivial things as *work*, if his wife had not prepared lunch-time meals for students in order to provide a family income. And Fichte could hardly have held his famous republican *Speeches to the German Nation* if he had not been a successful writer as well. Friedrich Schiller, a philosophy professor, supported himself entirely with his dramatic works; it comes as no surprise that he has gone down in the annals of history as a poet and dramatist, not as a professor.

As our example shows, the German university was progressive and reformist on the eve of the modern age, or at least potentially so. This could even be said, albeit with substantial qualification, of Humboldt's model university in Prussia. Compared to the rigid confines of the Prussian king's concept of education, the (new Humanist) form of higher education advocated by Wilhelm von Humboldt, unfettered by any Church influence and imbued with the idea of developing the individual, was progressive and directed towards the future. On the other hand, it remained the preserve of the elite, and contained little or no reference to any form of universal emancipation. To that extent, it fitted in well with the notion of 'Enlightenment' as officially decreed by the Prussian king at the end of the eighteenth century (the century of the Enlightenment, after all):

> True Enlightenment is possessed undeniably by the one who knows his place in life within the circle that fate has placed him, and who is able to live according to that position ... The more one extends his academic learning, the more the germ of dissatisfaction with his estate will grow.[1]

Enlightenment as conformity and subjugation is the other dimension to the history of the German university. To what extent this authoritarian view of affairs prevailed throughout most of the nineteenth century is shown not only by the draconian repression of the progressive student fraternities, the *Burschenschaften*, after the famous Wartburg festival in 1817, and the murder of August von Kotzebue, the arch-reactionary poet, in 1819 by a rather fanatical theology student, but also the fact that one of the 'rebels of Jena', namely Hegel, had meanwhile become a well-established philosophy professor in Berlin, who saw in the feudal Prussian state a manifestation of 'Absolute Spirit'. Even in the so-called *Vormärz* period, the phase leading up to the half-hearted bourgeois revolution in Germany in 1848, it was only a minority of courageous students and professors who resisted the conformist pressure exerted by their own institutions. Most of the professors who belonged to the first German parliament in 1848, in the Pauline Church in Frankfurt, were conservative and in the service of the state. Republican rebels were by far the exception.

The German university in the nineteenth century was above all an elitist institution, created for the male offspring of the upper classes and full of distinctions vis-à-vis the thirst for knowledge and education on the part of ordinary people. The most famous universities, in Berlin, Bonn, Heidelberg or Freiburg – where people like Theodor Mommsen and Heinrich Treitschke, Max Weber, Edmund Husserl, Heinrich Rickert and Wilhelm Windelband, Adolf von Harnack and Ernst Troeltsch taught – were places of exclusivity. These were far removed from the real social problems that existed, 'above' the industrial revolution, and the distress and the misery of the working classes. They were cut off from the emancipatory ideas that had moved the imagination and the thinking of many intellectuals a century before.

REFORM OR CONFORMITY?

The 1920s witnessed some ultra-cautious efforts at reform. Under the collapse of the Wilhelmine empire after the First World War, areas of revolutionary thought and action were able to develop – and the universities were no exception. Social democratic and socialist professors, mostly sociology and law professors, attempted to open the university to all-comers, including workers. Not only the famous Institute for Social Research was established at the University of Frankfurt, for example, but also the Academy of Labour, which was open to progressive trade unionists; in Berlin and Leipzig remarkable *folkhighschool* projects came into being which dedicated their efforts, in close cooperation with progressive university lecturers and professors, to those sections of the population that traditionally had no access to education.[2]

The German university as an institution was little affected by such developments, however. For all the revolutionary confusion of the post-war period and the shock waves of modernisation and Americanisation during the 1920s, it remained a traditional, essentially undemocratic and elitist institution – still the preserve of the educational elite and a predominantly male domain.

The extent to which the spirit of compliance and conformity prevailed over reformism is shown by the Nazi era. When large numbers of Jewish academics were forced to emigrate, German universities lost not only many of their leading researchers; they also lost that critical, reformist potential which had led during the 1920s to the first elements of a new and different type of university being designed and implemented. Universities shed nothing of their classical elitism under fascism; they were simply 'brought into line' with respect to Nazi ideology. The slightest sign of intellectual resistance to the latter was sanctioned with draconian punishments and even death at the hands of the Gestapo. The overwhelming majority of professors, including many of international repute, such as Martin Heidegger (to name but one example), had no shame in celebrating the new rulers and talking of the new age that had dawned.

The fact that German universities failed after the Second World War to face up to this period, but preferred the return to 'Business as Usual', is one of the sadder chapters in the history. The transformation, the institutional and ideological reforms that were needed, simply failed to materialise. Tradition and educational distinction served to blur and obscure the dreadful political collaborationism of the preceding years. Hermann Lübbe, the conservative social philosopher, praised this disturbing form of ignorance as late as the 1980s, calling it 'non-symmetric discretion' – by which he means the conciliatory attitude taken by prominent opponents of the Nazis at the universities and the considerable restraint exercised by ex-Nazis. This, claims Lübbe, was a model process of social de-escalation that enabled the establishment of a democratic polity.[3]

The flimsiness of this line of argument is shown by the present-day example of German unification. There is no talk now of 'non-symmetrical discretion' – despite it being everyday practice in other ex-Warsaw Pact countries, such as Poland, Hungary or the Czech Republic. The East German universities enjoy a luxury that money cannot buy, namely 'processing' (dismissing) a remarkable number of the professors and the overwhelming majority of the intellectuals in the social sciences and humanities. The cynical term 'processing' (*Abwicklung*) provokes immediate associations with Nazi terminology. And the process is risky not just from an economic point of view. Not only are politically undesirable persons being disposed of: a substantial body of experience is also being suppressed, one that is indispensable for understanding the problems that currently exist, an inestimable stock of social knowledge about the actual conditions that governed in East German society and which have adapted only superficially to those in Western Germany.[4]

The previous social scientific intelligentsia – not all of whom by any means were obedient members of the SED (Socialist Unity Party),[5] but often enough courageous critics of the official Party line – are being replaced by younger West German academics who would never have managed such a career had it not been for deliberate administrative colonialisation on the part of Western Germany. It would therefore seem as if a process typical of the post-war situation at German universities is repeating itself – this time with the political polarities reversed; superficial normalisation processes are displacing any debate on, or analysis of, key social problems, effectively throwing away any chance of fundamental reforms. Once again, conformity and compliance are winning the day.

AFTER UNIFICATION

If we are still able to identify certain opportunities that German unification has opened up for the universities, it is not because of some vague expectations that the communist era in the German Democratic Republic (GDR) might contain some hidden legacy. Universities in the GDR left very little space for free scientific discourse. Where lively debates and controversies *did* develop – such as after the twentieth Party Congress of the Communist Party of the Soviet Union (CPSU) in the mid-1950s – the Stalinist leaders of the SED were immediately provoked, and demonstrated to left-wing intellectuals, sometimes in absurd show-trials, where the limits to their intellectual freedom were. The response of prominent left-wing thinkers like Ernst Bloch and Hans Mayer was to leave the GDR in protest.

Even the crucial ideological aspect that the GDR had always set so much value by, namely the opening of the universities to the working class, did not materialise in any form. The degree of permeability of the education system that was undeniably achieved, and the targeted support for social strata with little access to education, led shortly after the war to dramatic changes in the student population.[6] But not for long. In the 1980s, the proportion of working class children among the student body was even less than the 17-18 per cent level that had been achieved in West Germany – a political statistic so delicate that publication was strictly forbidden.[7] The declining demand for education on the part of the lower social strata in the GDR therefore seems quite logical. The undisguised anti-intellectualism of the SED Party bosses and the lack of material incentives for academic professions – compared with the privileges enjoyed by the cadres in manufacturing industry – limited, understandably enough, the need for higher education among workers.

The cautious optimism one can entertain is rooted in the experience of over twenty years of educational reform in West Germany. The 'Western' origins are not the critical factor here, but the context of reform. The universities in the Federal Republic were not prepared for any kind of opening. The educational system was split into vocational training for simple people following basic primary education, and a higher general education for the elites.[8] This is where the universities came in; higher general education was the 'vocational training' of the privileged strata, so to speak.

At the end of the 1950s, this system of allocation became increasingly dysfunctional, because the capitalist labour market needed workers who were not only highly skilled, but who were also able to maintain a willingness to learn and flexibility throughout their entire working lives. It became increasingly unlikely that anyone would have any use for a fifty year-old worker whose vocational training dated back to when he or she was sixteen. 'Learning' had to be learnt. And that had something to do with economics, not just democracy. One of the major educational reformers of the post-war period, the founder of the Max Planck Institute for Educational Research in Berlin, Hellmut Becker, demonstrated this to industrialists and politicians as early as 1957 with a convincing example:

> Let me take the excavator crane in the open-cast mining industry in the Rhine area, which costs 20 million marks, extracts 100,000 cubic metres of coal in each 16-hour shift and is operated by seven people; this is a machine about the same size as a small frigate that used to need a master mariner and numerous other skilled people, never mind the crews themselves, whereas here there are only seven men, of whom even the crane driver has no other training than the general education of an

unskilled worker who has grown up in the factory. This means in the context we are talking about that we need people who possess a more developed sense of responsibility. This crane driver must realise at once when something is not functioning as it should ... This means ... that the modern human being requires a greater sense of responsibility and a greater degree of understanding that goes beyond what he actually needs to do. Now you may reply that such people are specialists. But they are not specialists; because when the crane operator was trained, this type of crane had not been developed yet, and when this type of crane came out, people were being trained who will actually be using very different equipment by the time they join the active labour force.[9]

Becker's argument was extremely powerful. It rallied the support of both 'modernisers' and the 'Enlightenment brigade'. By using a military comparison, Becker, himself the son of a Prussian Minister of Culture, even won over the most conservative of educational policymakers. In any case, the example cited anticipates a coalition typical for educational reform: 'Modernity *and* Equality of Opportunity' is the slogan. Ludwig von Friedeburg, another major advocate of educational reform, himself Minister of Culture in the progressive state of Hessia and an educational and industrial sociologist of some repute at Frankfurt University, later developed this coalition into a programme – not only for the educational reform phase, but also for today.[10]

A subversive political imagination in matters educational will say he is right, in that the universities were indeed opened up at that time. The number of students from working-class backgrounds has quadrupled, and the proportion of women at the universities has increased from 13 to 40 per cent.[11] In Germany today, we have a more democratic and modern university system than ever before. Of course, as in many Western European countries, we also observe contrasting effects as well. I should like to mention the two most important, to which Pierre Bourdieu, especially, has referred.[12]

> Educational titles show inflationary tendencies. A teacher or professor in Germany is no longer somebody special. The opportunity for many people from outside the old educational elite to acquire these titles means that they are devalued from the outset. This is undisputed. Is it dramatic in any sense? Or isn't it fantastic that a working-class girl can now become a sociology professor? Or that people no longer recoil in

deference if someone says he or she is a professor?

The problems that these 'new professors' might have among their peers, the 'irritations of habitus' to which Bourdieu refers, are obviously secondary in comparison. Secondly, many acquire the educational title, but there are no positions to apply for. Whereas the first generation profited from the opening of the social space and was able to translate the gain in 'cultural capital' (education) into available jobs, the cohort that follows is left empty-handed. Bourdieu calls them the 'cheated' generation: the nurse who decides to do a degree in social work, and who has to finance with night shifts in hospital not just her studies but also her family income after examination; the bank clerk studies sociology and drives a taxi or restores run-down apartments after the Masters Degree. Was studying really such a waste of time? Of course not.

Today we have a kind of educated 'protest elite' – people who understand social problems and know how to defend themselves against them, even if they do not have highly paid jobs. This is almost equivalent to an opening of the university, and to a secret liaison, on a high level, between Enlightenment and modernisation. For modernisation today also means building a car that only needs three litres per hundred kilometres (ninety-four miles to the gallon); producing energy that will not place a burden on our great-great-grandchildren, and learning communitarian behaviour that accepts the otherness of others while still maintaining contact with them. Such questions have long been of economic and not just ideological interest. But they reveal a new coalition between modernisers and enlighteners – both inside and outside the university.

An interesting contrast is developing among German universities. Whereas the western part of the country has seen a reversion to traditional structures within the university system over the last decade, the restructured universities in Eastern Germany are generally open to society and communitarian issues. This can be explained in very pragmatic terms – absurdly, for all their new elitism, universities in Western Germany have been mass establishments for some considerable time now. It is by no means uncommon to find more than 1000 students at a lecture. Large law faculties are even starting to hire circus tents for foundation lectures, because the university itself has no rooms capable of holding the sheer numbers of students. In Eastern Germany, on the other hand, the 'group university' is everyday practice, that project of educational reform where academic staff and students are supposed to develop a personal working relationship with each other.

This is changing the relative attractiveness of universities. Almost a third of the East German students moved west after unification in order to study at the 'right' establishment, but virtually no western students went East. Today, in contrast, there is a definite interest among the latter in the Eastern German universities on account of their simpler structure. Rostock, Greifswald, Frankfurt/Oder or again Jena are becoming popular choices. Another, less visible aspect is now starting to have an impact. The newly-appointed professors from the west are mostly 'children' of the educational reform and therefore more egalitarian than elitist in orientation. This creates a climate of communication and interaction – not only in the academic sense, but also socially and politically. German problems, German contradictions are being discussed and debated by east and west German students together. The university is turning into a model of social reconciliation and rapprochement – unmistakably a process of silent reform.

Before the fall of the Berlin Wall, Marx's 11th Thesis on Feuerbach – 'The philosophers have only interpreted the world in different ways; the point is to change it' – stood engraved in the foyer of the Humboldt University in Berlin, still a prominent establishment for mass education, although today somewhat elitist. It appears to me – in view of the dramatic changes in Eastern and Central Europe over the past decade, and in Germany as well – that a variation on this thesis that I recently read in a satirical magazine would be more appropriate: 'We have made enough changes to the world. The point now is to interpret it.' The silent practice of the minor universities in eastern Germany comes very close to this demand.

Of course, the right to, and the instruments for, interpretation and analysis should be available to all, not just the intellectual elites. But that would mean opening the universities for anyone who feels an interest and a need to participate in this process of political interpretation. *Intensive cooperation and accessibility* – that would be the real Utopia. Antonio Gramsci expressed it thus:

> For a mass of people to be led to think coherently and in the same coherent fashion about the real present world is a 'philosophical' event far more important and 'original' than the discovery by some philosophical 'genius' of a truth which remains the property of small groups of intellectuals ... it is not a question of introducing from scratch

a scientific form of thought into everyone's individual life, but of renovating and making 'critical' an already existing activity.[13]

It would be an amazing achievement in post-unification Germany if East German universities, in particular, were successful in taking this challenge seriously. This outcome is not at all certain, however. But, if the learning process bears fruit, at least at some universities, then this would provide an impulse for the rest of Europe, over and beyond the German situation – if you like: from the deserted coalfields of the Bitterfeld mining areas to the South Wales Valleys.

NOTES

1. L.Friedeburg, 'Bildung zwischen Aufklärung und Anpassung' in Peter Alheit et al. (eds) *Von der Arbeitsgesellschaft zur Bildungsgesellschaft? Perspektiven von Arbeit und Bildung im Prozeß europäischen Wandels*, University of Bremen Press, Bremen 1994, p50.
2. D. Hoffmann, *Gemeinschaft in der deutschen Erwachsenenbildung. Historische Analyse und Perspektiven für die Praxis*, Frankfurt, Berlin, Bern, New York, Paris, Wien, Peter Lang 1995, pp239ff.
3. P. Alheit, *Zivile Kultur: Verlust und Wiederaneignung der Moderne*, Frankfurt, New York, Campus 1994, p205.
4. P. Alheit, 'Social demobilisation through the German reunification. Challenges to popular adult education' in Peter Alheit *et al* (eds) *European Adult Education, Societal Change and Culture*, Roskilde University Press, Roskilde (in print) 1995.
5. The Socialist Unity Party (SED) was the East German Communist Party, in power prior to unification.
6. Lötsch, 'Intelligenzproblematik in der DDR' in Wolfram Fischer-Rosenthal and Peter Alheit (eds), *Biographien in Deutschland. Soziologische Rekonstruktionen gelebter Gesellschaftsgeschichte*, Opladen: Westdeutscher Verlag 1995, pp177–188.
7. A. Meier, 'Bildungssoziologische Daten zur DDR-Gesellschaft der 1980er Jahre' (unpublished paper, Bremen) 1989.
8. L. Friedeburg, 1994, *op.cit.*, pp51ff.
9. H. Becker, *Weiterbildung. Aufklärung – Praxis – Theorie (1956–1974)*, Stuttgart, Klett 1975, p55.
10. L. Friedeburg, *Bildungsreform in Deutschland: Geschichte und gesellschaftlicher Widerspruch*, Frankfurt/Main: Suhrkamp 1989; Friedeburg, 1994, *op.cit.*
11. M. Vester, *et al*, *Neue soziale Milieus und pluralisierte Klassengesellschaft*, Forschungsbericht, Hannover, University of Hannover (agis) 1992, pp169ff.
12. P. Bourdieu, *La distinction. Critique sociale du jugement*, Editions de Minuit, Paris 1979.
13. A. Gramsci, *Quaderni del carcere*, Edizione critica dell'Istituto Gramsci.

A cura di V. Gerratana (4 Vols), Torino, Einaudi, Vol. 2, Quaderno 11, XVIII, § 12, 1975, pp1378, 1383.

5

THE UNIVERSITY-COMMUNITY INTERFACE IN EUROPE – THE CASE OF 'TRADITIONAL' UNIVERSITIES IN THE NETHERLANDS

Barry J. Hake

The continental European universities, with the exception of the 'new' universities built in the 1960s and 1970s, are not usually located 'on campus'. Their faculties and departments are scattered around the cities and towns to which they sometimes owe their names. This does not necessarily mean, however, that these spatially dispersed universities share intimate relations with local communities and neighbourhoods. Patterns of interaction between universities and surrounding communities have been marked historically both by tensions and constructive relationships. In Leiden, for example, there is an apochryphal story which relates that at the end of the nineteenth century students from the student corps *Minerva* threw heated coins into the streets and watched with great hilarity as the poor attempted to collect these 'pennies from heaven'. On the other hand, students from the same corps, supported by a small number of university professors, were involved during the same period in efforts to develop University Extension and University Settlements for the working class.[1]

This chapter makes the case that the interface between universities and communities is indeed problematic and characterised by fundamental contradictions. These contradictions reflect the variations in the 'relative autonomy' of universities as institutions within the social formation, and their role in the reproduction of social relations. This chapter focuses on the structured social location of the 'traditional universities' and their relationships with the environment. The term 'traditional' refers here to those universities which consciously formulate their core contributions to society as the production of knowledge through research and the dissemination of this knowledge, and the means of its generation, through the teaching of undergraduate and postgraduate students. Their identity as 'traditional universities' is manifested in the so-called Coimbra Group of thirty-four of the oldest European universities. The notion of 'traditional university' has to be understood, furthermore, within the context of the binary systems of higher education in most continental European countries. Rather than seeking to break down the binary divide, current policy discussions actually envisage strengthening the distinction in some countries, such as Austria and the Netherlands. Despite the recent creation of a unitary system of higher education in the United Kingdom, British readers will recognise the very real distinction between the 'traditional universities', as an elite core of research-based universities, and the 'new universities' in the form of the erstwhile polytechnics.

The reflections of this chapter are coloured heavily by my experience at Leiden University which is the oldest university in the Netherlands – it was established in 1575 – and is a leading member of the Coimbra Group. In a recently published document setting out the mission statement for the university in the twenty-first century, the core tasks of research and teaching were reiterated, and the selection of the best students available was emphasised.[2] Although this report has been warmly received, both within and outside the university community, it failed to mention, for example, the contribution of the university to continuing professional education, let alone the needs of non-traditional students.

In the light of this, the chapter will focus on a number of key areas in understanding the articulation between universities and their environments, with particular reference to those institutions referred to here as 'traditional'. These are: i) notions of 'environment', 'community' and 'publics'; ii) the core functions of 'traditional' universities as research and education; iii) the extension of these functions in forms of service to non-university publics; iv) contradictions in the current policy debate in the Netherlands which inhibit the development of a service function to the community and a clear conception of the university as promoting lifelong learning.

ENVIRONMENT, COMMUNITY AND PUBLICS

Ideas about the relationships between universities and their environments are based upon extremely varied, if not contradictory, geo-political, spatial and organisational understandings of that environment.[3] Substitution of the term 'community' for 'environment' only serves to illustrate their ambiguities and heterogeneous character: does it refer to the immediate geographical area of the university in the sense of the 'local community', or is it the broader regional or national area? In the recruitment of students, for example, the university may simultaneously see itself as serving the needs of the local community with regard to part-time students while at the same time recruiting full-time students at a national level. In attracting foreign students, universities may operate at the European or world level. As to their research function, they may undertake research in conjunction with nearby firms, for local government authorities, or national governments, while researchers may regard themselves as part of the world community of scholars. 'Community' is above all characterised by a lack of precision and determined by the specific contexts in which it is used. This chapter regards the 'community' as a distinct set of 'publics' which are addressed by and which may address the university as an institution. These may be unorganised 'publics of individuals' or they may be organised 'collective publics'.

It is possible to distinguish at least seven broad understandings of potential 'publics'. First, universities often understand the public in terms of the potential or actual individuals involved in existing or new activities. As regards the teaching task of universities, this has traditionally been understood in terms of students enrolled in undergraduate or postgraduate programmes. Second, an increasingly distinctive public comprises the part-time, mature student and those catered for by the continuing professional education provision of universities. A third understanding of the public refers to adults who enrol on short courses of liberal adult education provided by the universities. Fourth, an important 'proto-public' is constituted by 'non-traditional' categories of students and the promotion of the wider access for these groups.

In contrast with the focus on the 'individual publics' of the university associated with the first four categories, it is also possible to distinguish three broad categories of organised 'collective publics' whose interests may be served by the university. These include, fifth, professional organisations with an interest in the provision of continuing professional development for their members, but also organised groups, voluntary associations and social movements in civil society. Sixth, a further connotation of the term 'public' – and one frequent in current usage – is that of the firms and employers comprising the so-called 'business community'. Last, there are the 'representational publics', whether they are elected or not, in the form of local, regional and national governments, advisory bodies and research councils, and increasingly the international (including the European) level. The following analysis traces some of the emergent patterns in the interaction of the traditional university with this broad range of potential individual and collective publics.

RESEARCH AND UNDERGRADUATE TEACHING AS CORE FUNCTIONS OF 'TRADITIONAL' UNIVERSITIES

Research

University-based research is currently subjected to growing societal pressures. The key role of the university as the producer of scientific knowledge is challenged by the tendency to locate research in para-university, semi-public and indeed private research organisations outside the university sector. Sometimes, as increasingly in the United Kingdom, semi-private and private research organisations compete with universities for public research funds. There are changing public priorities with regard to the balance between fundamental and applied research, as manifested in the decline in resources available in universities for fundamental research and the growing role of government agencies and the business sector as sources of university research funding. Consequent disquiet within universities is focused on the threat to traditional autonomy this represents.

These developments vary significantly from country to country, and reflect the nature of the unitary or binary systems of higher education in place. In Germany, the Netherlands and the Scandinavian countries, all with established binary systems, the universities have been able to maintain a relatively strong position, and their autonomy, with regard to the share of public funding for research and the encouragement of fundamental research. In these countries, the polytechnics are not regarded as research institutions as such but as professional training schools. The Netherlands, for example, where there is still a very strictly observed binary divide, has a distinctive tripartite system channelling research funding, and this specifically excludes the polytechnics. In this tripartite system, public research funds form an important part, in the first place, of the block grant allocated by central government to the universities which they re-distribute according to their own priorities. Second, national research councils allocate funding for fundamental research on the basis of open competition. Success in securing such funding is regarded as the *sine qua non* of the 'good researcher'. Both of these sources of funding are subjected to an external research quality audit. Third, research funding is also secured from other sources, such as government departments, business and trade unions and the like, for applied and policy-related research. This form of applied research is excluded from the external quality audit and the reports produced thereby are not even included in the measures of research output based on publications.

The emphasis of this system on fundamental research as 'real' science raises the question of the university's relationship to 'public service research' addressing the interests of specific publics outside the university. Many of the traditional universities do not include this in their mission statements, and it is not always recognised in relevant legislation nor as a distinct funding category. How is their research articulated with the disparate publics in the outside world? At the level of the university, a number of main forms of articulation can be identified as described below. Applied research tends to be institutionalised in para-university institutions which are effectively cut off from mainstream funding channels for fundamental research. These institutions are financed through contract research and employ researchers short term. Their major contractors are public agencies, such as central government departments, regional and local governments, health and care institutions, transport and housing agencies. The dissemination and application of their work are largely determined by political decision-making processes which are in turn influenced by the intricate interplay of political bodies, interest and pressure groups. Applied research also articulates with organised interest groups in society, private industry and the business world as increasingly significant publics. In addition to their direct research for industry and business, universities have increasingly moved in the direction of creating institutionalised 'transfer points' in order to establish structural forms of communication between university-based research and its potential users. The creation of Science Parks is the shining example of the 'high-tech' version of this particular structuring of the relationships of the university with its environment. In addition, there is the public service function based on the transfer of research findings, primarily through the servicing of large national or international concerns which operate in global markets. These are not directly associated with regional or local interests except via the creation of local employment opportunities. There is a problem in the lack of transfer of knowledge to small and medium-sized firms which traditionally have neither close links to universities nor manifest a research base in their production processes.

A highly problematic dimension of the public service aspect of university-based research is its relationship with potential publics other than organised interest groups such as public authorities or businesses. One understanding by universities of this relationship is their focus on the 'general public'. This can manifest itself in efforts to educate this public at the local level to an appreciation of science by way of organising Science Fairs and open days. More problematic, however, is the endeavour of placing the research capacities of universities at the disposal of disparate and less organised publics. Even in those universities with a strong social democratic identity, particularly in the Scandinavian countries which have traditionally established strong links with organised labour and the trade unions, there is still the extension of public service research to other informally organised publics to consider. These publics include the myriad of voluntary associations in civil society which voice the interests of 'community' groups, such as tenants' and neighbourhood associations, womens' groups, environmental activists, ethnic minorities, workers and the unemployed. These often do not have a tradition of making use of the resources of universities and do not know very well how to secure access to them.

During the late 1960s and early 1970s, student activists in a number of European countries were instrumental in developing alternative forms of the transfer function which sought to place research-based knowledge at the disposal of these publics. In the Netherlands, for example, 'Science Shops' were established to mediate between the practical concerns of 'ordinary people' and research support from the universities. At first organised in socially relevant projects by small groups of students, these has since been institutionalised in most Dutch universities as 'University Science Shops'. They are financed by a combination of core funding from the central university for a small, permanent staff of mediators, the salaries of researchers on the university staff, and, increasingly, contract research. Individuals and groups are encouraged to contact the Science Shop with their specific problems. Mediators then contact researchers in the departments who may be interested and prepared to take on the research involved. Two recent cases of such public service research at Leiden University have involved, on the one hand, a local environmental group who were concerned with the environmental pollution caused by the laboratories of the science departments of the university itself; on the other, the Medical Faculty, on behalf of the Federation of Dutch Trade Unions, has investigated the effects upon workers of chemicals used in the bulb-growing region close to Leiden. The latter example illustrates the potential influence of public service research in that it eventually led to legislation on protective clothing and set limits on the chemicals permitted. Science Shops occupy, however, a very marginal position within the overall research activities undertaken at Dutch universities.

The dependence of Science Shops on interested members of university staff, often together with their students, raises the issue of the role of the individual researcher in developing a public service dimension in research. Often informed by ideological commitments to specific social groups and ideas about the social responsibility of science, some individuals have always been involved in a measure of public service research. It was the tradition at Dutch universities until recently, for example, that members of staff were expected to devote their time to research, teaching, and public service activities, and they were indeed assessed, however marginally, on this basis. Given the current pressures exerted by external audits of research and teaching, the major emphasis is now placed on the research performance of academics, with teaching well back in second place, while public service activities have disappeared from the assessment agenda. In a recent international comparative report, Dutch academics were notable for the high relative priority they allocated to the research component of their tasks compared with the teaching and public service components.

In the traditional university, the relationships between university-based research and diverse publics in most continental European countries are still predominantly focused upon, on the one hand, fundamental research and the maintenance of university autonomy, and, on the other, the growth of applied research for highly specific organised publics such as official and quasi-governmental authorities and the business world. In the Netherlands specifically, the recent long-term policy statement by Leiden University paid significant attention to research and teaching as the core functions of the university while failing to mention the public service task. The traditional universities in the Netherlands appear to be well on the road towards the emphasis on 'excellence' and 'quality' in fundamental research, the point of reference for these activities being the international research community. Despite public debate about the need for the 'entrepreneurial university' in the late 1980s, Dutch universities are still more dependent upon public funding of their research than those in almost any other European country.

Undergraduate teaching

Traditional universities are also confronted with the issue of the publics to which their teaching is directed. As regards the teaching of undergraduates, a major question is whether the universities will continue to address their traditional public of school-leavers, or whether they will extend their teaching at this level to other publics. European universities must confront the issue of making provision for the 'traditional' and 'non-traditional' student, including in the latter primarily the mature student whether in full-time and part-time study.

By way of comparison, more than half the students registered at British universities in 1994-95 can now be classified as non-traditional or mature students. Such comparisons nevertheless illustrate how complex and diverse is the situation for there are wide variations in the length of university study and the average age of graduation. While British students usually study for three or four years and graduate in their early twenties, students in other countries take a much longer period and hence graduate in their late twenties. Furthermore, most other countries do not have a system of selection to university study, with entry instead open to all who secure the appropriate secondary school diploma. Continental European universities have historically admitted a larger percentage of the age group to university study than the UK, although the drop-out rate is significantly higher as well. In the Netherlands, for example, half the students who enter university fail to graduate.

Nonetheless, the student population at Continental European universities is still dominated by the traditional secondary-school leaver in full-time study, rather than the non-traditional, mature, part-time student. Expansion of student numbers at universities in most European countries in the past decade has not significantly changed this. Growth in numbers has largely involved the enrolment of an increasing number of young women school-leavers. And, in binary systems of higher education there has been no significant change in the social class composition of the student population at universities, despite the expansion. Working-class youngsters still tend to choose to follow a course of professional training at the polytechnics. Coping with the large traditional student population entering the universities is now widely regarded as the major policy issue for this sector in most countries, rather than the encouragement of access of non-traditional students.

Continental European universities tend thus to attract a relatively small percentage of part-time mature students. Indeed, legislation in those systems commonly still does not recognise the part-time student as a distinct category and no special provision is made for them, such as teaching in the evenings or on Saturdays. In the Netherlands, the formal recognition of part-time study for a university degree was only introduced in the early 1980s. Although the number of students registered in this mode of attendance increased 300 per cent by the early 1990s, still less than 2 per cent of all students at Dutch universities are part-timers. Current policy measures in the Netherlands even threaten to increase the barriers for mature part-time enrolment. While a little under a third of part-time students in Dutch universities already possess a professional qualification gained at a polytechnic, these measures are intended to prevent polytechnic graduates from subsequently enrolling for a university degree course with the support of public funding. Should they do so, they will receive no mandatory grant support, and, given the absence of discretionary grants, they will have to pay much higher fees – as much as 300 per cent more – than those of regular full-time students. This goes in the face of all the evidence that following up a polytechnic education with a university course is the main route through which working-class students gain access to a university qualification. These policy measures are already exerting this form of negative influence, and not only on those university departments which have made provision for part-time, mature students. They obviously restrict the educational opportunities available for non-traditional students, in particular specific publics such as returning women.

Possession of the appropriate secondary-school diploma continues to dominate entry to university degree courses in most continental European countries. This effectively operates to prevent any significant changes in the composition of the student population and the extension of university study to non-traditional publics. Potential students without the appropriate diplomas may sometimes qualify for university entrance by taking an alternative examination, but the numbers opting for this route are small. In most European countries, access courses leading to university entrance for poorly qualified candidates remain only a very hesitant development. As University of Dundee research uncovered during a recent comparative study of access strategies, Dutch civil servants and university officials had great difficulty in even comprehending the concept of 'access courses' for unqualified students in relation to university entrance. Such rigidity of thinking is also manifested in social benefit regulations, which permit the unemployed and single mothers to follow 'appropriate' vocational training courses with maintenance of benefits, but which actively prevent them from enrolling in higher education courses even when they are suitably qualified. Extension of university study to the less qualified adult population is also prevented by the failure in many countries to move towards the recognition of the principle of, let alone the development of national systems for, the accreditation of prior learning in general, with reference to university entrance in particular.

CONTINUING EDUCATION AND THE 'TRADITIONAL' UNIVERSITY

Despite their limited numbers among the student populations at traditional universities in most countries, part-time mature students tend to use university degree courses to contribute to their continuing professional education and career development. This contribution of undergraduate degree courses to the continuing education of professionals goes largely unrecognised. This is because there is still a very clear distinction drawn between the university-trained professions and those trained at polytechnics. From the viewpoint of the traditional universities, the latter are widely regarded disparagingly as merely 'para-professionals' for whom their type of institution carries no responsibility. Traditional universities thus make no provision as such for the continuing education of professional groups such as nurses and nurse educators, midwives, architects, librarians, social workers, primary school teachers, adult educators and community workers. Insofar as they do provide continuing professional education, this is largely restricted to the needs of those professions that demand a university education as a criterion of entry – doctors and medical specialists, the legal profession, engineers, natural scientists, and, to a limited extent, university-trained secondary school teachers. These are characterised by strong professional associations, both national and international, which establish the entry criteria and the requirements for continuing professional education. In most countries, the organisation and provision of continuing education for these professions is managed by the relevant faculties and is not necessarily organised across the university by a central unit for continuing professional education. A significant exception can be found in those countries where there is a formal distinction between the 'traditional' and the 'technological' universities. The latter are notable precisely in the degree to which they do give priority to the continuing education needs of their graduates and organise provision through a central unit across the institution. This finds expression, for example, in the work of the European University Continuing Education Network (EUCEN), which is dominated by those universities providing continuing education for these professional groups.

Continental European universities, furthermore, do not share the role taken by many in Anglo-Saxon systems in making provision for the educational needs of adults who are not registered as students on degree courses. Despite the well-documented interest in many European countries in University Extension at the turn of the last century, most universities in these countries did not develop the provision of liberal adult education traditionally associated with the British universities as 'responsible bodies'.[4] This form of provision was largely rejected as the 'popularisation of science' and hence not a legitimate task of the traditional university. Provision of liberal adult education was developed by the quite distinct 'popular universities' in the form of the *Volksuniversiteit*, *Folkeuniversitet* and *Volkshochschule*, and they have no formal relationships with the universities.

There are indications, however, that the traditional universities are now hesitantly recognising the demand for continuing professional education and university-level educational provision among non-traditional student groups. Although they have yet to take on 'lifelong learning' as a core task, they are beginning to embrace new areas of activity. The Coimbra Group, for example, recently decided to investigate the provision of continuing education by the traditional universities. In the Netherlands, for example, there has been a growing trend in recent years to enable adults to enrol as *à la carte* students on courses that are part of the normal educational programmes offered to undergraduates. Marketing is in general based upon appeals, on the one hand, to the contribution these programmes make to professional development, and, on the other, to the general needs and interest of adults for liberal adult education. As such, they can scarcely be described as the initiation of new provision for adults, let alone for radically new publics. A yet further significant development is the discovery of 'older learners', somewhat belatedly, as a potential category of consumers for university provision. The emergence of another public has become manifest in the growing number of special courses for older learners at the traditional universities in the Netherlands ('Higher Education for Older Adults'), while a private university for older adults has been recently announced in the province of Baden-Württemburg in Germany. It must be recognised that these are often the hobby activities of retired professors and remain marginal to the core tasks of the traditional university.

CONCLUSIONS

Despite the rhetoric of the European Union's *Memorandum on Higher Education*, that report was accurate in its reference to the lack of involvement and commitment on the part of universities to the development of continuing education and for their need massively to expand their provision to meet the needs of adult learners on a broad front. As the EU memorandum rightly observes, there is considerable variation in the measure to which the institutions of higher education currently exercise these responsibilities. Since the challenging and far-reaching OECD report in 1982, little has fundamentally changed in the position of the traditional universities with regard to their social responsibilities for non-traditional publics.[5] Indeed, there are indications in a number of European countries that they are now looking inwards to their core functions of research and teaching, in response to the emergence of mass systems of higher education. This is above all determined by their efforts to cope with the influx of large numbers of young adults, mostly middle-class, who have come to regard university study as one of the 'rites of passage' into adulthood, and who increasingly regard the university diploma as one of the only ways of securing a place in increasingly uncertain labour markets. In line with this, traditional universities become more not less concerned with restricting access, and they interpret the issue of quality as the restoration of the academic identity of the university within binary systems of higher education. The maintenance of the university as an 'academic community' predominates in current policy debates to the exclusion of other conceptions of the university-community interface.

This has become manifest in a number of recent reports contributing to the current debate about the future of the university in Dutch society. They all concentrate on the maintenance of the binary system, the restructuring of the initial degree course to maintain academic standards, and the limitation of access. The Association of Dutch Universities is likely imminently to publish a policy document re-iterating the perpetuation of the present standard formula for university study, i.e. a full-time, four-year initial degree course! Coupled with recent measures to reduce considerably the level of student grants, the introduction of loans in place of grants for all students, and the doubling of student fees, the prospects are poor for even that small percentage of Dutch university students who do come from working-class backgrounds. These, together with the growing restrictions upon part-time mature students, mean that the public served by Dutch universities will increasingly be limited to its traditional one of middle-class school-leavers. Despite these retrograde trends, however, the critical question cannot be ducked: 'How long will the Humboldt-like "traditional university" continue to survive in these post-Fordist and post-modern times?'[6]

NOTES

1. X. de Vroom, 'Adaptation of an Educational Innovation: the introduction of university extension into the Netherlands, 1890–1920', in B.J. Hake and S. Marriot (eds), *Adult Education between Cultures: Encounters and identities in European adult education since 1890*, Leeds Studies in Continuing Education, Leeds 1992.
2. *Keorsen op kwaliteit [En route to Quality]*, Leiden University, Leiden 1995.
3. OECD/CERI, *The University and the Community: The Problems of Changing Relationships*, OECD, Paris 1982.
4. T. Steele, 'A Science of Democracy: an outline of the development of

university extension in Europe, 1890–1920', in B.J. Hake and S. Marriot (eds), *op.cit.*
5. J. Field, 'Transformation and Renewal in Continuing Higher Education in Europe', *International Journal of University Higher Education*, XXXII, 2, 1993.
6. OECD/CERI, *op.cit.*

6

KNOWLEDGE, INNOVATION, AND TECHNOLOGY TRANSFER: UNIVERSITIES AND THEIR INDUSTRIAL COMMUNITY

Hans G. Schuetze

The relationship of higher education institutions to their society and the economy is a matter of permanent and intense discussion. The shift from 'elite' to 'mass' higher education has led to a re-thinking of the functions of higher education, the boundaries between traditional universities and other post-secondary institutions, and the internal working – the 'private life' – of higher education.[1] The focus of this chapter is the relationship of universities with a special type of community-industry. 'Technology transfer' is the term commonly used to describe this relationship and in particular the activities by which university research is used and applied for commercial use.

Universities are frequently characterised as fulfilling three major functions, all of which contribute to the advancement, application and dissemination of knowledge. The primary, and oldest, function is the education of students, providing both the foundations of culture and civilisation, and the preparation for professional life and leadership roles through advanced forms of education. It has traditionally been aimed at the young and the bright; only more recently has the education of adults come to be regarded as more than a marginal university activity.[2]

The second function, research, has emerged more recently and only gradually came to be seen as a major university activity. So accepted is it now, however, that it is almost heretical within the contemporary university in many countries to separate teaching from research.[3] Yet, at the same time, much of the original research function is now located, depending on the system, in specialised non-university research institutions (research societies, government laboratories), while a significant part of higher education is now provided in non-university institutions whose emphasis, at least when they were set up, has been specifically on teaching (community colleges, polytechnics, *Fachhochschulen*, *Instituts Universitaires Technologiques* (IUTs), etc.). The latter were created or expanded largely in the 1960s and 1970s to meet the dramatic increase in demand for higher education.

The third activity, traditionally less developed in Europe than in North America, is service to the community, both local and universal. Such service functions have covered a broad spectrum of activities, from technical assistance to various community groups on issues of organisational and social development, to co-operation with the health sector for the improvement of hospital care and other forms of community health care, through to, more generally, a range of activities concerning cultural and intellectual enrichment. Assistance in scientific and technical matters to industry – technology transfer – has become a recognised function of individual university researchers and university-based research institutes as a whole.

As the term 'technology transfer' suggests, it is usually seen as a process that is both technical and commercial. In its narrow interpretation, it describes a process whereby a piece of technology or of technological know-how produced in a university department/laboratory is passed on 'downstream' from the generator to a receptor/user. Thus, it is typically defined to involve 'the transfer from one organisation to another of any artefact or knowledge relating to a product or potential product and its manufacture. The transfer is a commercial transaction in which one party buys the right to use intellectual property held by another'.[4]

This chapter regards this process as more complex than do the above formulations. In particular, the view is challenged that 'the transfer of an artefact of knowledge' properly describes the process by which universities contribute to technical change, industrial innovation and economic development. The creation of new knowledge that is relevant for industrial application does not take place in isolation in university laboratories, but is closely linked to its design, application and commercialisation by multiple loops of feedback, involving many parties and multiple stages of learning and development.

TECHNOLOGY TRANSFER AND INNOVATION

University/industry co-operation can be regarded as a longstanding as well as ongoing interaction; historical examples include the close involvement of university departments and professors in the dramatic rise of the German chemical and pharmaceutical industries in the nineteenth century, and, at about the same time, the American Land Grant university which had the explicit mission of assisting the agricultural sector through R&D and other technical assistance, as well as training a specialised workforce. However important these early models of university/industry relationship, such co-operation was considered almost taboo in universities in the 1960s and 1970s. This was in part a result of the student unrest and criticism of old-style universities and their autocratic structures, in part it arose from a more critical, if not hostile, appraisal of the role of the sciences and technology as a whole.[5] Yet, only ten years later, attitudes had changed dramatically. Not only had universities started actively to engage in industry liaison and co-operation activities but governments came increasingly to see this as an important basis for economic development and international competitiveness, and sought to support it in diverse ways.

Thus in the 1980s, 'technology transfer' came into fashion. After the earlier broad-brush promises of 'human capital theory' – economics of education rationales at the core of much of the expansion of higher education in the 1960s and 1970s – the potential of technology transfer from university labs to industry application gave rise to new expectations about the economic impact of higher education. Many universities as well as other R&D institutions set up transfer or industry liaison offices (ILOs); science and research parks flourished as incubators for spin-off companies built on ideas by university professors or graduate students. Enthusiasm about the potential for the economic application of a wealth of untapped knowledge available from university laboratories and professors sprang from the insight that the key economic forces were now based on knowledge and information rather than, as in the past, natural resources and the availability of transportation.

A new literature grew. Mostly descriptive rather than analytical, it concentrated on successful examples where proximity and collaboration of universities and 'high-tech' companies, many of them spin-offs by university researchers or graduates, had led to clusters of knowledge-based firms, generating new know-how and further spin-offs. Knowledge and learning, co-operation and networking between firms and institutions, developing applications and applying knowledge in innovative ways, came to be seen as the ingredients of economic success. Route 128 around Boston and Cambridge, Silicon Valley south of San Francisco, the Cambridge Science Park in the United Kingdom were much-heralded examples of such co-operation and regional economic development that were driven by close university/industry linkages.[6] 'Growing the next Silicon Valley' became the objective – or the obsession – of both regional planners and university presidents.[7]

By the 1990s, much of the initial enthusiasm has given way to more realistic assessments of the potential of technology transfer and the conditions under which it can be realised. 'Technology transfer' refers to various forms of transfer mechanisms and activities, including consulting, research or science parks, other incubator facilities, contract research and development, transfer offices, special institutes outside of, but associated with, universities, industry liaison offices (ILO), regular liaison programmes, and many others.[8] Too many of these, set up in the original wave of enthusiasm, have not produced the expected results.

Given the waves of appraisal and opinion, it is timely now to evaluate technology transfer critically and from a broad perspective. This can be done by focusing on three aspects of the relationships: first, the process of industrial innovation in which university/industry co-operation plays only one, albeit potentially important, part; second, there is the university side of the relationship, looking here at the larger picture, not only at specific technology transfer arrangements; third, there is the industry side of the relationship. A major concern for policy makers in the latter case are the links, mostly under-developed, with small and medium-sized enterprises (SMEs), which occupy an increasingly important place on both policy and research agendas.[9]

MODELS OF INDUSTRIAL INNOVATION

Technology transfer is part of a larger system of science and technology and of innovation more generally. Models of such systems, explicit or implicit, describe how the pieces of the system fit together and interact with each other. These models change over time, whether because of emergent new insights, or changes in dominant perspectives, or in response to the contextual changes in the world the models address. Each of these factors has influenced the conceptualisation of industrial innovation, and its role in economic growth and the creation of jobs and income.

The conceptualisation of innovation in the 1960s, 1970s and early 1980s was largely based on a linear model. Broadly, basic research was taken as the initial phase of all innovative activity, leading in linear fashion to applied research, then to experimental development. This, in turn, forms the base for innovative activities in firms, leading eventually to innovative products or processes of production, and their commercialisation. Although there was some recognition at the time that these stages were not entirely independent and sequential, innovation was seen primarily as a uni-directional process; the linear approach focused attention on each stage in relative isolation from the others.

The linear model came in three variants: 'science and technology push', 'technology pull', and 'market pull'. They differ by the 'players' regarded as the moving force in innovation – the scientist, engineer, or the marketing analyst (representing the consumer). These differences notwithstanding, the three variants shared the idea that knowledge is discovered in research institutions (universities, government laboratories, some large private-sector laboratories), and passed on to firms by various transfer mechanisms before appearing in the market as new or improved products and services.[10]

Over the years, the shortcomings of this model of the innovation process became increasingly apparent. One lies in the separation of the process of innovation into a system of distinct activities, beginning with a single source of knowledge creation. Another is the assumption of a single direction of development. In all, scientists, engineers, designers, marketing analysts and consumers were regarded as playing on different, largely unconnected fields. This is now widely recognised as inadequate to reflect the complex, multi-dimensional nature of innovation. This recognition derives in part from changes in the ways businesses organise themselves in an increasingly competitive and rapidly-changing world. The traditional view of separate stages between discovery or invention, innovation and diffusion becomes blurred, with multiple feed-back loops representing co-operation among scientists, engineers, designers, marketing personnel and consumers.

The complex nature of R&D activities and the interdependent and multi-directional flow of knowledge are more accurately described by chain-linked models of innovation. Such interactive models emphasise the central role of design, the feedback effects between the 'downstream' and the 'upstream' phases of the earlier linear model, and the numerous interactions between science, technology, and the process of innovation in any phase of the process.[11] Five main characteristics of technical change and innovation stand out.[12]

- A system approach emphasises the importance of multi-directional linkages, a well-developed communications infrastructure, and transfer mechanisms to facilitate networking – the circulation of information and the sharing of knowledge among the various actors and institutions involved.

- Innovation is seen as a series of cumulative, self-reinforcing processes towards the gradual development of areas of technological expertise among individuals, firms, regional clusters of firms, and public institutions.

- There is a central role played by knowledge and learning. Technical change and innovation are dependent on the capacity *inter alia* of individuals, private firms and public research organisations to accumulate knowledge, know-how and skills through learning from codified sources of information, direct experience, or from others.

- There is a unique development pattern for each innovation, reflecting a particular set of historical, geographical, industrial and other factors; communication and transfer mechanisms, support programmes and institutions should thus distinguish between the needs related to specific technologies, and more generic needs related to a wide variety of technologies.

- A systems approach emphasises the systemic nature and interdependency of technical change: activities in one area can affect a wide range of activities in other, even seemingly unrelated, areas.

The 'linear model' also fails to grasp another dimension that has since come to be seen as equally as important as research and development – the social dimension. This covers the social, organisational, institutional and financial factors that are prerequisites for successful innovation. Technological change is above all a social process, and can only really be understood as the interdependence of technical, economic and social activities. Neither the technical nor the economic potential of new technologies can be fully realised without concomitant, even anticipatory, social and institutional changes throughout society.

From this understanding of innovation, has developed the concept of national systems of innovation. This no longer places the sole or primary emphasis on the generation of knowledge; instead there is proper recognition of its development, application, transformation and distribution:

> The rate of technical change in any country and the effectiveness of companies in world competition ... does not depend simply on the scaleof their research and development, [it] depends on the way in which the available resources are managed and organised, both at the enterprise and the national level. The national system of innovation may enable a county with limited resources ... to make very rapid progress through an appropriate combination of important technology and local adaptation and developments.[13]

Thus, innovation in a knowledge-based economy crucially depends on industrial clusters, knowledge networks, mechanisms for efficient knowledge and technology transfer, a techno-infrastructure consisting of various public and private institutions and agents, adequate financial institutions, mechanisms for financing innovations, public policies that support innovations by providing an innovation-friendly climate, and well-educated people. Universities can play a key role in all of these, but not primarily through technology transfer:

> It is certainly true that the contemporary major research universities are distinguished by a great emphasis on science, and increasingly on technology as well. But ... they remain primarily teaching institutions, and their chief role is to develop and train human talent. The vital link between ... universities and the advancement of science and technology ... therefore can be discovered mainly in the pool of talent which the universities both harbour and produce.[14]

This from the long-time president of the Johns Hopkins University, one of the leading research universities in the United States.

THE UNIVERSITY PERSPECTIVE

Thus, universities represent an important part of innovation systems, as contributors to a complex, multi-layered process. Recognition of the collective nature of this process has important implications for the organisation of technology transfer; the forms this has taken in universities have been mentioned already. There is no 'one-best' formula or universal model. It follows from the nature of universities as 'loosely coupled systems' that central offices or units are only partially effective in the process of establishing linkages and harnessing concrete collaboration with industry. More centrally, individual departments, institutes and laboratories will be at the centre of the co-operative arrangements with private enterprises while central offices more appropriately concentrate on such tasks as finding suitable partners, managing the legal side, filing patent applications, commercialising and marketing patents and other know-how, and the like.

Despite the considerable organisational efforts that have been undertaken by universities in the last decade for better realising their potential for assistance with innovation in the private sector, it is questionable whether these have realised the potential that exists in universities. Three of the most significant sets of factors behind this under-achievement are discussed in the rest of this section.

The prevalence of the linear model

In spite of the advances in the understanding of the process of innovation, universities continue largely to adhere to the linear view. This reflects attitudes and a self-image which follow from a particular conception of the nature of knowledge, namely:

> ... [the] notion that there exists a set of theories and principles – some known, some waiting to be discovered – that can be applied rigorously to well-defined problems and lead to correct solutions. Application, in this conceptual framework, is no more than the act of putting theory to use and, therefore, not in and of itself a potential source of new knowledge. Hence the flow of knowledge is linear and uni-directional, from the locus of research to the place of application, from scholar to practitioner, teacher to student, expert to client.[15]

This view of knowledge as a 'quasi-static commodity' underpins the 'technology push' model, for which such mechanisms as transfer offices and incubator centres are identified as appropriate to hand over (or 'down') the knowledge (or technology) to 'receptors' to put to commercial use.[16] The metaphor of a river is here an apt one, with a 'source' of knowledge and 'downstream' activities, from the mountain of pure theory down to the muddy seas of practice.

If instead knowledge is seen as dynamic, complex, multi-faceted, and context-specific, requiring multiple interaction and constant feedback, then the nature of the university contribution changes substantially. For one thing, universities as institutions and, more importantly, their 'understructure', (laboratories, departments and individual researchers) must more actively interact with practitioners.[17] Enterprises are thus not 'receptors' being offered ready solutions – although that might occasionally happen as when licenses are taken out for patents, copyrights, or trademarks held by a university or an individual researcher. Instead, enterprises become an active part of, and partner in, the entire process, involved both in the definition of the problems addressed and in the process of research and development towards their solution. This type of active involvement is difficult for most academic researchers even to accept, let alone to implement in a university setting. They mostly have little experience of the 'messy' world of practice – customers, competitors, banks, deadlines and 'bottom lines' – and how all these shape needs and priorities. Problems are rarely either neatly defined or embraced within the narrow specialisation of an institute, department or individual academic.

If collaborative research and development are no longer seen as one-shot events but rather as a continuum, other consequences follow for universities. Rather than waiting for firms to contact the transfer office, the department or the individual researcher, universities must be in regular contact with those firms, industrial associations and other mediating organisations to learn about problems, and how they might contribute to their solution. They must become part of networks where information and knowledge flows in a permanent and systematic fashion. Nor should such networks be confined to individual universities and firms, but should include other institutions in the same region or field, such as other universities or institutes, government laboratories, community colleges, regional economic planners. They should include others who perform R&D, provide education and other learning opportunities, or information, or contribute in other ways to the innovation of firms. Recognition by universities that they must engage in such activities has in general been forthcoming very slowly in comparison with other, more practice-oriented institutions such as polytechnics, technical colleges, or *Fachhochschulen*.

A final example concerns academic reward systems, which offer little recognition or incentive for faculty activities other than research. In most traditional universities (technical or polytechnic universities provide contrary examples), published and peer-reviewed basic research are still the principal, if not the sole, qualification for hiring, promotion and tenure.[18] They remain the most valued element of institutional prestige, translating in turn into research grants, faculty salaries, equipment, support and working conditions. True scholarship, on this view, is reserved primarily for acts of scientific discovery, with other academic pursuits as derivations from this.[19] If co-operative, transfer and outreach activities are to be increased, they must become more than second rank and marginal, and to this end, esteem and rewards must be accorded to dissemination and application activities. To realise this will involve the reform of deeply ingrained value systems and perceived hierarchies based on a traditional understanding of scholarship. Yet, it can be done; there are other successful, application-oriented models of universities, such as the American Land Grant institutions, or the German *Technische Hochschulen*.

The lack of multi-disciplinarity

At present, many universities engage in management research and organise courses in technology management; philosophy faculties may address ethical topics relating to new scientific developments and the impact of new technologies; labour market economists, sociologists and industrial psychologists explore different aspects of their impact. On the whole, however, the humanities and social sciences are not involved in concrete research projects conducted by departments of science and engineering for, and in collaboration with, industry. At one level, this seems simply to support C.P. Snow's still contentious observation of the polarisation between the 'two cultures' of the sciences and the humanities; it is more directly the expression of the essentially fragmented nature of the university.[20]

> A university is not a coherent institution, nor – in spite of all the rhetoric to the contrary – a community of scholars. It is ... a collection of

substantially autonomous individuals, loosely organised into departments or equivalent units – themselves often fragmented ... Although
Clark Kerr's dictum about parking problems and salary being the only
issues of interest shared by all faculty may be something of an
exaggeration, it is rare to find in an university any substantial level of
discourse about collective purposes.[21]

Universities might seem, through bringing together a wide range of
disciplines under the same organisational roof, the most appropriate, if
not the only, societal institution to offer a genuinely multi-disciplinary
perspective; in reality such multi-disciplinarity is rarely discussed and
achieved. Departmental structures and disciplinary orientations
prevent universities from expanding into applied areas in response to
social demands for new interdisciplinary areas of knowledge.[22] Nor
are their structures conducive to the co-ordination of activities
conducted by the various departments, such as continuing education,
health care services, or field research activities. To be sure, universities
have started to set up interdisciplinary programmes and centres, and
these are indeed valuable components in the recent development of
academic research.[23] Yet, they remain, like interdisciplinarity on the
whole, exceptions to the rule. The rule continues to be the
'fragmentation of the academic community into discrete disciplinary
sub-cultures' and their corresponding impact of 'reducing the internal
sense of community across academic fields'.[24] This clearly militates
against university institutions becoming 'common enterprises'.[25] Clark
has shown how attempts by universities and state administrators alike
to link together the fragmentary disciplines and sectors in order better
to accommodate the demands by consumer groups, industry and
professional groups, are frustrated 'by the logics of discipline, expertise,
and professionalised disorder'.[26]

Knowledge and learning

'Technology transfer' is often, as seen, narrowly defined as commercial
transactions through the transfer of artefacts of knowledge embodied
in patents, trade marks, copyrights, prototypes, research reports, and
other tangible products of university R&D. As such, it is distinct from,
and regarded as unrelated to, other university activities, especially
teaching and learning. There is nevertheless some recognition that the
process 'demands some form of technology software, information or

knowledge which is disembodied from the physical artefact. Disembodied technology transfer is associated with ... information through the media of documents ... discussion seminars, technical training and education.'[27]

'Disembodied technology transfer' is actually fundamental to the process of innovation, not a marginal annex to other core activity. Learning and communication are critical elements in the process of matching different kinds of technological and business cultures and in innovation generally. Learning occurs in many ways, as adult educators *par excellence* know. Experimentation and learning from enterprise experiences, while not highly codified and systematic perhaps, are just as important for mastering technical and organisational change as more formal ways of learning.[28] Neither is the learning limited to firms themselves. Networks among different 'actors' in overall innovation systems are a means of communicating knowledge not just information. 'Learning by interacting' is thus a pivotal way by which people learn – customers from clients, smaller sub-contractor firms from larger ones, users from producers, competing firms from each other'.[29]

Yet, there is a need for organised, systematic learning as well. Continuing education departments, for example, and, increasingly, mainstream faculties are offering professional education, and courses for graduates or practitioners from other fields.[30] The general theme of university continuing professional education is complex and beyond the focus of this chapter. Two points are, however, relevant here. First, is an organisational matter: in most universities, technology transfer and continuing education are the responsibility of different units which have little connection with each other. This makes coherent, systematic programming, let alone anything customer-tailored, difficult or impossible. Industrial participants must themselves look for courses or programmes appropriate to their particular situation. Second, there is a pedagogical issue related to the earlier discussion of the university's hierarchy of functions. Experienced participants in continuing education programmes sometimes complain about the lack of relevance of the course content to their professional background/expertise and to their particular learning needs. Like complaints from employers about lack of preparation even of graduates from engineering or management schools, this results in part from the teaching being excessively theory-led as a derivative of research, and in part from the lack of real-life contact and experience of many of the professoriate.[31]

TECHNOLOGY TRANSFER AND THE SMALL FIRM

Innovation, with knowledge and learning at its core, depends on the capacity of individual 'actors' to accumulate and use knowledge through different forms of learning. Larger firms normally can analyse their information and knowledge needs, and identify corresponding sources and methods. While many small firms are just as dynamic and innovative as larger ones, especially in 'high-tech' and knowledge-based fields, their problems are of a different order. Here, innovation needs tend not to emerge as neatly-defined R&D questions. In contrast with larger firms with specialised staff and a division of labour permitting a more rational and focused approach, innovation problems come usually as a mixed bag – of management and work organisation, finance and marketing, lack of workforce skills, and sometimes technical problems. The most pressing need is often for an analysis of such problems and the identification of solutions (and partners to those solutions). Hence, networks and diverse intermediaries have an important role: industrial advisors and innovation counsellors of industrial associations; engineering and management consultants, regional/local development officers; financial advisors and business accountants.

University transfer/industry liaison offices are rarely very useful partners to small firms in this, for they cannot, for the most part, respond to the mix of problems associated with major innovation projects. This is summed up in the paraphrase from the OECD study on universities and the community: 'Small firms have problems – universities have departments'.[32] By contrast, the specialisation and division of labour of larger firms can reflect the university's disciplinary divides. The greater facility with which universities co-operate with larger firms is reinforced by the play of other factors. The R&D problems of larger firms typically call for more basic research and therefore are more familiar and of interest to the university researcher, compared with smaller firms where the emphasis tends to be more on the 'D' than the 'R'. Contracts for co-operative projects are typically large-scale, making them more attractive than assisting small firms resolve their problems. As research is expensive, particularly in medicine, the sciences and engineering, research grants from industry become an increasingly important source of revenue compared with public budgets, and thus the expectation grows that 'intellectual work must be supported by an economic surplus'.[33] For all of these reasons, co-operation between universities and small firms tends to be problematic.

Technical colleges/institutes and other non-university institutions, insofar as they undertake research and development at all, may well thus be more appropriate than universities to assist smaller firms with their needs, given their applied, inter-disciplinary approach and emphasis on development rather than 'pure' research. This raises particular problems, consequently, in countries where the higher education system is less differentiated than, say, in the UK or Germany, with few HE institutions outside the universities to provide this kind of assistance. Community colleges in Canada, for example, are teaching-only institutions with no mandate to carry out R&D.

As we have seen, technology transfer is part of a larger system of knowledge creation and application, and of relationships between universities and the community; there has also been a tendency to interpret it excessively narrowly. Central to innovation through the application of new knowledge is learning – systems of innovation have been called 'learning systems'.[34] As the advancement of knowledge through teaching and learning is a central responsibility of universities, each knowledge transfer ought to include education, targeted to the needs of innovators and practitioners involved in the changes, whether technological, organisational or managerial. Universities are thus far only marginally involved in co-operative research and organised learning as twinned activity, for there tends to remain a strict organisational division of research and technology transfer and of continuing education activities in the university.

NOTES

1. M. Trow, 'The Public and Private Lives of Higher Education', *Daedalus* 104, 1976, pp113–27; S. Blume, 'Problems and Prospects of Research Training in the 1990s', in OECD (ed), *Research Training – Present and Future*, OECD, Paris 1995.
2. OECD, *Adults in Higher Education*, OECD, Paris 1987; H.G. Schuetze (ed), *Adults in Higher Education – Policies and Practice in Great Britain and North America*, Almqvist and Wicksell International, Stockholm 1987.
3. S. Muller, 'Research Universities and Industrial Innovation in America', in J. Coles (ed), *Technological Innovation in the 80s*, Prentice Hall, Englewood Cliffs, N.J. 1984, p15.
4. W. Faulkner, J. O'Connor, M. O'Gallagher, M. Thompson, *The Technology Transfer Process – A Pilot Study on the Role of Intermediaries*,

Scottish Enterprise Foundation, Sterling 1988, p8.

5. L. Cerych, 'University-Industry Collaboration – A Research Agenda and Some General Impacts on the Development of Higher Education', *European Journal of Education*, vol. 24, 1989, pp309–13.

6. A. Saxenian, *Regional Advantage: Culture and Competition in Silicon Valley and Route 128*, Harvard University Press, Cambridge 1994.

7. Thus the title by Miller and Coté, 1991.

8. N. Reimers lists ten typical linkages with industry, beside the production of graduates: academic consulting, doing research, philanthropic contributions from industry to institutions, industry affiliates programmes, research consortia, publications and conferences, exchanges of scientists, shared equipment use, science or industrial parks, and technology licensing ('The Government-Industry-University Interface – Improving the Innovation Process', in J. Coles (ed), *op.cit.*)

9. See for example W. Sengenberger, G. Loveman and M.J. Piore, *The Re-emergence of Small Enterprises – industrial restructuring in industrialized countries*, International Institute for Labour Studies, Geneva, 1990; R. Rothwell, 'Innovation and the Smaller Firm', in W. Brown and R. Rothwell (eds), *Entrepreneurship and Technology – World Experiences and Politics*, Longman, Harlow, Essex 1986. For an overview, see L. Hommen, K. Rubenson, H.G. Schuetze, *Innovation, Skills and Learning in Small and Medium-sized Enterprises – Theory, Research and Policy Perspectives*, 1996 (forthcoming).

10. J. de la Motte, 'Canada and the National System of Innovation, in A. Holbrook (ed), *Resource Book for Science and Technology Consultations*, vol. 2, Industry Canada, Ottawa 1994.

11. OECD, *Technology and the Economy – The Key Relationships*, OECD, Paris 1992, p26.

12. *Ibid.*; L. Coete and A. Arundel (eds), *An Integrated Approach to European Innovation and Technology Diffusion Policy*, Commission of the European Communities, Luxembourg 1993.

13. C. Freeman, *Technology and Economic Performance – Lessons from Japan*, Pinter, London 1987, p3.

14. S. Muller, *op.cit.*, p9.

15. E. Lynton, 'Internal Conditions for Effective University Engagement in Knowledge Transfer and Other Forms of Outreach', *Metropolitan Universities*, (forthcoming, 1996; in mimeo, p6).

16. *Ibid.*, p7.

17. B. Clark, *The Higher Education System – Academic Organization in a Cross-National Perspective*, University of California Press, Berkeley 1983.

18. E. Lynton and S. Elman, *New Priorities for the University – Meeting Society's Needs for Applied Knowledge and Competent Individuals*, Jossey-Bass, San Francisco 1987.

19. The hierarchy of academic esteem is itself open to change, as several authors have called for a reconsideration of the meaning of scholarship. Boyer, for example, has distinguished four different types of scholarship, interdependent and of equal value and importance: the scholarship of teaching, integration, application, and of discovery, (E. Boyer, *Scholarship*

Reconsidered – Priorities for the professoriate, Carnegie Foundation for the Advancement of Teaching, Princeton, N.J. 1990.

20. T. Becher, *Academic Tribes and Territories – Intellectual Enquiry and the Cultures of Disciplines*, Open University Press, Milton Keynes 1989; C.P. Snow, *The Two Cultures and the Scientific Revolution*, University Press, Cambridge 1959.

21. Lynton, 1996, *op.cit.*, p13.

22. R. Geiger, 'Organized Research and American Universities', unpublished paper 1987, quoted by T. Becher 1989, *op.cit.*, p136.

23. *Ibid.*

24. R. Barnett, 'Limits to Academic Freedom', in M. Tight (ed), *Academic Freedom and Responsibility*, Open University Press, Milton Keynes 1988.

25. Lynton 1996, *op.cit.*

26. Clark, 1983, *op.cit.*, p207.

27. Faulkner, *et al*, 1988, *op.cit.*, p9.

28. See L. Hommen *et al, op.cit.*

29. B. A. Lundvall, 'User-Producer Relationships, National Systems of Innovation and Internationalization', in D. Foray and C. Freeman (eds), *Technology and the Wealth of Nations – The Dynamics of Constructed Advantage*, Pinter London, 1993, pp297–99; see also B. Lundvall (ed), *National Systems of Innovation – Towards a Theory of Innovation and Interactive Learning*, Pinter, London 1992.

30. OECD 1987, *op.cit.*

31. Lynton 1996, *op.cit.*

32. OECD, *The University and the Community – The Problem of Changing Relationships*, OECD, Paris 1982.

33. S. Rothblatt, 'The Notion of an Open Scientific Community in Scientific Perspective', in N. Gibbons and B. Wittrock (eds), *Science as a Commodity*, Longman, Harlow 1985.

34. Lundvall, 1992, *op.cit.*

7

COMMUNITIES, UNIVERSITIES AND CHANGE: RECENT NORTH AMERICAN EXPERIENCE

William S. Griffith

Many of those who seek to acquire or refine their understanding of the changing continuing education functions of universities in their communities resemble the five blind people coming upon an elephant. Each felt one part of the beast and proclaimed to have discerned its nature. One felt the trunk and reported that an elephant is very much like a snake. A second, feeling the ear, stated that an elephant is like a fan. A third, touching a sturdy leg, announced that an elephant is like a tree. A fourth, running both hands along the side of the beast, affirmed that an elephant is like a wall. The fifth, grasping the elephant's tail, asserted that an elephant is like a rope. All were reporting what they had sensed, but each was unable to envision the whole animal because each had direct experience with only one part of the animal. Similarly, many of those who make strong assertions about the changing relationship of universities to their communities speak from a limited acquaintance with one or a few aspects of that relationship. Differing concepts of the field in part provide an explanation for the shift in predominant emphasis from individual and community development to an economic motivation.

CONCEPTS OF UNIVERSITY CONTINUING EDUCATION AND EXTENSION

The concept of the universities' adult education work in communities has exhibited a major shift – from earlier perceptions of extending the intellectual resources of the university to those who were unable to become traditional university students, to a conception of continuing education that restricts the intellectual fare to economically favoured sectors of the community. This change, which ought not be equated with development, is reflected primarily in the programmes available; it is tellingly illustrated by the renaming of the associations of university people with responsibilities in continuing education, both in Canada and the United States. Divergent views of the future of the work of universities in their communities are likely to mean that a primary economic motivation for university continuing education is maintained.

Based on a comprehensive study of the history of the work of American universities in adult education, John Morton, a twentieth-century pioneer in university extension, conceptualised it as embracing all of the educational work of the university aside from resident instruction.[1] At mid-century, the concept of extension was broad, encompassing a wide range of services to diverse populations and collectivities.

In 1960, Peterson and Peterson wrote a guide to policy for university adult education. Rather than referring to 'extension functions', the Petersons preferred 'community services' and included under that label all manner of educational endeavours as well as sports and recreation. University presses, broadcasting, lending libraries, placement services, concerts, plays, consulting services to governments and business, and an incredibly wide array of programming activities were covered, some of which scarcely seemed to belong within education.[2] In the 1960s, emphasis was placed on 'community services', with that term as the umbrella for such activities provided by universities as well as by the burgeoning community colleges.

The community services approach spawned sub-groups, each of which chose a name they hoped would be descriptive of their special interest. In 1962, members of the National University Extension Association defined 'community development' as 'the process of community education and action democratically organised and carried through by the people themselves to reach goals they hold in common for the improvement and enrichment of the entire community.'[3] They saw the university's role as that of actively assisting this process through education and training of concerned citizens in the community. A basic principle is that the university makes its resources available to the community but leaves to it the decision-making. The emphasis on community improvement flourished, being nourished by injections of federal funds. Political priorities more than academic dialogues provided the direction of the universities' relationship to their communities.

Efforts to classify the adult education functions of universities in a systematic fashion were made by Shannon and Schoenfeld, who described three types of extension: geographical, which extends regular classes to other times and places; chronological, which provides continuing education for those who already have completed their formal higher education; and functional, which deals with community development rather than focusing on individual learners.[4] However, this attempt to regularise the terminology, and prevent the substitution of one term for another without a clear definition of either, failed, like a number of others, to attract substantial support beyond a small group of adult education scholars. Philosophical considerations were given significantly less attention than government programmes offering funds. Rae Rohfeld, addressing the nature of the community work of universities in the United States, decried their abdication from this pioneering work with communities.[5] Convinced that the universities had gone overboard in catering for the individual, she called for a return to an emphasis on improving the functioning of communities as social units. She expressed her commitment to the education of the social mind rather than concentrating only on the individual mind.[6] Driven by economic considerations, the trend toward serving educational demands of individuals appears to be supplanting the historical concern for the development of the community as an entity. Continuing professional education, focused on the individual learner, thus occupies a position of prominence previously enjoyed by community-focused work dealing with social groups.

Continuing professional education is for those who have completed their formal degree work and are now engaging in learning for the purpose of preventing obsolescence or to comply with relicensure requirements. They do not form a geographically-defined community; they are linked, for instance through Internet or other electronic means. Professional groups have the financial resources to cover the costs of the educational participation they choose.

Further complicating the conception of university work in adult education is its perceived utility in the minds of those who are the administrative leaders in major universities, such as the University of California. Pitman, in reviewing Rockhill's history of university extension in California, noted that instead of viewing such work as an extension of the mission and resources of the university, the system now focuses on bolstering the popularity of the university through developing and strengthening ties with business and industry.[7] Financial pressures have moved the extension work toward serving elite, affluent audiences.[8] Public relations and pecuniary gain have become the justifications for the universities' involvement in much of adult and continuing education today.

Not only has the financial support provided by the federal government been eroding since the 1960s, but the interest and involvement of state governments has also declined. Rockhill observed that the loss of federal funding had a tremendous impact on extension programmes. Social programmes that appealed to other than a monied audience required government subsidies. Those programmes rooted in humanitarian values or oriented toward social problems are not economically viable. Serving the self-interest of monied markets has become the primary justification for extension programmes.[9] Entrepreneurial concerns and economic considerations have eclipsed educational sensitivities.

The emphasis on marketing for profit has significantly altered the nature of university extension education. A clear and unmistakable movement toward markets with money has supplanted programming directed toward people who cannot afford high extension fees. It has come to dominate the concerns of extension programmers.[10] Accordingly, the work of the university in adult education further widens the gap between the educationally disadvantaged and those who have earned at least one degree.

As the nature of the priorities in extension, community service, and continuing education has shifted in North America, a corresponding transformation in the associations of the university adult educators has taken place.

CHANGES IN THE ASSOCIATIONS OF UNIVERSITY EXTENSION AND CONTINUING EDUCATION

The national associations of adult educators working in universities in Canada and the United States have changed their names through the years, reflecting not merely a shift in terminology but a change in their focus.

The Canadian situation

Prior to 1954, university adult educators in Canada had no national association that focused on their specific concerns. But in that year, the Canadian Association of Directors of Extension and Summer School was founded, indicating that the adult education function was perceived to be served both through the courses and workshops offered during summers and through various off-campus activities as well. In 1974, the Association changed its name to the Canadian Association for University Continuing Education. This change was significant because it reflected both the increasing prominence of continuing education and the loss of influence of those who would promote community development and other services to adults who had not had access to higher education.

Counter-influences may, however, be emerging. Harold Baker of Saskatchewan, analysing trends in university adult education, has noted that economic factors are favouring an expansion of distance education and, because of decreasing government funding, local people are being encouraged to take control of their own community, regional, and enterprise developments. Through these experiences, Canadian communities are reportedly learning to demand increasing educational services from their universities.[11] So, while the universities are apparently dancing to the tunes of economic pipers, Canadian communities are becoming aware of the potential value of university resources and are beginning to express their own legitimate demands.

Individual adult education units within universities in Canada have used a variety of names. Brooke and Morris, reporting on a study of policies and practices in continuing education units in Canadian universities, stated that six of forty-four units had used the word 'extension' in the title of their unit while two used the word 'community', which may indicate that both community and extension have less of an attraction to university adult educators than was the case in the past.[12] Nevertheless, twenty-two (50 per cent) of these continuing education units reported that they regularly provide community service programmes on a subsidised basis. In terms of the major functions undertaken by the continuing education units, however, the most frequently reported activity is the provision of university degree courses; this is followed closely by non-degree and university certificate courses. Less frequent as a major function are research, community public relations and community development.[13] So, despite the professed interest in serving communities, the typical unit focuses its efforts first and foremost on providing the standard campus menu at hours convenient to adult learners and in locations more readily accessible than the university campus.

Economic forces have become increasingly important in shaping the universities' educational menu. In 1989, a Committee for University-Industry Co-operation in Continuing Education submitted its report entitled: *Investing in Learning: The role of Canadian universities in economic renewal*. The Committee defined continuing education as comprising both credit and non-credit courses offered to part-time learners at a university, a college, a workplace or other locale, or by correspondence, significantly narrower in scope than the traditional definitions discussed above. The report stated: '... the very fact that universities have, until recently, not been major players in providing continuing education to meet the specific needs of employers and employees was the problem that gave rise to the Committee's existence'.[14] The assumption in all this is that a major function of universities is to provide continuing education to satisfy the demands of employers and employees for economic renewal.

Members of the Committee, representing universities, employers, and employees, examined fundamental issues, including the different views held of the objectives of education and training by industry and universities. The industry view was stated to be: 'To develop competencies defined as desirable by the organisation in response to its particular organisational needs and requirements'; the university view was reported: 'To develop knowledge in and through people, in the interests of the individual and society as a whole'.[15] It was hoped that the inevitable tension between these two views would be reduced by emphasising industry's perception!

In addition to calling for closer co-operation among all parties involved in continuing training, two recommendations demonstrate the approach favoured by the majority of the Committee: 'The Association of Universities and Colleges of Canada should co-operate with the Canadian Labour Market and Productivity Centre in an ongoing process of encouraging the planning of demand-driven continuing education [and] the federal government should provide incentive funding to industries and universities that co-operate in the area of continuing education, in support of the development costs of new programmes'.[16] In other words, the universities ought to be functioning as service stations, providing the educational resources specified by industry, rather than giving priority to other educational goals.

By the mid 1980s, the Canadian federal government was dealing directly with private and non-profit training organisations and was reducing its commitment to the institutional training programmes of the higher education infrastructure in the Provinces. As even greater emphasis on new technology and trade restrictions grew in the 1990s, an increasingly large proportion of federal training funds were allocated to the private sector. The federal government shifted its preference toward third party purchases of training favouring the private sector. Training agreements emphasised that programmes be more accountable and responsive to local needs through increased planning, reviews, evaluations, assessments, data bases of participation, approvals and reports. The increased involvement of the private sector, labour unions and regional and local governments allowed programmes to respond to local labour force needs.[17] The universities were seen to be slow to adjust to the new directions emphasised by government, so a shift in the funding mechanisms was introduced to ensure federal dollars could be used by industry to purchase only those programmes they desired. A corresponding decrease in the funding for basic research and community-based programming accompanied this shift.

In 1993, Hein reported on a survey of fifty-two deans and directors of the universities belonging to the CAUCE.[18] Based on a 75 per cent return rate, respondents from the member institutions ranked the relative importance of six purposes for university continuing education as follows: 1) Vocational; 2) Liberal Arts; 3) Personal Development; 4) Status Quo; 5) Social Reform; and 6) Radical Reform. The emphasis on the vocational purpose was more than twice as strong as the liberal arts in second place, with both social and radical reform given a barely measurable level of importance. Hein also addressed the dichotomous classification of the orientation of university continuing educators:

'university first' *versus* 'community first', observing that the community-first group consisted of two quite distinct sub-groups: advocates for the community and those who are motivated by financial considerations, providing programmes tailored for the community as a means of running a profit-making enterprise. Even an apparent community orientation may mask objectives that are driven more by economics than educational objectives.

Taylor and Sutherland analysed the impact of Canadian federal legislation on university adult education. They characterise adult education as being changed from a social movement to professional practice with a service orientation. It has become alienated from the public policy process. The agenda is now set for, rather than by, adult educators.[19] Prior to 1986, federal training purchases were made directly with universities. New agreements called for a portion of the funds to be given to a third party, such as an employer, who can decide what training to purchase. This process has become of increasing importance in the Ministry of Employment and Immigration, placing pressures on the universities to serve needs defined by the sponsors rather than designing programmes on the basis of their own assessment of needs.

In this context, Cruikshank has criticised the extension departments, charging that instead of providing some degree of advocacy for those adults who are not normally served by universities, they now focus on adults who can bear the high fees necessitated by self-support policies.[20] Consequently, university adult educators are marketing programmes to two distinct target groups: a) business and industry; and b) those who can pay. Instead of focusing on serving community learning needs, energies are devoted to bringing in money. She holds the leaders of extension programmes responsible for this situation, as deans and directors tend to adhere to business values. Cost-recovery is being used as an excuse for avoiding social activism. This business orientation of departmental leadership locks extension departments into a one-sided marketing approach.[21]

So, the debate continues, with the financially responsive currently holding the upper hand, shaping provision to suit economically advantaged clients.

Some comparisons with the United States

In the United States, the first organisation for those in the universities concerned with the education of adults was the Association for the Extension of University Teaching, founded in the late nineteenth century. It originated in Philadelphia and reflected a blend of both university people and other citizens. According to Pyle, the Society did not cater to vocational interests or needs.[22] In 1915, its successor – the National University Extension Association (NUEA) – was founded and university personnel took charge, introducing an emphasis on the practical and applied aspects of extension, departing from the English model that had served as a template for the earliest university extension developments.[23] At that founding meeting, Charles Van Hise, then President of the University of Wisconsin, made the following, scarcely-dated observation; 'Extension, if made truly educational along the highest lines and with the best results, like any other educational work, will inevitably become a source of expense to an institution'.[24] The leaders of university-sponsored adult education today have succumbed to the economic imperative and embraced the notion that such work must be not only self-supporting, but also contribute funds to the general university budget.

In 1980, NUEA members voted to change the name of the association to the National University Continuing Education Association. This change was justified on the grounds that the continuing education activities of the association's member institutions encompassed by then far more than extension courses.[25] By 1980, the prevailing concept of extension within the NUEA had become extremely narrow, and was equated with the provision of regular university courses to external audiences. Continuing education, which previously had referred only to the universities' continuing work with graduates, was redefined to include all that had before been regarded as extension work.

A shift from the liberal education of individuals and communities to a focus on other goals is reflected clearly in the 1989 report of the Extension Director of the San Diego campus of University of California: 'The primary outcome of extension programmes is stimulating local and regional economic growth through a number of links that result from extension programs, including increased access to technology and information, increased productivity, and increased relevance of university research and teaching to the practical needs of the community'.[26] Such perceptions of the university role as being targeted on economic growth inevitably results in a downgrading of provision that aims to enlighten individuals as citizens, parents, and community members, whatever their financial status. It is an ample illustration of the shift toward operating profit centres rather than educating individuals and communities for the common good.

THE FUTURE?

Prognosticators differ in their views on the probable changes in the future for university continuing education. In North America, strategic planning, the formulation of mission statements, and an urge to perceive visions, are currently popular activities. In 1990, a NUCEA Task Force issued a *Statement of Visions and Values*, a 'vision' that contains no reference to the word 'community', but instead focuses on the relationship of the continuing education unit to the parent university. It concludes that 'Continuing education is emerging as "the other way" to run the university.'[27] This function is thus being absorbed into the operation of other sectors of the university structure without a corresponding increase in the influence and visibility of the traditional extension or continuing education units.

Opinions differ concerning the most appropriate posture to adopt regarding the current economic situation. Writing from a social activist posture, Cruikshank urges that:

> We must develop a clear, long-term vision of the potential of university extension, a vision which includes social change as a key goal. We cannot allow cost-recovery to continue as an excuse for failing to address social justice issues. We must bring the struggle for social change into the adult education mainstream in order for it to become an integral part of university extension. If we fail to do this, we simply become 'neutered' technicians who help to maintain and reproduce the existing power relationships within society.[28]

Others express quite different viewpoints. Edward Scissons, of the University of Saskatchewan, believes that: 'Continuing educators have argued their worth on the basis of exclusive knowledge of people and practice – and are being proven wrong by professional colleges on both counts.'[29] In examining the relationship between the central continuing education unit and the several professional faculties, Scissons believes that: 'the role must be based on the non-mainstream elements of the continuing educator's skills: expertise in needs assessment, instructional design, and larger scale instructional evaluations.'[30] He argues that these are important, not because professional colleges cannot do them, but because they will not – at least not in the short term. Each requires a form and level of skill beyond that which most professional schools academics attribute to themselves, often only called for on an irregular, project-related basis.[31] In his view, the future for those employed in university continuing education units will be bleak unless they learn to embrace a specialised role that is required and valued by their university colleagues. Accepting and promoting this specialised role may be a key to survival in financially stressed universities. The price of becoming expert consultants to other academics does not, however, reflect a high priority for traditional liberal education or community development programming.

The university continuing education that will be of greatest value to society may well not be provision directed primarily to economic growth – educational efforts to improve the community in other ways are often of greater need. In this regard, Saindon and Holt have criticised the current social malaise and the cult of individualism: 'developing one's potential has become an excuse for narcissistic self-absorption. This is reflected in a tendency to value autonomy and freedom of expression above all other values, especially one's social concerns.'[32] Excessive individualism combined with an unwillingness to acknowledge social responsibility may be a greater threat to the quality of life for all people than economic stress. The shrinking of the middle class in North America poses threats of divisiveness and the destruction of a sense of community that is not being addressed effectively by educational leaders.

Saindon and Holt reported that the recent economic trend toward the polarisation in income distribution – the growth of low income and part-time employment and the social trend towards a widening gap between the highly educated and the educationally disadvantaged – presents major contemporary problems. They believe continuing education has placed insufficient emphasis on civic education in general and on the involvement of the educationally disadvantaged in civic literacy programmes.[33] Provision that addresses only economic considerations may well aggravate the problems of deteriorating communities rather than contributing to their solution.

Yet, economic considerations cannot be ignored if continuing education units are to survive. Milton Stern, addressing the University of California situation where extension programmes have gone from a

90 per cent subsidy status to one in which all direct and indirect costs must be recovered, acknowledges the power of economic forces: 'No matter what in our academic hearts we declare to be our proper program goals ... we must still do the marketing job required of us to survive, and more ... to provide a surplus for our masters'.[34] So, the persisting question is: 'how can those in university continuing education promote a growing awareness and concern for social and civic problems and their solutions in an environment in which their own financial survival is threatened?'

Under present economic conditions in Canada and in the United States, the role of universities has been transformed. Where once the university existed to provide educational opportunities for all of the motivated and intellectually alert citizens of a Province or State, in circumstances where it was assumed that the government would be responsible for providing the funds to underwrite the educational enterprise, a new role is perceived – that of economic engine, producing discoveries that can readily be transferred to production and thereby increase the competitive situation of the nation. Short-term economic goals dominate, and continuing education units are even more susceptible to the influence of this philosophy than are the academic departments and faculties involved exclusively in teaching and research. Even the academic departments are being shaped by the pressures to produce patents, products that will bring royalties to the universities, and contracts with business and industry.

Joe Donaldson of Missouri offers a trenchant observation regarding the present status of extension within contemporary universities in the United States:

> The continuing education function is being absorbed and 'main-streamed' in many of our institutions ... Perhaps today, more than at any other time within the history of continuing higher education, we and others with whom we work lack an understanding of who we are and what we do ... The larger and more prestigious institutions have been characterized by some as large, international profit-seeking organisations in which individual faculty members are being asked to become small business persons responsible for bringing in outside resources.[35]

Narrow conceptions of the university role in extension, community service and continuing education are inadequate to cope with the complex forces both within and outside universities. The tendency to react rather than to act has produced a public perception of university continuing education as a narrow-gauged, single purpose instrument. It is thus urgent to ask what university continuing educators are doing to counter this false impression?

University adult and continuing education is not insulated, nor should it be, from the problems and challenges of the society in which it is embedded. Strong forces are shifting the perception of such work in North America from one of serving a wide range of needs and purposes to that of serving primarily, if not exclusively, as the engine of growth and prosperity both for its parent university and the larger society. If we, who are immersed in adult and continuing education, individually and collectively, cannot ourselves see the entire elephant and the value of a broad perspective, and if we cannot convey that perception to others who have perceived only one part, who, then, shall we expect to transmit the grand vision, the great tradition?

NOTES

1. J.R. Morton, *University Extension in the United States*, University of Alabama Press, Birmingham 1953, p131.
2. R. Peterson and W. Peterson, *University Adult Education: A Guide to Policy*, Harper and Bros., New York 1960, p96.
3. R.W. Rohfeld, 'Community Development and University Extension: Involving the University in Social Change', *Continuing Higher Education Review*, 1992, 56, (3), p182.
4. T.J. Shannon and C.A. Schoenfeld, *University Extension*, The Centre for Applied Research in Education, New York 1965, pp3–5.
5. R.W. Rohfeld, 'Searching for University Extension's Role in the Community', *Continuing Higher Education Review*, 1994, 58, (1&2), p91.
6. Rohfeld 1992, *op.cit.*, p181.
7. V.V. Pitman, 'Review of *Academic Excellence and Public Service: A History of University in California* by Kathleen Rockhill', *Continuum*, 1985, 49, (1), p66.
8. *Ibid.*, p67.
9. K. Rockhill, *Academic Excellence and Public Service: A History of University Extension in California*, Transaction Books, New Brunswick, N.J. 1983, p216.
10. *Ibid.*, pp220–21.
11. H.R. Baker, 'A History of CAUCE: Its Formation, Development, and Role', *Canadian Journal of University Continuing Education*, 1993, 19, (2), p58.
12. W.M. Brooke and J.F. Morris, *Continuing Education in Canadian Universities: A Summary Report of Policies and Practices – 1985*, Canadian

Association for University Continuing Education, Ottawa 1987, pp6–7.

13. *Ibid.*, p3.
14. Canadian Association for University Continuing Education, *Investing in Learning: The Role of Canadian Universities in Economic Renewal*, (Report of the Committee for University-Industry Cooperation in Continuing Education), Canadian Association for University Continuing Education, Ottawa 1989, pp5–7.
15. *Ibid.*, Appendix B:5.
16. *Ibid.*, pii.
17. M.C. Taylor and J. Sutherland, 'The Decade of Change in Canadian Adult Training: A Description of the Federal/Provincial Training Agreements Between 1982–1992', *International Journal of University Adult Education*, 1994, 33, (3), pp68–9.
18. L.I. Hein, 'University First or Community First? The Orientation of University Continuing Education Deans and Directors', *Continuing Higher Education Review*, 1993, 57, (3), pp115–29.
19. Taylor and Sutherland, *op.cit.*, p55.
20. J. Cruikshank, 'Cost-Recovery: The Current Challenge', in M. Brooke and M. Waldron (eds), *University Continuing Education in Canada: Current Challenges and Future Opportunities*, Thompson Educational Publishing, Toronto 1994, p77.
21. *Ibid.*, p81.
22. H.G. Pyle, 'History of the National University Extension Association', in S.J. Drazek, N.P. Mitchell, H.G. Pyle and W.L. Thompson (eds), *Expanding Horizons ... Continuing Education* (Golden Anniversary Publication of the National University Extension Association), National University Extension Association, Washington D.C. 1965, p3.
23. *Ibid.*, p6.
24. R.W. Rohfeld, *Expanding Access to Knowledge: Continuing Higher Education NUCEA – 1915–1990*, National University Continuing Education Association, Washington D.C. 1990, pii.
25. *Ibid.*, p138.
26. As quoted in Rohfeld, *op.cit.*, p197.
27. NUCEA Task Force on Vision and Values, 'Statement of Visions and Values in Continuing Higher Education', *Continuing Higher Education Review*, 1990, 54, (3), pp146–7.
28. Cruikshank, *op.cit.*, p83.
29. E.H. Scissons, 'The Role of the Continuing Educator in University Professional Colleges', (paper presented to the 1982 meeting of the Canadian Association of University Continuing Education, Vancouver), mimeographed, 1982, p2.
30. *Ibid.*, p5.
31. *Ibid.*
32. J.J. Saindon and M.E. Holt, 'The Tragedy of the Commons Revisited', in *Continuing Higher Education Review*, 1987, 51, (3), p55.
33. *Ibid.*, pp63–4.
34. M.R. Stern, 'University Continuing Educators Should be Entrepreneurs – Ambivalent Activists, Uneasy Entrepreneurs – and the Search for Truth',

Canadian Journal of University Continuing Education, 1992, 18, (2), p24.
35. J.F. Donaldson, 'New Opportunities for a New Marginality: Strategic Issues in Continuing Higher Education', *Continuing Higher Education Review*, 1991, 55, (3), p123.

8

RE-CONNECTING THE ACADEMY? COMMUNITY INVOLVEMENT IN AMERICAN AND BRITISH UNIVERSITIES

John Mohan

UNIVERSITIES: PART OF, OR APART FROM, THEIR COMMUNITIES?

> Nothing more closely resembles a monastery (lost in the countryside, walled, flanked by barbarian hordes, inhabited by monks who have nothing to do with the world and devote themselves to their private researches) than an American university.
>
> Umberto Eco, *Travels in Hyperreality*

Relationships between universities and their communities are in a state of flux on both sides of the Atlantic. The context for this is one of economic decline and social polarisation in many urban areas in which universities are located, juxtaposed with continued physical expansion of universities. Much treatment of the relationship between university and community focuses on economic issues and, significant though this is, we should not neglect the social contribution universities might make to their communities. The purpose of this chapter is therefore to consider various ways in which (at least some) universities in the USA are making a greater social contribution to the welfare of their communities; whether and to what extent this implies a revised conception of the university's purpose; and the lessons which might be learnt from this. The chapter concentrates on three types of initiative: schemes to promote student community service and to link it into the undergraduate curriculum; partnerships with public schools; and university involvement in urban development.[1]

Numerous initiatives are seeking to rethink the relationship between large urban universities and their immediate communities in the USA. Among the baser motives for involvement are: guilt for past actions (urban universities have often adopted an arrogant, insensitive approach to physical expansion); institutional self-interest (due to rising crime); and accountabilities to local and state governments (as non-profit institutions many universities seek to show reasons why they should be granted tax exemptions). More positively, universities are: responding to criticisms that they lack a social purpose;[2] seeking to create partnerships to shore up urban education systems; and beginning to act as vehicles for neighbourhood stabilisation and economic development. Universities (and other non-profit institutions) are, by default, the only significant players in many inner city areas, due to capital flight, and they therefore have a significance to the community and local economy which goes beyond their direct physical presence. The sense of social crisis facing America's large cities, and the absence of a strong university response, is well captured by Harkavy and Puckett, who deplore the contrast between the 'deconstructionist bickering, mandarin practices and islands of horticultural beauty' that characterise some large research institutions, and the 'inland seas of violence, dereliction and despair that surround them'.[3] Apocalyptic as this may sound, it will resonate with many familiar with large American cities.[4]

In Britain, a reappraisal of university-community involvement is being driven less by adverse socio-economic conditions than by major changes in the education system, notably the end of the 'binary divide' between universities and polytechnics, the rapid expansion of the participation rate, and the institution of national competition for research funds. These processes are changing the identities of institutions, while the expansion of student numbers means that institutions have a dramatic physical impact on their local communities. These impacts are quite different from those made by the new universities created in the 1960s, which were often located on greenfield campuses on the fringe of cities, and which developed almost as communities separate from their host cities.[5]

For different reasons, then, universities on both sides of the Atlantic are asking whether universities can continue to maintain their distance from their immediate communities. However, the responses to those questions are somewhat different. Drawing mainly on the activities of American universities, I attempt to draw out lessons which institutions could learn in both countries and to point to the kind of institutional changes likely to be necessary to make a reality of community involvement and to make it central to the mission of the urban university.

MAJOR CURRENT DEVELOPMENTS IN UNIVERSITY-COMMUNITY INVOLVEMENT

Student volunteerism and study service

No visitor to the USA could fail to be impressed by the scale of volunteerism currently sweeping American campuses. Accurate and comparable statistics are difficult to obtain, but some institutions report that up to two-thirds of graduating seniors are engaged in community service and at least one study reported that this proportion could be generalised across all post-secondary institutions;[6] national coalitions such as Campus Compact and Campus Outreach Opportunity League have an expanding membership covering a growing proportion of post-secondary institutions; and some institutions have engaged in lengthy debates about whether or not to mandate community service.[7] Given the participation rate in American higher education, volunteerism on this scale must, by definition, engage a substantial proportion of America's rising generation. The proportions involved in the UK are much smaller: although student tutoring initiatives are expanding rapidly, this is from a small base; the numbers involved totalled some 5000 by spring 1995 with around 180 post-secondary institutions having established some kind of tutoring scheme.[8] This is probably the largest single element of student volunteerism in the UK – yet these numbers represent less than one per cent of the student population, in stark contrast to the USA.

If these kind of developments are to gain more widespread acceptance in Britain a number of lessons will need to be learnt to avoid reinventing wheels.[9] Debates will have to be settled about whether to mandate volunteerism, about how to integrate community service into the curriculum, and about providing an infrastructure to institutionalise it. In addition, British higher education has historically been dominated by the single-honours degree, in which students specialise in one subject at an early stage in their university education. Advocates of some form of study service therefore have greater difficulties incorporating it into this system, by contrast with the broad-based undergraduate education offered in American universities. Moreover, as a rule, British universities place less emphasis on acquiring the skills for civic participation than do American ones; institutions would not regard it as their duty to provide opportunities for students to engage in volunteer service and might legally be prevented from using public funds for that purpose. As a consequence student volunteerism is generally left to the students to fund and organise. There have been eloquent arguments for the integration of study service into academic programmes but they have made relatively little impact on the UK. Among the reasons for this are the quite distinctive research-led focus of the 'old' universities (even prior to the research assessment exercises) and the lack of effective mediating structures, which could bridge the gap between 'community' and 'academic' definitions of topics for investigation.[10]

There are nevertheless some small-scale initiatives which seek to integrate community service and academic study. Some government-funded initiatives (such as the Enterprise in Higher Education programme) have linked students with community organisations for internship-style activities.[11] There are also reasons for believing that such programmes will expand: there are strong vocational arguments for them; whatever party is in government, the role of the voluntary sector will increase, and this is one way to help individuals prepare for that; and, as in America, there is a degree of alienation from the political process and cynicism about the capabilities of government, so that some commentators are calling for a wider programme of civic education involving all students in their final year at school. This has also led to proposals for a national service initiative, partly modelled on the Clinton scheme (which provides some financial aid to students in return for their undertaking a year's community service), although in practice the proposals focus on school-leavers, particularly at-risk youth, rather than on college students.[12]

Partnerships with schools

The publication of *A Nation at Risk*[13] provoked a debate about falling education standards in the USA which continues today, and one response has been a rapid expansion of partnerships between American universities and schools.[14] Other reasons for this growth include: the mass access to (if not completion of) higher education in the US (and hence concern with the quality of recruits); the need for integration of minorities and developing culturally-sensitive pedagogies and support networks to ensure that they can succeed in higher education; and the failures of the public school system.[15] Schemes range from very small-scale mentoring and tutoring schemes, through programmes designed to raise aspirations and achievement among schoolchildren, to state-wide initiatives sometimes extending to school reform programmes. However there have been criticisms of the *ad hoc* proliferation of schemes: even on the same campus one can find programmes which overlap and replicate activity; schools closest to campus receive substantially more attention than those – perhaps equally needy – which are some distance away; and there is as yet only limited evaluation of the efficacy of partnership schemes.[16]

Arising out of these concerns, there is a growing recognition of the need for co-ordinating structures to ensure that university-school partnerships go beyond the rather *ad hoc*, altruistic activity that characterises collaboration at present. For example the American Association for Higher Education (AAHE)/Pew Trusts' initiative, Community Compacts for Student Success, seeks to bring together educational, business and community leadership in a long-term plan to improve educational outcomes for all school students.[17] These entail a critical examination of existing partnership activities to review what initiatives actually work, to ensure that duplication is avoided, and to focus resources where they would have the greatest impacts. The central role of universities in these collaborations is unknown in a British context. Also novel from a British perspective is the extent to which partnership activity can be legislatively mandated; universities in various jurisdictions have been required to collaborate with school boards.[18] Good corporate citizenship aside, it may be the case that local governments have leverage over universities when reviewing their taxation status, and they can therefore require greater collaboration.

Indeed the whole area of school-university collaboration is developed only on a very small scale in the UK. Typically it would incorporate small-scale 'taster' courses, designed to stimulate students' interest in academic subjects; student tutoring programmes; some *ad hoc* and informal linkages between Local Education Authorities (LEAs) and universities, which might involve limited support to pupils from schools in disadvantaged areas to help them obtain a place at university, as well as granting university admissions officers some discretion with regard to admission requirements. Of course there is collaboration in terms of educational research, but on the whole school-university collaboration, as understood in the USA, is limited.

The most obvious reason for this may simply be that, by contrast with the USA, Britain does not suffer from the social challenges – the disparities in funding between school boards in particular – which face urban schools in the USA.[19] Another reason may be the perception that the American school system is in need of fundamental reform (it is widely perceived as cumbersome and inflexible), so greater collaboration with universities is seen as a crucial way of translating innovative ideas direct to the classroom. In recognition of this, for example, Wayne State University (Detroit) has gone so far as to establish a university-owned and operated middle school, which will serve as a vehicle for implementing and evaluating curricular innovation; other institutions are also involved in school reform initiatives.[20]

Universities and community development

Urban development in the USA is the responsibility of a great many institutions and partnerships, in which universities often play an important role. Some of this is part of a well-established urban mission, in which university research efforts are targeted at the needs of local organisations. This is being complemented by some efforts to make universities' resources available to community organisations. In addition, as a consequence of urban decline, some institutions are becoming increasingly involved in neighbourhood stabilisation efforts.

In respect of community-based research, both British and American systems face the same difficulties: how to reconcile the long-term commitment necessary to develop a beneficial partnership with a community, with the national and international demands to publish high-quality research. There are no easy answers to this dilemma, short of a reconsideration of faculty reward structures. However, there are interesting initiatives in both countries which seek to democratise access to university resources; various foundation and government-sponsored programmes in the USA (such as the Urban Community Service grant programme) do so, while in Britain the Community Research Exchanges in Liverpool and Manchester, or the Northern Ireland Science Shop, offer good illustrations.[21] The latter are essentially 'clearing-houses' for matching community needs for research with the skills of faculty and students within universities. Such activities are generally working against the grain of the competitive, publication-driven higher education system. Among their characteristics are a collaborative model of inquiry, which aims to facilitate matching the skills and resources of researchers with the needs of community organisations; and a participatory and action-research approach, in which research and teaching activities are oriented towards – indeed partly driven by – community concerns. There are some signs, in the USA, of a move away from the 'urban observatory' approach of earlier university-city collaborations, in which the university's role was that of a detached, technocratic observer rather than that of an active participant.[22] Some suggest that this kind of collaborative activity is vital because, 'unless research is informed by the needs, knowledge and questions of the wider community, the quality of research will ultimately suffer through declining public support'.[23]

The involvement of American universities in neighbourhood stabilisation efforts has no obvious parallels in the UK. Such efforts include: financial backing and technical assistance to community-based organisations, to enable them to attract finance for low-cost housing; creation of umbrella partnership organisations, seeking to pull together all the major players in a locality; and geographically-focused purchasing and recruitment strategies. Foundation and government support has been forthcoming for these measures, as capital flight means that some urban areas have few major economic stakeholders apart from non-profit organisations. There are few parallels with such activities in Britain, despite the recent expansion of the system which has produced considerable capital investment. British institutions are typically much smaller than American universities – the billion-dollar budgets of certain American private institutions place them in a different league altogether. As a consequence even carefully targeted schemes for focusing purchasing or recruitment would have little impact.

The role of the university here is basically as a neutral agent concerned with the vitality of its immediate community, or as an 'entrepreneur in the public interest, serving as a catalyst for mobilising resources ... (this role requires) an institutional base so that a strategy of constructive change can be pursued for a long time'.[24] Major urban education institutions arguably can fulfil this role to a greater degree than any other actor in the American inner city. In the absence of major government initiatives and expenditures, the condition of America's large cities arguably makes university engagement not an optional extra but an institutional imperative.

One lesson which may be learnt from these efforts is that there is little point in institutions engaging in partnerships which depend too heavily on the institution itself. Without attempting to build the capacity of the community to solve its own problems, community groups will always be in a position of dependency; however remote it may seem, there is always the possibility that major urban universities could merge, close or relocate. This is where forms of knowledge imply and reinforce existing power relations: disinterested technocracy or political advocacy do not enable a community to do research on its own, just as physical redevelopment which depends on continued injections from the university's endowment and on the continued voluntary advice of university specialists will not enable a community to stand on its own in a competitive financial climate. However, universities still operate in a market, and the extent to which they can, consequently, open access to their resources to low-income groups is limited; there are clear constraints on the democratisation of knowledge and its use.[25]

CONCLUSION: RE-INVENTING UNIVERSITIES?

There is a great deal of energy and commitment behind these attempts to change existing academic practices, but before we get too carried away with enthusiasm for university-community involvement we should put it in context. The impact school partnership projects make, when set against the social circumstances of many at-risk children, may be limited; neighbourhood stabilisation efforts contend with the continued suburbanisation of economic activity and inner city decline. Inevitably, they represent a drop in the ocean when compared with the present conditions of many inner city areas, and with the reductions in Federal aid to cities of some $50 bn during the 1980s. Nevertheless at least some Presidents of prominent universities are convinced that the urban problems facing the USA are so substantial as to require a 'reinventing' of the American university. Sheldon Hackney of the University of Pennsylvania argued expansively (and, I think, optimistically) that this would produce a 'humanistic, morally inspired, civic institution, with an inclination and ability to help

America fulfil its promise as a fair, decent and just society'.[26] The emphasis on the civic character of universities is important here and is stressed more heavily there than in, say, British universities. A prerequisite for such developments would be changes to the academic reward system, giving much higher priority to types of scholarship other than that of discovery.[27] However, part of the problem here is a restricted definition of what is meant by public service: the mission of academic institutions is often viewed as a tripartite one involving teaching, research and service, but usually service (conceived narrowly as intra-university administration, or as service to learned societies) receives a much lower priority than the other two. By contrast, what may be needed is a model of academically-related public service, in which research and teaching activities are focused on the needs of an immediate geographical community. The benefits of integrating teaching, research and service, into a wider conception of academically-based public service, focused on the complex social problems facing America, could be considerable. For some years now there has been a vigorous debate in the USA on faculty roles and rewards, a debate which is rather more advanced than in the UK. At present, given the quadrennial competition for research funds instituted by the government, British institutions are engaged in an unseemly scramble to sign up those whose publication records are thought most likely to improve a department's ranking in the next rating exercise (in 1996). Scholars who have dedicated their work to community collaboration are unlikely to have the publication records that will find favour in that sort of struggle.

This raises the question of the contrasting funding bases of higher education in the two countries. Much work in the USA draws upon alumni and other charitable support, which permits institutions a degree of autonomy unavailable, by and large, to UK universities. The monolithic funding bases of UK higher education are inimical to innovation; endowment and other sources of funding are far more limited. This means that institutions who conceive of themselves, rightly or wrongly, as research universities, are highly unlikely to develop meaningful community links beyond symbolic gestures, since their financial viability depends almost entirely on how well they perform in research terms. Even the former polytechnics (which were established with part-funding from local authorities, with a clearer community focus) may be in danger of losing some of their strong local orientation as they strive to compete with the more established research institutions. Community involvement seems highly unlikely to infuse the research and teaching activities of most traditional British universities in this Darwinian environment. And it is highly unlikely that institutions will unilaterally develop the kind of initiatives reported here – a classic prisoner's dilemma. It is significant, for instance, that institutional reports and plans make much of the volunteer involvement of students, despite the fact of minimal institutional support for such activities and the almost total absence of their integration into the curriculum. If this is the best they can do, community involvement has not got very far.

A reading of the most recent statement on university-community involvement in Britain would not give grounds for optimism that this situation will change.[28] The report, published by the Committee of Vice-Chancellors and Principals (CVCP), concentrates on the economic aspects of university-community engagement: economic multiplier studies of the impact of institutions, impacts on the physical environment (particularly those resulting from the recent wave of new construction in higher education), discussion of the role of universities in technology transfer, and so on. Teaching is barely mentioned and community service, on the part of students, barely rates a footnote. The tenor of the report is that relationships between universities and communities are something which, by and large, are a good cause activity – that as responsible corporate citizens universities should be involved in the affairs of their locality – and that appropriate structures should be created to manage that interface, such as fora in which senior management can meet their equivalents from local government and business. Memberships of governing bodies or statutory agencies, breakfast meetings between chief executives and senior university personnel, *ad hoc* task forces – these are all very well, but community links can easily reduce to symbolic gestures and talking shops which salve more consciences than they solve social problems. But there is no analysis of how the central components of university activity (teaching and research) might be refocused to increase responsiveness to community concerns. I would suggest, however, that there are three ways in which greater community involvement could benefit higher education institutions.

Firstly, through a stress on service as part of an education for citizenship. If properly integrated into academic programmes, service learning, with its emphasis on problem-solving and reflection, may help equip students with transferable skills. As universities increase in size, engaging students in this kind of activity could make a substantial impact on schools and voluntary organisations. Secondly, orienting research and other efforts towards the needs of the community requires different ways of working than those driven by government research assessment criteria. If a university is to be more engaged in its community it might be characterised by a greater emphasis on participatory research (rather than the unidirectional linkages typical of much academic work) and on cross-disciplinary collaboration (rather than disciplinary and departmental fragmentation). In the UK at present this poses a dilemma: the new universities may have to consider whether, in seeking to improve their research ratings, they will lose their strong local grounding and links with community organisations; the older universities may have to consider whether the lack of perceived strong local links will detract from their identity.

Finally, the more universities' internal operations are driven by an intense competition for research funds, the less likely they are to foster a sense of communal involvement and co-operation and the more likely they are to promote a competitive individualism which pays little regard to a wider notion of community. The most positive lesson to be learnt from America is that, if properly organised and supported, community involvement can become a vital part of – if not yet central to – the university's mission. Engaging faculty and students with problems on an institution's own doorstep can provide a means of integrating teaching, research, and service, as well as a way of revitalising the education of the next generation and socialising them in a spirit of service. In this era of globalisation, perhaps we need to start by thinking and acting locally, and, to descend into Kennedyesque rhetorical antithesis, we might ask not what universities can do for their communities, but what community involvement can do to invigorate the universities. It is in this sense that I argue that universities might find themselves rooted more firmly in their immediate community and thus in a rather different position to that satirised by the quotation from Umberto Eco.

NOTES

1. I should like to acknowledge the support of a Harkness Fellowship of the Commonwealth Fund of New York in 1992-3. I was based in the Center for Community Partnerships, University of Pennsylvania, where I was generously hosted by Ira Harkavy. In the course of this fellowship I was able to visit a number of universities in various cities; even so, this work

was somewhat impressionistic and I caution against generalising across a higher education system containing some 3000 post-secondary institutions. An earlier version of this chapter appeared in *Metropolitan Universities*, vol. 5 (4), 1995, pp85–94. I am grateful to the editor, Ernest Lynton, for permission to reproduce material from that article.

2. See, for example, D. Bok, *Universities and the Future of America*, Duke University Press, Durham, NC, 1990; E. Boyer, and F. Hechinger, *Higher Education in the Nation's Service*, Carnegie Foundation, Princeton 1981.

3. I. Harkavy, and J. Puckett, 'Universities and the inner cities', *Planning for Higher Education*, 20 (4), 1992, pp27–33.

4. See Milken Institute, *The Challenge from Within: a National Commission on University-Community Interaction to harness the potential of America's cities*, Milken Institute, Santa Monica, CA, 1993. This publication draws attention to the high proportions of people living in poverty on the doorsteps of America's wealthiest private universities such as the University of Chicago, Columbia University, New York, the University of Southern California, Yale University, and the University of Pennsylvania.

5. M. Cross, and R. Jobling, 'The English New Universities: a preliminary enquiry', *Universities Quarterly*, 23(2), 1969, pp172–82; R. Jobling, 'The location and siting of a new university', *Universities Quarterly*, 24(2), 1970, pp123–36.

6. A. Levine, 'Editorial: service on campus', *Change*, 26(4), 1994, pp4–5; D. Hirsch, 'Politics through action: student service and activism in the 1990s', *Change*, 25(5), pp32–6; A. Levine, and D. Hirsch, 'Undergraduates in transition: a new wave of activism on American college campuses', *Higher Education*, 22, 1991, pp119–28.

7. J.F. Mohan, 'Making a difference? Student volunteerism, service learning and higher education in the USA', *Voluntas*, 5(3), 1994, pp329–348.

8. J. Potter, 'New directions in student tutoring: the UK experience', paper presented to *International Conference on Student Tutoring and Mentoring*, London, April 1995.

9. Note that in some countries there are initiatives which engage very substantial proportions of students in education-based community service. For an international review see S. Goodlad (ed), *Study service: an examination of community service as a method of study*, NFER-Nelson, Windsor 1982.

10. For British arguments for education-based community service, see *ibid.*, and also S. Goodlad (ed), *Education and Social Action*, George Allen and Unwin, London 1975.

11. In Britain the best example of this is the Community Service Volunteers (CSV) scheme, *Community Enterprise in Higher Education*, the purpose of which is to help develop courses in which students are assessed on their application of knowledge to community needs. See S. Buckingham-Hatfield, *Higher Education Meeting Community Needs*, Community Service Volunteers, London 1989.

12. J. McCormick, *Citizens' Service*, Commission on Social Justice, London 1994; J.F. Mohan, 'What can you do for your country? Arguments for and

against Clinton's national service legislation', *Policy and Politics*, 22, 1994, pp257–66; I. Briscoe, *In Whose Service?*, Demos, London 1995.

13. US National Commission on Excellence in Education, *A Nation at Risk: The Imperative for Educational Reform*, National Commission, Washington DC 1983.
14. See F. Wilbur, and L. Lambert, *Linking America's Schools and Colleges*, American Association for Higher Education, Washington, DC 1991.
15. L. Albert, 'Introduction and overview: the partnership terrain', in *ibid.*, summarises these arguments.
16. C. Stoel, W. Togneri and P. Brown, *What Works: School–College partnerships to improve poor and minority student achievement*, American Association for Higher Education, Washington, DC 1992.
17. Information on these schemes is available from the American Association for Higher Education, 1 Dupont Circle, Washington DC.
18. For example the Boston Higher Education Partnership was established in 1975 following a court desegregation decision which required school reform proposals to be prepared with an input from the city's universities. Albert (*op.cit.*) mentions 13 states known to have funded partnerships and it is likely that substantially greater numbers of school boards have given some funding to collaborative ventures.
19. J. Kozol, *Savage Inequalities: Children in America's Schools*, Doubleday, New York 1991. See also Urban Institute, *Confronting the Nation's Urban Crisis: From Watts (1965) to South Central Los Angeles (1992)*, The Urban Institute, Washington, DC.
20. J. Mohan, *American Universities and Their Local Communities: Service-Learning, School Partnerships and Community Development*, Harkness Fellowship Report to the Commonwealth Fund, New York 1994.
21. A. Irwin, *Science at the Service of the Community? The Nuffield Foundation Science Shop Initiative*, Nuffield Foundation, London 1995.
22. I. Harkavy, and J. Puckett, 'Lessons from Hull House for the contemporary urban university', *Social Service Review*, 68 (3), 1994, pp299–321. See also a collection of papers in *Teachers College Record*, 95(3), 1994.
23. A. Irwin, 'Creating the citizen scientist', *Times Higher*, 21.7.95, p20.
24. R. Hanson (ed), *Rethinking Urban Policy: Urban Development in an Advanced Economy*, National Academy Press, Washington, DC 1983, p179. On the need for such institutional support for community development see also H. Husock, 'Bringing back the Settlement House', *The Public Interest*, 1992, pp53–72, who argues that non-profit institutions can help play the same kind of role in community development as did the original settlement houses of the 19th century.
25. H. Wainwright, *Arguments for a New Left*, Blackwell, Oxford 1994.
26. S. Hackney, 'Reinventing the American University: towards a university system for the 21st century', *Teachers College Record*, 95 (3), 1994, pp311–316; see also the contributions to the same issue of that journal by the presidents of the (public, but research-led) institutions of Wayne State University, SUNY Buffalo, and the University of Alabama at Birmingham.
27. C. McCallum, 'The bottom line: broadening the faculty reward system', *Teachers College Record*, 95(3), 1994.

28. Committee of Vice-Chancellors and Principals (CVCP), *The University Advantage*, CVCP, London 1994. The CVCP comprises all chief officers of university-level institutions in the UK.

9

COMMUNITIES, UNIVERSITIES, AND THE WIDER EDUCATIONAL SCENE

John Andrews

This chapter seeks to put into broader focus some of the developments which we are currently seeing in the field of continuing education in universities in Britain. It argues that there is a pattern in the changes which we have recently seen in higher education and at the same time it reaches out to a new challenge for the university world of the future. In the context of these changes, the cause of continuing education and the role of departments of continuing education are factors of increasing significance.

Some of the points made below would have been regarded as heretical only a few years ago. Some of the changes highlighted are still a cause of tension and anxiety within the higher education world and a few have occasioned some hostility.

Many of the problems result from the origins of the European university system. To suggest that we have been getting it wrong for the last millennium is a rather over-bold statement. The fact is, however, that, whilst the university world of medieval Bologna, Cracow, Paris and Oxford, is very remote from the responsibilities which we are now properly seeking to put on our university system, its influences have been enormously pervasive.

The European university tradition is bound up with the European ecclesiastical tradition. The scholastic tradition of the university world is very much exegetical – that is the exposition and analysis of text, especially text with scriptural authority. The study of the text was a vital part of a university tradition, which has taken on many apostolic features. We should not overlook the fact that the words disciple and discipline share a common root and, whilst few university teachers today are likely to affect the spiritual arrogance of regarding their students as disciples, we still believe ourselves to be playing a pivotal role in the advancement of our discipline: which in some ways is to recast the same thesis in a more circular form.

In summary, a monastic aspect has dominated the university world and is illustrated by some of its most fundamental phenomena. Essentially it has been male only, residential and excessively introspective. It once required religious tests for admission; it has on occasions encouraged a near diaconal or even priestly tradition in its scholars; it has embraced a very limited subject range, forming something of a scholastic calendar; and it has given rise to an academic cycle coinciding with the ecclesiastical year.

If we look to our more immediate inheritance, we can see that the establishment of the civic universities was an important break with this tradition. These brought major developments including admitting women, catering for local students and offering part-time provision; they significantly increased vocational provision with the old disciplines of medicine and law acquiring significantly more relevant syllabuses, and to them were added training for the teaching profession together with engineering and the new sciences.

Associated with this was the early development of a wider civic educational programme, which eventually came to be delivered under the title 'Extra-Mural Studies'. Thus the tradition of academic exclusivity was preserved; the innuendo of this unfortunate title being that university studies properly so-called took place within the palisade.

These municipal foundations were illustrative of the best tradition of universities working with, in, and for, their own community. They were a source of civic pride and were in receipt of considerable municipal support and beneficence. The tradition continued through until after the second world war, but was then largely driven out by universal maintenance support and the increasing tradition of students going away from home and taking advantage of the university experience as a full residential experience. The old civic foundations developed campuses, frequently moving from the centre of town, or artificially identifying a campus by creating a precinct around themselves. Courses changed and part-time study became very exceptional. The newer university foundations of the 1960s were, of course, almost without exception of a campus style.

What had happened to the civic universities subsequently happened to several of the Colleges of Advanced Technology. Fortunately the polytechnics did not follow suit: it was no wonder that Government should show such fondness for them in the 1980s. Not only did they expand readily when expansion was sought, but they maintained their diversity and in particular continued to provide a range of part-time, user friendly, vocationally relevant programmes.

It might be said that this exaggerates and over-generalises. After all many universities drew their courts of governors locally, they often provided concerts and lectures for the local public, their teaching hospitals cured the sick and university research was not always irrelevant to the needs of industry and the economy. Some would argue that the exclusivity factor does not matter anyway. Universities are, it might be said, institutions apart from everyday affairs and attendance at them is an experience apart from the normal daily round. This is certainly a common view, but as an answer to the charge of excessive exclusivity, it is not good enough. The problems which were caused by this tradition have had very serious implications. Not least, they have had serious implications for continuing education. The whole title 'Extra-Mural' seemed to suggest that what went on under that title was outside of the main or proper functions of the university.

But the problems go beyond that. The nature of our universities has tended significantly to determine the professional structure of our society. It is not surprising that a tradition which was monastic and elitist would educate doctors but not nurses. It is interesting to reflect how that has affected not merely the sociology, but also the practice of health care. Engineering and science were in, but many of the professions which were developing in the nineteenth century were out: including architecture, surveying, pharmacy, accountancy. We developed a distinction between graduate and non-graduate professions, a distinction which has only recently been broken down with the contribution made by the Colleges of Advanced Technology and the Polytechnics to the 'degreeing-up' of many of these subjects.

The second aspect of this tradition has been the nature of many of the subjects which have been regarded as 'academic' within the full range of meaning which that loosely textured word can take on. They are frequently centred on scholastic disciplines with only an indirect relevance to the world of work. This has given rise to the principle of 'amateurism', which has tended to dominate public and diplomatic service and much of industrial and commercial management in the United Kingdom for so many years.

Within this, a cycle has repeated itself several times over. Institutions drift from part-time to full-time teaching, from sub-degree to degree and, if possible, postgraduate degree teaching, from providing for local to providing for in-coming residential students.

It could be said that so long as the higher education world was catering for a tiny, elite minority, this did not matter. The great majority of people enjoyed a more 'relevant' education through apprenticeships, professional programmes, higher technical training, through diploma programmes and professional qualifications.

But as we have moved from the six per cent participation rate of the early 1960s to the thirty per cent plus participation rate of today, it is understandable that many employers and many students with an eye to employment, look for more than just a degree. The vast increase in intakes to Law and Business related degree schemes has illustrated this and the drift to more career oriented courses has become more apparent as a result of a combination of economic recession and a rapid technological development which has reduced the number of middle skilled jobs.

Society no longer funds higher education simply because it is regarded as a 'good' in its own right. Given that Government now, and any likely Government in the intermediate future, will need to control public spending, it is inevitable that we will be involved in the prioritisation of public funding. One can see this very directly in Wales where higher education is funded from the Welsh Office block vote. This means that, in seeking funding for higher education, the Higher Education Funding Council for Wales (HEFCW) is in competition with other heads of Welsh Office spend – Industry, Roads, Housing, Health, Environment, Schools etc. It is not surprising that university colleagues in Wales find HEFCW encouraging institutions to contribute to economic development and particularly to the Welsh economy; or indeed that, when the then Secretary of State, John Redwood, was persuaded to provide additional funding to improve research in Welsh higher education institutions, he asked the Council to have regard to his policies in Wales, including in particular his economic policies, in distributing the funding. In summary, it is in the interests of higher education institutions in Wales to play a major role in economic and social development in Wales, as well as in the wider national and international scene.

Whilst recognising the value and importance of many of the changes which have taken place and which are taking place and which will take place, in higher education, it is unfortunate that they have had to coincide with a period of intense pressure on public funding and have, therefore, been pushed forward in coincidence with heavy efficiency gains and increasing demands for accountability for resources, which have increased the administrative demands on institutions.

The most important of these changes has been the widening of higher education: widening in the sense of the removing of the binary line, so that we now have one spectrum of higher education institutions, with the important implication that has for equality of esteem of different institutions, different degree subjects and different modes of study. I make no apology for underlining the importance of this change. We no longer have an elitism of post-school three year residential degree students set against the rest. Widening again in that we now have thirty per cent participation of school leavers and, when that is coupled with the striking increase in mature students, this has resulted in a near exponential growth in the higher education sector, going beyond anything that was forecast as recently as 1985.

These macro changes are obvious to everyone. Behind them lie a number of other very important changes, some of which this paper can only touch on, but I hope both to give a flavour of the change, and to underline my thesis that, whatever the criticisms made, there is a pattern to it and that pattern is logical, and good. I reflect on three areas of change:

First, the growth of the polytechnics and the subsequent abolition of the binary line, together with other forces, has meant that a whole range of new subjects have come to be recognised as properly and fully belonging in the higher education firmament. These include teacher training, pharmacy, architecture, surveying and planning, construction, environmental occupations, nursing, tourism, food science and management in a thousand and one forms.

It is sometimes fashionable to criticise some of these subjects as providing too narrow an education. Given the track record of medieval exegesis in university studies, often conducted through into the nineteenth century and beyond with an attention to casuistry which beggared belief, this is a somewhat incongruous criticism. These new subjects do not have a rich literature in the way that Divinity or History has, they may not match the analytical and rationalistic demands of Law or Philosophy, nevertheless they have a rich relevance to modern life and their study is far superior to the apprenticeship or crammed learning techniques which were often the training methods in these areas in the past.

Higher education has made a major contribution both to the economic life of the country and to the individual career base by these developments and by the bringing of the new universities and college sectors fully into the firmament of higher education.

Secondly, as Chief Executive of a Further Education Funding Council I have been increasingly impressed by the enormous range of further education provision and the way in which much of it is developed to meet the needs of students for user friendly delivery. The Further Education Funding Council for Wales (FEFCW) has led the way among funding councils in developing a funding methodology which is not concerned with the full-time/part-time distinction or day or evening study. We fund on the basis of learning units. We have funding units for admission and guidance, for the teaching and learning process and for attainment. It is a highly flexible form of funding with steers within it encouraging institutions to provide part-time courses and outreach programmes to attract women returners, the unemployed or the employed, for whom education is not so easily accessible, as well as those with educational disabilities or those from areas of social and economic deprivation and so on. Would it not be a challenge for the new millennium that the university world too should provide in all its richness a programme of higher education, vocational and academic, inspired by the same wish to bring education to students in a form which educated for life and for career, in an environment in which no student was handicapped by circumstances? The polytechnics that were, the new universities that are, have given an impressive demonstration of what can be done. Many of these have contributed powerfully to the learning environment of their areas.

Thirdly, there is an important tradition of wealth-creating research in the UK, but unquestionably university scholars have been encouraged to the view that research is something to be pursued for its own sake and for the personal satisfaction of the scholar. If it leads to major discoveries and publications furthering the reputation of the scholar and advancing mankind, so much the better. But, the idea that because research is pursued at public expense there is a public interest in its direction and its outcome, is something which has not been readily accepted into the comprehension of the university world in Britain.

This is changing, and a lead was taken in Wales when the Secretary of State asked the HEFCW to have regard for his economic policies in the distribution of the additional research funding which he made available in 1993. This initiative was taken up and pushed forward on a broader front in the White Papers on *Competitiveness* and *Realising the Potential* in 1994. The result is that a significant amount of research funding will in future be determined by what is perceived to be relevant to targeted national economic interests as a result of technology needs forecasts. A very significant amount of Research Council funding is likely to be determined in that way and a significant element of funding council funding will no doubt reflect this initiative.

HEFCW has been enthusiastic to encourage Training and Consultancy work in universities. We believe that Training and Consultancy development with links with local and national industry and employers and employees will become increasingly vital to the institutions as communal beings. We also believe that it will become increasingly important to the economy of institutions.

In essence the pattern of these changes is to bring forward the concept of the university as a responsible being, responsible to students, employers and the community. Many institutions that do not respond to these new influences will probably be left behind. A few universities will continue to be able to appeal more exclusively to a traditional clientele and will change rather more slowly, although even those universities will find that on the research front they need to respond more rapidly. For the vast majority of institutions their ability to command public funding and public attention, will increasingly depend upon their public attraction, their public appeal, their public contribution.

There will be enormous challenges arising from the increasing demand for higher education. At the present time the participation rate is just over thirty per cent for the post-school generation. But the National Training and Education Targets propose a growth in the number of students reaching the two A levels/NVQ 3 level from thirty per cent at the beginning of the 1990s to sixty per cent of twenty-one year olds by the millennium. Given that is the level for entry into higher education we are likely to see a significant increase in the demand for higher education at the turn of the century and beyond. Another of the targets is very much concerned to develop the lifelong learning achievements of those in work, to sixty per cent reaching two A levels/NVQ 3 level by 2000; this is bound to increase demand from mature students.

This will have a major impact on higher education. But no Government is likely to increase the funding to the level which would be necessary to enable a proportionate increase in the number of school leavers and mature students taking three year full-time residential courses. The extension of the loan system will inevitably lead to more students looking for opportunities to pursue higher education in a less costly way. A shift to a Tax or National Insurance premium repayment system will be more user-friendly, but not necessarily cheaper to individuals in the longer run. The growing enthusiasm amongst mature students for lifelong learning will also affect the demand for courses in higher education which offer most value for money.

This will put enormous pressure on the system to diversify itself in a way that caters for new student needs. There will be continued pressure on further education colleges to provide higher education courses locally, particularly at HNC level. They have a very rich local estate and cater in a sensitive and user friendly way for school leavers and adults who chose to develop through the further education stream rather than the traditional school stream. For many of these students HNCs and HNDs and top up courses leading to degrees are a natural way forward.

In addition, many students will want to take advantage of higher education, not to take the traditional degree, but to obtain the knowledge, training and skilling which will be available from higher education courses. Already a very large proportion of the postgraduate taught course provision is provided on a part-time basis, with a strong vocational element.

The higher education students of tomorrow will require flexibility in provision and increasingly are likely to look for provision which is relevant to their world of work. Part-time courses, distance learning, outreach provision, collaboration between institutions, targeting the needs of special groups, women returners, unemployed men, students with disabilities, employees needing up-skilling, and so on, will become major features. Part-time, outreach and distance learning packages will become crucially important.

In this, colleagues who have traditionally been involved in the world of continuing education will have a lead role to play. But this can only be achieved if the whole idea of continuing education is perceived to be central to the mission of universities and not something which is 'without its walls'. This is an important factor in the enthusiasm to

114

mainstream continuing education. One hopes that, in mainstreaming continuing education, we shall not so much be taking continuing education into the appropriate subject departments in the university world, as taking those subject departments out and streaming them into the programme of continuing education. It is important that continuing education, like careers and like industrial liaison and other activities, which in the past have been seen as ancillary functions in the universities, should clearly be seen to be part of a continuum of function and responsibility. I have argued elsewhere that I believe the seams in our educational system are too thick.[1] To continue this metaphor, instead of a cloth with different colours, shades and patterns across its width, our educational system is like a patchwork quilt, made up of independent pieces stitched together by seams, whose very thickness seems to emphasise the separateness of each part of the cloth. We need to move away from this. I am not arguing that we should substitute a grey garment for a richly patterned one. On the contrary, the whole emphasis of what I am saying is on the need for continued and increasing variety. As we struggle to meet socio-economic needs, whether in Wales or elsewhere, we need to provide a greater range of training and education at full-time and part-time levels, to meet an ever increasing and widening range of students. In essence, we need to increase the colour and patterning of the garment, whilst removing many of its seams or at least reducing the barriers they represent.

Above all I am not arguing for an increasing level of alikeness in higher education institutions. On the contrary I regard it as vital that diversity is maintained. Many of the former Local Education Authority higher education institutions already have rich local roots and are used to working in the community with industry and with a wide range of organisations and agencies as well as providing for their neighbourhood students. It is important that they maintain this mission. They have little to gain by seeking to climb the research ladder. It is steep, the funding is limited and the level of selectivity is high. The research ambition for many institutions is likely to prove a mirage if their aim is to become increasingly involved with basic and strategic research, to seek ratings in the assessment exercise and funding from the Councils. Rather their opportunities are likely to lie in developing a wide range of consultancy and training programmes for local and national industry, organisations and agencies which make use of their special aptitudes and relevancies. Many of these institutions already have a most important tradition in this area and one of the encouraging features in Wales is the way in which institutions have maintained diversification and adherence to their mission. It is these institutions again which often have the strongest tradition of part-time teaching and providing continuing education programmes. It is easy to understand why. They have not been hidebound by the conventions of the old university world, but have had to be flexible and nimble to find and develop their own niche in the higher education world. But even though these institutions are well equipped to face the new generation of demands which are being imposed on the higher education world, they do not have sufficient capacity, experience or range of provision to cope by themselves nor can the more traditional institutions afford to be left behind. The whole higher education sector will need to face up to a new range of responsibilities.

In essence, the idea of universities as communal beings needs to be redrawn. The old sense of community, the monastic tradition, is introspective and exclusive. It is too narrow, too elitist, and too ignoring of responsibilities. Whilst it might have sufficed for charitable institutions funded by endowment, donation and fee, it is unreasonable for institutions to expect such a tradition to be preserved by inputs of public funding without recognising a concomitant public responsibility. The idea of universities as communal beings must be redefined to embrace not simply responsibility to the community within, but responsibility to the community without. For many institutions this may be predominantly its neighbouring geographical community. For other institutions it may be a wider community made up of individuals, enterprises, organisations and agencies drawn to it by geography, professional interest, shared pursuit and an ever widening range of links.

This challenge to the university world is one appropriate for the new millennium. Not only does it go well beyond the vision of scholars of the medieval universities of Europe, it goes well beyond the vision that our colleagues had less than a decade ago. The challenge is that universities should play a central role in revitalising our communities and our economy. We need to develop provision for those who in the past have been excluded from the world of higher education, whether by disability, prejudice or economic fortune. We need to take the university world to the outside world and to bring the outside world into the university. In short the challenge is that universities should become central and vital to our economic, social and individual well-being. In that way the knowledge and experience, the scholarship and the skills which they nurture, will be seen as vital, living and available, and not things possessed behind the walls or on the campus, with that sense of remoteness and mystique with which the ancient priests kept their tablets to themselves.

NOTE

1. John Andrews, 'The New Funding Context for Further and Higher Education', in *The New Agenda for Further and Higher Education in Wales*, University of Glamorgan, Pontypridd, 1992.

10

BALANCING EQUALITY AND DEVELOPMENT IN UNIVERSITIES AFTER APARTHEID: A FOCUS ON ADULT AND CONTINUING EDUCATION

Shirley Walters

Nelson Mandela issued a proclamation for the establishment of a National Commission on Higher Education on 3 February 1995. The broad aim of the Commission is to investigate all aspects of higher education and make appropriate policy recommendations. This chapter is therefore being written at a time when the South African higher education system is undergoing a thorough review. The debates about the future of higher education have just begun in earnest amongst a broad range of stakeholders.

The issues of access, finance, and democratic governance are three of the critical issues for universities in post-apartheid South Africa. These issues are not new, but contestation around them is taking new forms at the different institutions. The issues, of course, cannot be seen in isolation, but need to be seen in the context of the broader debate within the society and within the institutions of higher education. These debates centre around two poles, the one concerned with 'equality', and the other with 'development'. This chapter is in three parts: a brief overview of universities in South Africa; the key elements of the equality-development relationship; a CACE study to illustrate university adult education and the equality-development debate within it.

A BRIEF OVERVIEW OF UNIVERSITIES IN SOUTH AFRICA

There are twenty-one universities, with gross inequalities between historically black (HBUs) and historically white universities (HWUs). In 1959 the Extension of Universities Act was introduced which created universities for particular ethnic groups. The majority of the HBUs are located in the rural areas and the HWUs in urban areas. Vast discrepancies exist in financing, material resources, staffing, undergraduate teaching loads, quality of students, availability of courses, and so on. As Badat *et al* state:

> The functional differentiation of HBUs and HWUs has its origins in the different conceptions of the roles of these institutions. The HWU's were conceived of as providing the human resources and knowledge required by the advanced industrial, social and dominant political order enjoyed by the white population. By contrast, the HBUs were shaped to provide the human resources deemed to be necessary for the occupations available in the urban areas to black people and to the 'development' of bantustans – this being unrelated to any broad conception of the knowledge and skills required for their 'real' economic and social development.[1]

For example, HBUs have heavy concentrations on courses in public administration, education, religion, and the humanities, with little in the natural sciences, engineering and related disciplines. Also post-graduate programmes, research, and publication remain poorly developed in these institutions. Neither the HBUs nor the HWUs have prioritised adult and continuing education, for which there has been no state support. University education is geared to school leavers although at the HBUs the students are older than at HWUs; for example, at the University of Zululand 49 per cent of first-time entrants to undergraduate studies are over twenty-three years old, while at the University of Cape Town there are only 3.5 per cent over twenty-three.

While there is a growing literature which presents differing analyses of universities in the country, there is no dispute that the universities reflect the social-structural inequalities of a race, class, gender, institutional and spatial nature, that have been generated by a particular trajectory of economic and social development during both the segregationist and apartheid periods, and which are deeply embedded within the institutions. The major challenge for universities is to restructure and transform the institutions in ways which tackle the range and severity of the inequalities within and amongst the universities, while moving in critical alliance with the Government of National Unity towards equality, democracy and new paths of economic and social development.

A crucial debate amongst the universities revolves around two poles: the attainment of equality in relation to access to institutions, and the quality and hence the resourcing of institutions and the range of disciplines, graduate programmes and research within them; the developmental role of higher education in producing human resources and knowledge relevant to economic development and political management.[2]

The equality pole, grounded in conceptions of equal social rights and redress, finds strong expression among black students and parents, the democratic movement and within historically black institutions. The right to education has been and remains a powerful claim in South Africa and has been explicitly stated in the Freedom Charter of the African National Congress, which proclaims: 'The doors of learning and culture shall be opened!'

Through the years of the struggle for democracy there were regular calls for the right to education, training and skills upgrading. The institutions of higher education were challenged by students, academics, and community organisations, to change their student and staff compositions to reflect the race, class and gender composition within the broader society, to obtain resources for historically disadvantaged social groups, and for increased funding and qualitative development of the historically disadvantaged institutions. It is clear, however, that given the many calls on the national budget, the financial and other resources which will be required to redress the effects of the apartheid-capitalist system at the higher education levels are not likely to be available.

The 'development' pole is rooted in an emphasis on the role of the higher education system in producing the human resources and knowledge relevant to economic development and political management. It finds expression in the view emanating from some of the HWUs, which argues that, given their research, professional and post-graduate teaching programmes and capacities, and their reputations as centres of excellence, they constitute vital national resources, and any diversion of resources away from them would be detrimental to economic and social development.

THE EQUALITY-DEVELOPMENT RELATIONSHIP

There is much debate about the relationship between equality and development both within South Africa and internationally.[3] 'Equality' as used here refers to redress of social structural inequalities, and 'development' refers to socio-economic, political and cultural development. In the literature, some of the questions posed are: what is the relationship between the two? must one wait for economic development to ensure democracy? can the democratic process not impact positively on the development process? is democracy a constraint on economic development?

While this is not the place to answer these questions, a rejoinder by Ake is pertinent:

> Africa's failed development experience suggests that postponing democracy does not promote development; and even if it were true that democracy is competitive with development it does not follow that people must be more concerned with improving nutrition than casting votes or more concerned with health than with political participation. The primary issue is not whether it is more important to eat well than to vote but who is entitled to decide which is more important.[4]

There is a strong argument in South African debates that the higher education system must recognise the competing claims of both equality (redress of social structural inequalities) and development (socio-economic, political and cultural development and human resource development to effect this). On the one hand, it is imperative to accept that equality demands cannot be relegated to some future period when development has occurred. As Badat *et al* stated, there are at least two reasons for this: the goal of equality motivated the struggle against apartheid, and continues to be an extremely persistent and pervasive demand; and there is no guarantee that 'development' will also entail redistribution and a secular trend towards general equality.

On the other hand, human resource development, even where this entails the privileging of a certain layer of the educational and occupational structure, cannot be neglected, because in both the short term and the long term, economic development constitutes a necessary, if not a sufficient, condition for the possible enhancement of the conditions of the people, even if this does not also generate greater equality.

Wolpe asserts that the two poles of equality and development are always in tension.[5] If one accepts this then clearly a range of tensions exists between the equality-development objective, and within equality and development goals; trade-offs are implied, and difficult political choices entailed. For Wolpe the critical question is, 'How is the relationship ... to be determined?'

The question cannot be answered in a vacuum, but must be located within the broader Reconstruction and Development Programme of the Government of National Unity, so that the efforts in higher education are not piecemeal, but are part of the national political and socio-economic processes. The meanings of equality and development need also to be unpacked. It is not necessarily helpful to assume that the meanings of 'equality' and 'development' are unproblematic. For example, achieving equality across gender, race, class, and cultural differences, will require different strategies and will be prioritised differently by various interest groups. It is likely that black, urban, middle-class men's interests will have more prominence in the equality stakes than those of working-class, black, rural, women. How the tensions within and between the equality and development relationship are resolved will be the outcome of political contestation.

It is important to recognise that no matter how rational the approach of balancing equality and development policies may appear for the formulation of higher education policy, policy change is a fundamentally political process. Indeed, as Scouffe states, 'the assumption that education policy could be the result of simply identifying and choosing the alternative that is "best", that is relevant or not wasteful, ignores the obvious political fact that "best" has to be determined in the political crucible of competing interests'.[6] It will be very important to get all the constituencies involved in the policy debates on higher education, particularly the students. Securing their support is no easy matter, emphasising again that what may be 'rational' will still have to weather interest group claims and challenges, long after the trade-offs and compromises have been negotiated.[7]

In concrete terms, balancing equality policies and development policies will involve both the assessment of the human resources needed for political, economic and intellectual/cultural development and the operation of policies geared towards equality within and between institutions. The simultaneous consideration of equality in relation to the human resources required to reconstruct South Africa leads to a new model of the higher education system.

In the next section, adult education at the university will be discussed within the framework of the equality-development tension, using the University of Western Cape as an illustrative case study.

UNIVERSITY ADULT AND CONTINUING EDUCATION: A CACE STUDY

Only five of the twenty one universities have departments of adult education. Some others have administrative centres concerned with forms of continuing education. The Centre for Adult and Continuing Education's (CACE) at the University of Western Cape (UWC) prioritised adult education. Funding from the state for adult education was only possible when it related to courses of study that fell within the traditional parameters relating to entry and level. Adult education has depended primarily on private funding, and adult education activities have most often been marginal to the mainstream university activities.

The UWC is an historically black university set up in 1961 under apartheid legislation to serve people classified 'coloured'. From the late 1970s, UWC developed a proud history of anti-apartheid struggle. It became particularly well known in the late 1980s for its defiant stance of open support for the then banned liberation movements. It has a student population of over 14,000 with half being women, nearly half black, the rest mainly 'coloured', with a sprinkling of white students. The majority of students are from poor, working-class homes, with many being first generation students.

CACE was established in 1985 and within its first ten years it prioritised issues of 'equality'. The institute, which is located within the Faculty of Education, was born at a heightened period of anti-apartheid struggle and its mission was shaped very much by the politics of the time. Its 1988 brochure states:

> CACE aims to promote adult and continuing education which serves the poor and the oppressed individually and organisationally, with an

overall commitment to the attainment of a non-racial democratic society. This it hopes to achieve through

- informal, non-formal and formal teaching,
- ongoing research,
- provision of appropriate resources to adult and community educators.

There seem to have been three distinct periods in CACE's short history. The first is represented by CACE's unambiguous location within the 'people's education movement' from 1985 to 1989. The second is a period of transition captured by the slogans developed in 1989: 'preparing to govern' and 'moving from resistance to development'. The third period begins in May 1994 and is concerned with 'learning to govern'. In the first two periods, the communities served by CACE were defined mainly by their community and worker organisational bases, broadly within liberation politics. The third period has seen a shift from service to organisations within civil society to a mix of parastatal, state, and community-based organisations. There is also a far stronger focus on the community of professional adult educators and trainers.

The call for People's Education was first made at the National Education Crisis Committee conference of December 1985. It was a response to the deep crisis in education, which in turn reflected the political and economic crises of the time. People's Education was concerned both with mobilising all constituencies within education to participate in the struggle against the apartheid state and with building the foundations for a future democratic education system.

People's Education was taken up at UWC by students and staff. CACE staff participated actively through running nonformal and formal courses for community activists; the establishment of a small resource centre, in which posters, pamphlets, newsclippings, formal and informal publications on radical educational and organisational theory and practice were stored; a contemporary history project which captured developments within the popular social movements of the Western Cape; a research project to monitor developments within People's Education; and the production of popular publications. The primary constituency with which CACE worked was the vast network of community organisations which formed part of the broad democratic movement. The students on campus were also regarded as part of this constituency as many of them were both student activists and community activists. A Senate Committee was established which reflected these constituencies and to which CACE was accountable.

During this period the three formal courses – the Certificate and Advanced Diploma for Educators of Adults and the B.Ed module on Adult and Continuing Education – were established. The first two resulted from lengthy consultations with community educators and activists, and aimed to provide space for critical reflection by practising educators and activists. The certificate programme was designed to enable rural participation and to give practitioners with a standard eight education access to the university. It was a ground-breaking design within the context of South African university adult education, and is now an important reference point for national developments in the professional training of adult educators. The certificate was most concerned with access. It was meeting the most urgent training needs of practitioners in the field, and was not subsidised by the state.

In 1985 there was not a 'field' of adult education. There were many organisations and institutions 'doing' adult education, but few would have identified themselves as adult educators. The primary reference point for adult educators was the political struggle against apartheid. There was little self-identification as 'adult educators'. The context of educational practice was emphasised, rather than the theoretical or micro educational issues. While the government at the time actively hindered adult education through harassment of individuals and organisations, within the democratic movement there were the early stirrings of recognition of its potential relevance. Our prime concern was adult education as part of a broad movement for democratic transformation.

In late 1989 CACE co-hosted a conference with the Centre for Development Studies at UWC. It brought together activists from the democratic movement and it focused on 'Facing the challenges of the 1990s: Organising for democracy in the Western Cape'. One of the central themes of the meeting was 'preparing to govern'. For the first time activists were showing concern for the 'mess' that would be inherited once transfer of state power had been achieved. Some issues which previously would not easily have captured the attention of most activists began to emerge – for example, ecological concerns, AIDS, and the fact that millions of adult South Africans could not read or write. Not only the question of the destruction of the apartheid state but also the creation of a nonracial democratic society was placed firmly on the agenda for the next decade.

Adult education began to emerge tentatively in various fora as being important for achieving equity and redress. At the National Education Crisis Committee conference in December 1989 the slogan 'Literacy and numeracy for all' was used. More people began to ask what adult education was, and how it could contribute to the building of a democratic society. The period of transition was firmly underway with the unbanning of the political organisations on 2 February 1990.

At this time space opened up for people located within various sectors to begin to stake out their specific domains, and to begin to articulate their needs and interests as separate from the 'political'. Amongst adult educators a change was discernible. There was some movement towards the acknowledgement of adult education as an important field in its own right. Adult educators began to talk more confidently as 'adult educators', although the differences in their location meant there was little trust, for example, amongst those working in non-governmental organisations, community based organisations, trade unions, universities, or technikons.

The context shaped CACE's work in three key ways. First, we began to engage more specifically in policy orientated research. Secondly, we emphasised the development of indigenous approaches to anti-racist and anti-sexist training programmes for adult educators. Thirdly, we actively supported networking and the building of organisations specifically concerned with promoting the interests of adult educators, NGOs and women. The question of the professionalisation of the adult education field began to emerge more prominently.

In 1989 there were the first tentative moves to form an ongoing dialogue amongst the five universities in South Africa which were training adult educators. In 1992 a structure was established which linked the Universities of Cape Town, Natal, Witwatersrand and Western Cape to facilitate cooperative work in the field of adult basic education, and to act as a conduit for funding from USAID. By 1994 joint research projects between the universities were underway. In addition, a standing annual conference of university-based adult educators has been established since 1992, and an Association of Tertiary-based Adult Educators has been formed. This period saw the emergence of a more coherent community of university-based adult educators. By 1994 a central concern for these universities was the professional development of adult educators and trainers.

From 1991, with the anticipation of democratic government, there were competing bids to influence the formulation of future national policy options amongst adult educators, for example, working in literacy, trade union and workplace education, university-based adult education, and political and community education. Conferences and meetings were held to try to develop more coherent, unified positions. At this time it became clear to us at CACE that we needed to emphasise the close inter-relatedness that exists between organising the field of adult educators, theorising adult education, and practising it on the ground. Given the lack of a national system and the marginality of the field, the interdependence of all adult educators across sectors and organisational locations was clear. If adult educators were to make any headway they needed one another.

The momentum around education policy research increased dramatically at this time, and numerous policy documents were produced and critiqued, particularly those generated through the ANC. Within the political framework of transition towards the negotiated settlement, there was growing consensus that a comprehensive approach to adult education and training within an integrated system of lifelong learning was needed. Organised labour, employers and the state, all shared some agreement that widespread provision of adult basic education was crucial for economic renewal. Amongst the trade unions and community organisations, particularly, adult basic education was seen as addressing equity and redress issues. In 1993 questions of economic development were beginning to be placed more forcibly on our agendas through the alliance of the trade unions, employers and the state. The National Training Board produced substantial documents in late 1993 which affected profoundly the ANC's Education and Training Policy Document.

THE NATIONAL TRAINING STRATEGY INITIATIVE

Within the South African economy there has been a crisis for the past two decades, and growth rates have declined dramatically. There is about 50 per cent unemployment and widespread poverty. To create jobs and improve the living standards for the majority of people there needs to be massive economic growth. Within the Reconstruction and Development Programme there is an understanding that growth can be kick-started through the rapid provision of basic necessities such as housing, water-systems and electricity on a wide scale. However, to sustain growth over a longer period, industry will have to expand and be structured in order to meet the demands of new markets and new conditions.[8]

Faced with the economic crisis, employers, organised labour, the state and other stakeholders have developed some consensus on the need for, amongst other things, a major thrust in education and training which adopts an integrated approach and which is within a lifelong learning framework. In the National Training Strategy Initiative, which involved all the stakeholders, they state their vision as an approach to education and training which can meet South Africa's need for, 'a human resources development system in which there is an integrated approach to education and training which meets the economic and social needs of the country and the development needs of the individual'.[9] They state that this vision requires a paradigm shift from thinking about education and training as separate entities to thinking about learning as a lifelong process.

A set of principles has been adopted by the National Training and Strategy Initiative, which is central to the envisaged system.[10] They are:

- integration of education and training;
- relevance to national development needs;
- credibility internationally and nationally;
  coherence and flexibility within a national qualifications framework;
- standards should be expressed in terms of a nationally agreed framework and internationally accepted outcomes;
- legitimacy should provide for the participation in planning and coordination thereof of all significant stakeholders;
- access to appropriate levels of education and training should be provided for all prospective learners in a manner which facilitates progression;
- articulation should provide for learners, on successful completion of accredited prerequisites, to move between components of the delivery system;
- progression should ensure that the framework of qualifications permits individuals to progress through the levels of national qualifications via different appropriate combinations of the components of the delivery system;
- portability should provide for learners to transfer their credits or qualifications from one learning institution and/or employer to another;

- recognition of prior learning (RPL);
- guidance to learners.

An assumption of the integrated approach is that the country requires a highly skilled, flexible workforce which can apply new production and organisational technologies within post-Fordist production processes. The new production technologies enable the production processes to be highly automated, flexible, and smaller in scale. Workers in new automated enterprises have to be able to perform a wide range of both manual and mental tasks as part of close-knit production teams. It is recognised that the impact of post-Fordism is uneven. Its impact has been greatest in strategic export-oriented industries, and in these industries it has led to an increase in education and training levels. On the negative side it has also led to deskilling of work and displacement of labour. As a consequence, there has been the informalisation of economies, with growing numbers of low-wage firms struggling to survive.

A PARADIGM SHIFT

In 1994 there was a major shift in the adult education and training discourse. A shift from political and social movement discourse which highlights issues of equity and redress, to one which is driven by a training discourse which highlights economic development within a management framework. These developments coincide with South Africa's re-entry into international economic and political life. They are clearly related to global economic and political developments. The language of competency-based, outcomes-driven education is new to South African adult educators, whereas it has become part of the normal discourse of many adult educators in other parts of the world. South African adult educators and trainers are in something of a paradigm shift. Both are afraid of being dictated to by the other. The concerns of adult educators are captured in articles such as that by Griff Foley.[11]

The training discourse is being shaped by the organised labour and business sectors, which are urban-based and mainly male. The social movement adult education discourse is shaped by people in non-governmental organisations and tertiary institutions who have worked traditionally with economically impoverished men and women in rural and urban areas. The former are centrally focused on economic development and the latter on community development of various kinds. As I have argued elsewhere, there is a worry amongst some of the adult educators that the new system will still not meet the needs of the majority of marginalised women and men but will continue to privilege urban-based, employed, men.[12] Having said this, it is also acknowledged that the division between economic and community development is problematic, and it is imperative that adult educators and trainers take up the challenge of developing an integrated approach which addresses personal, economic and community development.

TOWARDS EQUALITY AND DEVELOPMENT IN UNIVERSITY ADULT EDUCATION

Whereas we have been primarily concerned in the last ten years with issues of equality, the central importance of economic development is recognised as part of the achievement of equality. The shift from being part of the anti-apartheid movement to being part of the process of reconstruction and development of the country has meant significant changes to both our theory and practice. We are still grappling with what it means on both these levels.

The universities as a whole have barely begun to think about the implications of lifelong learning, Recognition of Prior Learning and an integrated approach to education and training for their functioning. The universities are still geared to administering rigid entry requirements and mainly to servicing school leavers even though some of them have large percentages of older learners. The general policies and the orientation to teaching and learning do not put access to learning at the centre. Access is still framed in relation to entry requirements and finances, not epistemological access.[13] Within the context of the Reconstruction and Development Programme, it is reasonable to assume that the universities may be given incentives to rethink their approach to issues of access so that concerns for both equality and development are met.

The professionalisation of the field of adult education and training is being driven by a range of factors, including social reconstruction and economic development. Adult basic education is being developed at national and provincial levels. Systems need to be put in place in line with the emerging national framework which ensure coherence, career paths for practitioners, and so on. We are being called on now to assist certain Ministries of Education in provinces to do this. How these systems are set up will determine how the tension between equality and development is played out.

The concept of integration of adult education and training is being applied in our professional courses. Practitioners from multiple work sites, for example, industry, community organisations and state adult centres, are attending the courses. The profile of the constituency we serve has changed. While the majority of students are still from urban and rural settings where social development is primary, there are more students from state, parastatal and industrial workplaces. The curriculum is having to be radically rethought to adapt to the changes. The concept of 'integration' is forcing us to grapple with 'equality' and 'development' simultaneously. An important aim of the courses remains the development of adult educators and trainers who understand and can work with multiple oppressions within their contexts.

The importance of research, to engage with the many issues which the new paradigms and the new contexts are throwing up, is stark. The lack of resources to do this is equally so. But it is critical that research space is created. International linkages with intellectuals grappling with similar issues are recognised as critically important, and one way to try to ensure that we learn the lessons from others.

Active and continuing engagement with the policy-making processes provincially and nationally is ongoing. There has been a move away from conceptualising policy options to implementation and delivery. The harsh realities – of fiscal constraints, lack of political will at provincial levels, resistance to change, the ongoing marginality of the field, and the limited depth of trained black women and men to give leadership to adult education and training – have been dawning after the initial euphoria.

Funding possibilities for the work are changing. The donors who supported anti-apartheid activities have redirected their funds either to the government or to other areas of priority. New sources of financing have to be sought through both state and private means. Whereas before there was no possibility of accessing state funds, there may be some possibilities now. On the one hand, the argument has to be won through the National Commission on Higher Education that continuing education should be funded, and that the professionalisation of adult education and training should be supported. On the other, there may be opportunities to undertake joint ventures with state or other organisations.

CONCLUSION

University communities are having to learn to live in a democratic state. For the broad student population, access, democratic governance and finance will continue to be critical 'sites of struggle'. However, these issues are still seen in fairly narrow ways, as they do not yet challenge any of the fundamentals. They do not, for example, challenge the bias towards school leavers. Notions of lifelong education have only begun to be discussed as part of a national vision, but there is still little pressure being brought to bear on the institutions to service those older women and men who have not had the opportunities to undertake initial or continuing education. With the limited prospects of employment after completing school, we can anticipate that it will be the school leavers who will continue to exert the most influence on higher education policy. It will be left largely to the adult and continuing education interests, in alliance perhaps with organised labour and business, to advocate for access for older students on the basis of the need for equity, redress and economic development.

In the field of adult education the new discourse of outcomes-based education within a national qualifications framework is presenting positive pressure for us to clarify what is of value within our traditional approach, and to move out of the shadows of oppositional discourse to engage and contest the mainstream. Economic development is absolutely crucial for the achievement of effective equality in South Africa. Adult educators in universities are challenged to work more closely with people and concerns emanating from the formal and informal sectors of the economy, to work with government, and to continue to strengthen organs of civil society. The communities with which we work have expanded to include people from different sectors and from different organisational bases.

A determining factor in shaping the relationships between the universities and their communities will be prospects for funding. In the last fifteen years support from international agencies has enabled work to be done amongst poor, working-class, and highly politicised communities. The professional continuing education that occured had to be self-funding, hence it was out of reach for the majority of people. If the universities are to be able to serve the historically disadvantaged sectors, funding mechanisms will need to be developed. This may be in the form of an incentive from the RDP fund. But if this does not happen then the prospects for the universities in general, and adult and continuing education in particular, to contribute to equality and redress will be put under severe strain.

One of the ways in which universities are beginning to find alternative sources of funding is through partnerships with state, parastatal, business or other interests. An example of this is a partnership which CACE is entering with funders, NGOs and the Ministry of Education of one of the poorest provinces, the Northern Cape. CACE is being asked to deliver its courses for the professional development of adult educators and trainers into the remote and impoverished towns and villages of the province. This is part of the development of the provincial Adult Basic Education and Training system. This example holds promise for retaining capacity within adult and continuing education to continue to ensure that the resources of the universities are made available to rural, poor communities who live far away from the institution.

The pressures on the universities are enormous. On the one hand there are the interests from the industrialised, urban centres of mainly male power. On the other, there are the masses of school leavers who are demanding access to higher education. There will be very difficult political and educational choices to be made. Ultimately, it will only be in action that the balance between equality and development in the universities will be determined.

NOTES

1. Saleem Badat, Zenariah Barends and Harold Wolpe, 'The Post-Secondary Education System: Towards Policy Formulation for Equality and Development', in *Higher Education Financing Conference, Background Reading and Conference papers*, January 1995, p5.
2. *Ibid.*
3. See, for example: I. Wallerstein, ' "Development" lodestar or illusion', in *Unthinking Social Science: The limits of nineteenth-century paradigms*, Polity Press, Cambridge 1991.
4. C. Ake, 'Rethinking African Democracy', *Journal of Democracy*, 2, (1), 1991, p35.
5. H.Wolpe and Z. Barends, 'A Perspective from within the ANC on Quality and Inequality in South African Higher Education', prepared for South African Association for Research and Development in Higher Education Conference, University of Orange Free State, 1–2 October 1992.
6. G. Scouffe, 'The Assumptive World of Three State Policy Researchers', in *Peabody Journal of Education*, 62, (4), 1985, p116.
7. Badat *et al, op.cit.*, p13.
8. There is some concern as to whether the RDP's Commitment to growth

through redistribution will be able to withstand the pressures from the International Monetary Fund, which prefers the 'growth first re-distribution later' route. Both A. Olukoshi, 'South Africa: Another Ghana?', *South Africa Report*, Vol 10, No 1, 1994, p30; and V. Padayachee, 'Can the RDP survive the IMF?', *South Africa Report*, Vol 10, No 1, 1994, p25, highlight the need for South Africa to resist donor conditionality, in order to avoid the development paths of the majority of African countries.

9. National Training Board, *A discussion document on a national training strategy initiative*, NTB, Pretoria 1994, p10.
10. *Ibid.*, p2.
11. G. Foley, 'Adult education and capitalist reorganisation', *Studies in the Education of Adults*, Vol 26, No 2, 1994.
12. Shirley Walters, *Continuity not rupture: an analysis of adult education policy proposals emanating from the National Education Policy Investigation (NEPI)*, CACE Publications, Cape Town 1993.
13. See Wally Morrow, *Epistemological access in the university*, unpublished paper, UWC, Bellville 1993.

11

UNIVERSITY ADULT EDUCATION 'ON THE "BORDER" ': RECENT CROSS-BORDER AND EUROPEAN UNION EXPERIENCES AND ISSUES IN IRELAND

Peadar Shanahan

European Union power, state sovereignty, borders and cross-border co-operative efforts for development are, at the time of writing, major issues for many in Europe. They are raised in acute form in Northern Ireland (IRL-N) and the Republic of Ireland (IRL-S). This chapter starts from the assumption that sovereignty is of fundamental importance to many people. It further assumes that sub-states in the EU inter-state system have relinquished their sovereignty to the EU and, with Bodin and Hobbes as well as more recent thinkers, assumes that while sovereignty can be delegated it cannot – not easily at any rate – be shared. It assumes that inter-regionalism or cross-border co-operation for development within the EU is a positive activity, particularly in situations such as in IRL-N and IRL-S where there is conflict over the border. It is in the context of EU inter-regional policies and through the processes of integration generally in Europe that such conflict can be transcended and thus assuaged. The chapter illustrates the policies and 'leverage' activities of the developing power of the EU. More specifically, it documents the Europeanisation of

Irish universities in general and with particular reference to inter-regionalism, training and development, and policies for the integration of the 'excluded'. It illustrates the efforts of the EU inter-state system to cope with the socio-economic consequences of the global re-structuring of capital project, a project which entails an increase in the integration of resources, labour, markets, media, information and consumerism, in addition to the further exclusion of millions through unemployment and poverty. This global restructuring had its mirroring in Europe in the introduction of the *Single European Act*.

The chapter reflects on cross-border co-operation between university adult educationalists in Ireland, describing the activities of four university campuses: University College Galway (UCG) and Maynooth College (IRL-S); Jordanstown Campus, University of Ulster; and Magee College, University of Ulster (IRL-N). These four university adult education departments/centres, with their background of work in community development, formed *The Inter University Partnership for Community Development* (IUPCD). The smallest of the four institutions – Magee College, 'The University on the Border' – played an historical and politically significant role not only in cross-border co-operation but even in the development of the political issues in Northern Ireland in the 1960s, leading eventually to the re-emergence of militant Republicanism. It was also from Magee College that the innovatory, cross-border training project was carried out under EU auspices with Letterkenny Regional Technical College between 1987 and 1989, the project on which the inter-university venture was later based.[1]

Up to that time, most research had been founded on the idea that both states of Ireland were the natural result of historical evolution. However, it is often forgotten that the Irish border was imposed through conflict and this is acknowledged here as a fundamental starting point. It is useful to problematise the 'border' once again and consider adult education developments on either side as dual aspects of the society of the island of Ireland. This promises a more dynamic approach, as well as having implications for on-going efforts to find more peaceful ways of settling 'border' difficulties between the UK and IRL-S.

CROSS-BORDER CO-OPERATION IN UNIVERSITY ADULT EDUCATION IN IRELAND

A politico-historical perspective

In the nineteenth century, socio-economic change and industrial development occurred unevenly on the island of Ireland. The transfer of technology and forms of economic organisation from Britain to Ireland resulted in the early industrialisation of the North-east much as in other industrialising regions in Britain, Germany and Belgium. On the other hand, sustained industrial development did not effectively take place in the southern part of the island until the late 1960s. These were highly distinct patterns of development in that the two parts of the island represent different experiences not only of capitalist colonial and post-colonial domination and development but different experiences of the processes of socio-economic change at different points in time. In the contemporary world, Northern Ireland may be said to represent a peripheral region in a declining mature economy – the UK – while the Republic of Ireland reflects the experiences of certain countries of the capitalist post-colonial, Third World, and other late industrialising countries of the European periphery.[2]

The resurrection of the European colonial experience and, in this context, the capitalist colonial experience in this chapter on adult education is stimulated by Memmi's book, *The Coloniser and the Colonised*, for which Jean-Paul Sartre wrote the original introduction in 1957.[3] This book serves as a challenge to the European 'collective amnesia which would consign the colonial legacy to a past which no longer informs the present'.[4] History is never as simple as we might want it to be; transitions are not neat and definitive. Memmi's ideas on colonialism, the post-colonial critiques around the world, and the particular nature of capitalist colonialism, very usefully inform the historical perspective on the current Northern Ireland situation.

Since the partition of the island of Ireland in 1921, IRL-N remained under the jurisdiction of Britain with its own local parliament in Stormont, Belfast until its disbandment. To the south, IRL-S began the slow, national project of recreating and indigenising the state institutions inherited from the British. Moreover, the economic/industrial histories differ greatly. Because of the experience of capitalist colonialism, the whole society of the island reflects not only the divisions observable in other European societies like gender, class, race, peripherality, age, disability, etc. It also reflects divisions commonly observed in the post-colonial countries of the globe, particularly the problems of nationhood and state.[5] More recently, societal changes, consequential to the re-capitalisation of capital, have affected IRL-N and IRL-S differently. Consequently, these uneven and distinct historical developments that have occurred on the island since the early nineteenth century, have given rise to different histories of, and influential factors on, the contemporary adult education scenes in both parts of the island.

In a general sense, the origins of the traditions of adult and continuing education in both IRL-N and IRL-S may be differentiated in the following way: whereas that in IRL-N reflects the British secular, urban and isolationist tradition in adult education, the influential factors in IRL-S are indigeneity, the 'sacred', the rural, and pro-Europeanism.[6] However, having acknowledged these differences, we can also see that history also asserts the commonality of the people who inhabit the island of Ireland. The 'border', established in 1922 when Britain withdrew from IRL-S, thus remains problematic; hence our emphasis on problematising it.

Recent experiences, 1985–95

Over the past ten years, the EU has been actively intervening in cross-border university adult education on the island of Ireland. This has cost to date approximately £6,000,000 (55 per cent of cost, the other 45 per cent coming from the universities). The intervention has created the Inter-University Partnership for Community Development (IUPCD) between four university adult education partners which at its highest point of resourcing in 1992-93 involved sixteen full-time Training and Development Officers/Researchers, plus administrative back-up in the field. 690 students, mostly unemployed activists, graduated in community development.

University of Ulster, Magee College, is situated in Derry, the second city of IRL-N and located about two miles from the border with IRL-S. The College became part of the Royal University of Ireland in 1879 and was then larger than the colleges in Cork or Galway. In 1909, it associated with Trinity College in Dublin. Students began in Magee and, in true cross-border fashion, went to Trinity in Dublin to finish their degrees in theology and arts. In the 1960s, a second university was established in Northern Ireland. However, that university – New University of Ulster – was sited in Coleraine, a small market town forty miles east of Derry. This decision caused the first peaceful protest to take place two years prior to the outbreak of the 'Troubles' in 1968. Undergraduate degrees were removed from Magee to Coleraine in 1972. The cross-border connection with Trinity College was severed. Magee College, from 1968-84, was only an adult education appendage to Coleraine with fifty students. In 1984, Magee became one campus of the multi-site University of Ulster, the other campuses being Coleraine and Jordanstown, Belfast. It now has about 2000 full-time equivalent students and is by far the smallest of the three campuses with little administrative or decision-making power within the University of Ulster.

Many of the nationalist population in Derry hail originally from IRL-S and there are strong informal and cultural links between this natural hinterland and the city. Such links were broken, at least formally, with the establishment of the border in 1922. In 1968, too, the recent 'Troubles' began and the College had little to offer except a Foundation Studies Course for adults and community development led by Tom Lovett.[7] During this time, however, informal links were established between staff in Magee and University College Galway (IRL-S). In the late 1970s and early 1980s, Magee College adult educationalists were part of Galway's rural community development programmes in County Donegal.

However, it was the Anglo–Irish Agreement in 1985 which 'legitimated' cross-border work, leading to the more recent developments in cross-border co-operation which had their origins in Magee College, a university 'on the border'. The nature of this co-operation cannot be understood without considering the detailed forms it took.

In 1984, the Magee Community Development Studies Unit set up an Advisory Committee for its part-time Extra-Mural Certificate in Community Studies and invited on to it a staff member from the Regional Technical College in Letterkenny (IRL-S), twenty miles away. From this interaction, a number of meetings followed, culminating in a cross-border symposium on Community Development in December 1985. In 1986, UCG approached Magee College to suggest a Community Development joint training project on the Lifford/Strabane border as an exercise in cross-border co-operation without, at that stage, funding. This took place in the cross-border towns of Strabane (IRL-N) and Lifford (IRL-S) between 1986 and early 1987. In 1987, the European Social Fund (ESF) granted funding to the proposal from Magee College and Letterkenny Regional Technical College, whereby each was granted around £300,000 to develop a joint curriculum over two years. Eight full-time staff were appointed. The course in Magee developed a new curriculum with a mixture of skills and educational inputs and entailed both college and community training.

Following the success of the Innovatory Project, 1987-89 – the Magee Unit won the Shell UK Prize for Open Learning, Partnership Awards – the four campuses, (Magee, Galway, Jordanstown and Maynooth) successfully submitted four proposals to the ESF for inter-regional and inter-university education and training for people involved in community development. Joint training between Magee and Galway and between Jordanstown and Maynooth was established. This was funded until 1994.

In 1990, the four Colleges submitted a proposal to the INTERREG Fund (the EU programme to faciliate inter-regional co-operation) for rural regeneration. This project was delayed until 1993 and limited the time of the project to 18 months. In addition to this co-operative work on a local level, the four university adult education programmes on each of the campuses are involved in ESREA (European Society for Research on the Education of Adults) and the *ERASMUS* Studies in European Adult Education programmes. At the time of writing, however, the IUPCD is not in receipt of EU funding.

ISSUES FOR UNIVERSITY ADULT EDUCATION PRACTICE IN A MILITANTLY-DIVIDED SOCIETY

Who is being serviced and what is being served?

From South Africa to IRL-N and the UK, universities are being forced to respond to questions such as: who is being educated ? What, why and how are they taught? Adult Education is central to the exploration of answers to these questions. But, in Ireland, North and South, UAE is not fundamentally any different from that in other comparable settings, being mainly concerned with continuing education and with those who have sufficient resources to use university facilities in part-time courses to 'better themselves'. It is thus mainly for the 'haves' in society and the main beneficiaries are the universities, colleges and consultants serving their needs. As privileged institutions of the state, universities in the EU area, while more open than other institutions to democratic influences, reflect the structures of dis/advantage of society – such as class, gender, race, peripherality – in a particularly effective way. In the case of IRL-N, however, the most critical and visible structure of dis/advantage remains the politico-religious divide. Universities are not above these processes in IRL-N. Two reports of investigations into both of the universities in IRL-N have expressed anxiety at aspects of each in relation to the politico-religious structures.[8] It is thus necessary to clarify the kind of UAE being addressed.

Adapting James, we can distinguish four tendencies in UAE: Academic, Training, Professional Education, and Empowerment.[9] 'Empowerment' is concerned with the 'excluded'.[10] It is not isolated from the day-to-day practical concerns of excluded people but deals with and is integrated with their realities; it is geared to changing these realities directly by using the university's capital, both material and cultural. It is not only concerned with personal development but is also oriented toward collective analysis and action.

The work of the IUPCD described above may, in general, be categorised as reflecting the UAE tendency towards empowerment. This is particularly true of the IRL-N elements (Magee/Derry and Belfast) of the IUPCD where only the long-term unemployed were recruited. However, in the case of Magee, a number of issues added to the challenge of operating an effective UAE for empowerment response. These included: the border itself (being two miles from the College); the uneven distribution of unemployment between nationalist and unionist working-class neighbourhoods, with the nationalists being well over twice as likely to be unemployed; the differing traditional attitudes to Community Development in each type of neighbourhood, it being better developed in nationalist neighbourhoods; the dominance of nationalists in Derry (65 per cent); and the fact that this particular UAE project was essentially cross-border and thus identified with nationalist aspirations.

From 1982, Magee College adopted the policy that selection of community groups and recruitment to the programme would be based not on community relations principles but on that of potential for development and evidence of energy and activity. Both policito-religious communities were, however, always represented on the programme each year. Sometimes, people who some years earlier had been trying to kill each other were sitting down with each other in a course of 40 weeks, analysing common problems in their neighbourhoods and discussing solutions!

EU and state 'leverage' in higher education: the Europeanisation of Irish universities

From the initial Cross-border Innovatory Project in 1987 between Magee College and the Regional Technical College in Letterkenny, the entire work of the IUPCD illustrates the impact of EU leverage in higher education in Ireland. This process has been referred to as the 'Europeanisation of Irish Universities' and, according to Dineen, is characterised by: (i) less dependence on the national government for funding; (ii) more market-driven; (iii) more dependent on the EU; (iv) stronger links with industry.[11] These characteristics do not, I suggest, cover the range of the impact of Europeanisation and three more should be added: (v) greater sensitivity to the issue of exclusion, unemployment and poverty by higher education institutions; (vi) increased and stronger links between universities and local government, political and community bodies; and, above all, (vii) inter-regional co-operation between universities – such as cross-border co-operation in UAE – and, more broadly, inter-university co-operation within the European Union as a whole.

The project work also reflects the modification of the traditional elite institution into the mass university and the growing interest of the state in university life as well as its use in social and economic policy developments.[12]

UAE cross-border policy implementation: a problem-free development?

The 'legitimation' of cross-border co-operation in UAE in Ireland had an overtly political origin: the Anglo-Irish Agreement in 1985. As O'Malley has contended, this Agreement between the two governments was itself a direct response to the threat to constitutional nationalism in IRL-N by militant Republicanism.[13] This threat was a consequence of the alienation of nationalists following the deaths of ten Hunger-strikers in 1981 (including an MP) and the re-politicisation of militant Republicanism. The Anglo-Irish Agreement, with its 'legitimation' of cross-border co-operation, was rejected out of hand by the IRL-N unionist community.

Meanwhile, EU policies on inter-regional (cross-border) co-operation for development, while not formulated into a distinct programme until 1990, were in place. From the re-beginning of Magee College in 1984, it became clear to the University of Ulster authorities that cross-border projects between Magee and RTC, Letterkenny, would be looked on favourably by the EU for funding. By December 1985, a cross-border symposium on Community Development was held in which the North-West Cross-border Community Development Training Project was publicly proposed and at which representatives of the education authorities of both IRL-N and IRL-S participated.

Yet, running the IRL-N cross-border programmes with RTC, Letterkenny and UCG in IRL-S was scarcely free from frustrations. The following examples give a flavour of the difficulties.

After the Magee ESF-Innovatory Cross Border Project (1987-89) and a year of joint cross-border training with University College Galway and Maynooth in IRL-S, the IRL-N proposals to the EU no longer included a cross-border responsibility. To the South, on the other hand, IRL-S proposals did include responsibility for joint cross-border training! The cross-border joint training continued until the end of funding in 1994 only because of strong personal relations between the adult educationalists involved, particularly between Magee, UCG and Maynooth College.

To take other examples of the frustrations, in 1990 an INTERREG Proposal was put forward in Magee following the appointment of an IUPCD staff member as Academic Advisor to a major Conference under this programme sponsored by the Socialist Group in the European Parliament (the INTERREG programme being specifically for co-operation between *different* regions of the EU). It was initially aimed at cross-border co-operation for rural regeneration. A long delay followed the formal acceptance of the proposal and when eventually funded, the control of the project was switched from Magee, which is on the border, to Belfast Jordanstown, which is sixty miles from it and technically outside the programme area stipulated. The focus of the project changed too, and became Northern Ireland agency development rather than about cross-border initiatives. Cross-border development work by IRL-N academic staff was not eligible for support. Since 1987, IRL-N administrative restrictions on travel in IRL-S, despite its proximity to Magee College, inhibited, or at least frustrated, the inter-regional dimension to cross-border work. An

INTERREG 11 Conference in May 1995, partly organised by the University of Ulster, did not even include anyone from the IUPCD.

These are but anecdotal allusions to the genuine political drama represented by the efforts to promote UAE cross-border work from 1984 to 1995.

CONCLUSIONS – QUESTIONING THE FOUNDATIONS OF STATE AND EU POLICIES IN UNIVERSITY ADULT EDUCATION

After working in university-based adult education for community development with the 'excluded' sections of the population over the past twelve years, and that in a situation of militant insurgency, I am led to agree with Torres, that in order to grasp the inner rationality of adult education programmes and policies we must ask on what basis the capitalist state would be willing to undertake substantial reforms: 'Any mode of State intervention and most of the State's policies are therefore linked to a changing pattern of potential or actual threats to the political system, or to structural problems that emerge out of the process of accumulation of capital. The modes of state activity can thus be seen as responses to these social threats and problems.'[14] In the light of this, new versions of the old political questions that were asked in radical adult education circles for generations again become relevant.

To what degree should new policies in this relatively minor field of state support for education be related to the spectrum of political conflict in civil society? Should a new adult education strategy be viewed as a mode of national integration of the masses which dominant alliances use to mould the 'excluded' into a Nation State, or even a Super State? More specifically in relation to our project: What has this cross-border, university-based adult education with the 'excluded' been all about and why did it take place here rather than elsewhere? What social and political conditions lie behind the investments of IRL-N, IRL-S and the EU of approximately ten million pounds with the unemployed, through university adult education and collectivist self-help enterprises, including cross-border work? These questions cannot be ignored by attending only to the surface rhetoric, as opposed to the reality, of policies and programmes.

The conclusion here is that the interests of these states, including the inter-state system of the EU, in the 'excluded' are *not only* a consequence of the potential of the contribution of the excluded to the creation and accumulation of capital; *not only* a consequence of the need to introduce change and renewal to the bureaucracies and institutions of the state by engaging the radical ideas of professional adult educationalists; and *not only* a consequence of the need to develop new skills and new definitions of work. They are, *even more so*, an expression of state interventionism aimed at strengthening the legitimacy of the dominant alliances as a prerequisite to sustaining or developing the generation and accumulation of capital. In other words, change in state policy in relation to adult education with the 'excluded' in a market-driven society is more a function of, and a reaction to, the threat to the dominant alliances in society they represent, than of any other factor.

This must, however, be understood in context. Changes in state polices towards UAE require the recognition of the importance of bureaucracy and institutional politics, specifically the effects of intense intra-state, inter-state and intra-European state bureaucratic struggles for dominance. Intense inter-university competition for resources from Europe has also been a telling factor. The specific role of the vocational adult educator and project staff with the 'proper community credentials' and their historical employment in the university system must also be taken into account.

Given the historical analysis of the first part of this chapter, the importance of the Troubles to the development of the IUPCD can hardly be under-estimated. The on-going conflict in Northern Ireland became in part problematic to Britain within the global re-capitalis-tation project. It has also become problematic to the EU and to the policies emerging from the Single European Act. After many years of overt, covert and bloody conflict, the Downing Street Declaration has been signed, the present Ceasefires established and the Framework Document published. New programmes that, in effect, problematise the border in relation to inter-regional development and the support of peace have been set in place by the EU: The Special Support Programme for Peace and Reconciliation in Northern Ireland and the Border Counties of Ireland 1995-1999 and the European Structural Funds INTERREG Programme Ireland and Northern Ireland 1994-1999. The argument is being made too for 'Border Crossings: Developing Ireland's Island Economy' through increased state policy co-operation in industral development.[15] Recently, new cross-border university initiatives have been organised by sister colleges: Queens

University, Belfast (IRL-N), and University College, Galway and University College, Cork (IRL-S), all of which are celebrating their 150th anniversaries together. In addition, a Conference of University Rectors in Ireland (CRI) has been formed and has received special funding from the European Commission to support a staff and student mobility scheme in Ireland with the objective of enhancing co-operative measures between the universities all across Ireland. All these initiatives in inter-university co-operation auger well for the future. There is much potential too in Magee College – the 'University on the Border'. Its geographical position, history and its symbolism can play a key role in contributing to peace, inter-regionalism and inter-university partnerships in the future. The experience of the IUPCD over the past ten years can be regarded as a forerunner for that future.

NOTES

1. P. McClenaghan and P. Shanahan, *Report on the Cross Border Community Economic Development Innovatory Training Project*, Community Development Studies Unit, University of Ulster, Magee College, Derry 1989.
2. P. McClenaghan, *Dimensions of 1992 ILSCAE Conference Report Introduction*, Community Development Studies Unit, University of Ulster, Magee College, Derry 1993.
3. A. Memmi, *The Coloniser and the Colonised*, Earthscan, London 1990. (Translated by Howard Greenfield, with original introduction by Jean-Paul Sartre, new introduction by Liam O'Dowd). Crotty (*Ireland in Crisis: A Study in Capitalist Colonial Underdevelopment*, Brandon Press, Dingle 1986) makes the distinction between capitalist colonialism and other forms of colonisation. With the introduction of private property, he maintains, colonialism took a different form. He distinguishes between capitalist colonialism in situations where the indigenous population is migratory, as in North America, and where it is 'settled'. In the latter case, he further distinguishes between a capitalist colonialism in which the land is merely annexed, the indigenous leadership removed but the peasants left to till their land under the new stewardship (as in much of the southern part of Ireland in the sixteenth to eighteenth centuries), and that of a capitalist colonialism in which not only is the land annexed but it is transferred from the peasants to 'working-class' colonialists brought in for that purpose who otherwise would never have had the capital (much of the Plantation area in Ulster). In this case, the surviving indigenous population is driven off or accepted back as 'coolies' on the land they once possessed. Kenya, Algeria and parts of IRL-N exemplify the legacies of the latter category.
4. L.O'Dowd, in introduction to Memmi, *op.cit.*,p30.

5. L. O'Dowd, 'States of Ireland: Some reflections on research', *Irish Journal of Sociology*, 1, 1991.
6. P. Shanahan, 'Adult and Continuing Education in Ireland-North (IRL-N) and South (IRL-S)', in A. Kaiser *et al* (eds), *European Manual of Continuing Education EuHWVB*, Soderdrück, Luchterhand 1994. See also J. Field, 'Policy-Borrowing and Adaptation in the Development of Continuing Education in Northern Ireland, 1921–1950' in M. Marriot and B. Hake (eds), *Cultural and Intercultural Experiences in European Adult Education*, Cross-Cultural Studies in the Education of Adults, 3, Leeds Studies in Continuing Education, 1994. Field contends that although British patterns did constitute a model for policy-makers in IRL-N after the founding of the NI 'state' in 1921, the shape and the nature of provision which emerged differed in significant ways from the British adult education system, particularly in relation to its denominational character. Ties with Britain inhibited the emergence of genuine intercultural exchanges. It might be added that after the founding of the Irish Free State in 1921, the slow process of nation-building and indigenisation after British rule also had the effect of a mutually reinforcing process of distancing the historico-political expression of adult continuing education between IRL-S and IRL-N.
7. F. D'Arcy, 'Ten Years in Western Ulster', *AONTAS*, 4, 2, 1985; T. Lovett, A. Kilmurray and C. Clarke, *Adult Education and Community Action*, Croom Helm, London 1983.
9. Fair Employment Commission of Northern Ireland, *Report of an Investigation into the University of Ulster*, December 1989; *Report of an Investigation into the University of Ulster*, April 1990.
9. W. James, 'Where is Adult Education Going?', *CEDEFOP*, 9.
10. Commission of the European Communities, *Background Report Social Exclusion and Poverty: New Action programme 1994–1999* and *Report of Action programme 1989–1994*, SEC/B34/93, Jean Monet House, London 1994.
11. D. Dineen, 'Europeanisation of Irish Universities', *Higher Education*, 24, 3.
12. M. Trow, 'Uncertainties in Britain's Transition from Elite to Mass Higher Education', in T. Whiston and R. Geiger (eds), *Research in Higher Education*, The Society for Research into Higher Education and Open University Press, Buckingham 1992.
13. P. O'Malley, *Biting at the Grave: The Irish Hunger Strikes and the Politics of Despair*, Blackstaff, Belfast 1990.
14. C. Torres, 'A Political Sociology of Adult Education: A Research Agenda', *Education* (Malta), 4, 1, p31.
15. D. Hamilton, in *Border Crossings: Developing Ireland's Island Economy*, as reported in *The Irish News*, 1 September 1995.

12

THE WELSH LANGUAGE AND ITS RESTORATION: NEW PERSPECTIVES ON MOTIVATION, LIFELONG LEARNING AND THE UNIVERSITY

Steve Morris

One of the principal differences between continuing education provision in Wales and the rest of the United Kingdom is the Welsh language. The extramural departments of the University of Wales have a long and distinguished history of providing courses in their communities through the medium of Welsh whether they be literature classes, general culture, history or politics and for many Welsh speakers in the outlying (and not so outlying) communities of Wales, this provision was the only opportunity for them to receive any part of their education in their mother tongue. It is therefore not surprising in the sixties and seventies when the demand to establish an effective system for the teaching of Welsh to adults began in earnest, that the authorities and the public looked to the continuing education departments (or the old extramural departments as they were then) for this. During that period – an exciting and pivotal period in the history of the process of trying to save and restore the national language of Wales – the importance of schools in the process of transmitting language came to be realised but in addition to that, it was soon also realised that this would not be to any great avail unless these children's parents were to have the same opportunity: 'It is a mistake to try to restore the Welsh language only by means of the schools, without giving any attention to linguistically educating those who govern society, namely the adults'.[1]

THE HISTORY OF THE WELSH FOR ADULTS PROVISION IN THE DEPARTMENTS OF CONTINUING EDUCATION

Williams' study shows that the main reasons adults had at that time for learning Welsh were (i) to understand the news on the radio and the television (ii) to join in the social life with friends (iii) popular light reading and (iv) an interest in languages.[2] At the end of the 1960s and the beginning of the 1970s, the fragile situation of the language, following the substantial fall in the number of speakers in the 1961 and 1971 censuses (656,002 to 542,425 or 26 to 20.8 per cent of the population of Wales) brought a renewed interest in the Welsh language – amongst Welsh speakers and non-Welsh speakers alike – and a change in the way in which the teaching of the language to children and adults was regarded.[3] It was during that period that the network of Welsh for adults classes was developed through the extramural departments, further education colleges, WEA, local education authorities as well as numerous voluntary movements and *ad hoc* classes in pubs, chapels, schools and private homes and in the media. By the beginning of the 1970s, the first *Wlpan* classes had been held in Cardiff, Pontypridd and Aberystwyth.[4] This system was developed from intensive teaching in Israel originally – *Wlpan* is a Hebrew term which means *studio* or 'a place to which people are led', according to Mrs Shoshana Eyton who had taught on the first ever *Wlpan* in Israel in 1949, 'but in the world of education the best definition would be "a school employing intensive teaching methods where the result is guaranteed" '.[5] The intention of these courses in Israel was to linguistically – and culturally – assimilate non-Hebrew speaking Jewish incomers as thousands of them flocked back to Israel when the country won its independence in 1948 and to ensure that Hebrew would be the main language of the new state.[6] The intensive methods of the *Wlpan* were adapted for the purpose of Welsh and principles were introduced such as: intensive, functional-structural drilling; emphasis on oral skills; emphasis on Welsh as the principal teaching and class language (and the only language after a certain level); attending classes three or four times a week for a period of three to four months; it is only after fully mastering the basic principles and patterns of the oral language that students move on to the formal written language. This development was a very important step forward in the organisation of Welsh for adults in Wales, giving an opportunity to students to *succeed* in learning to speak Welsh in a comparatively short period – succeed not only in being able to speak the language but in being able to use it like first language speakers. A very strong motivation – and motives – were needed to succeed on an *Wlpan* course and the launch of these courses in the middle of the 1970s illustrates a fundamental change in students' reasons for learning from the period of the Williams 1965 report and the reasons noted by James.[7] Motivations can be seen that are more typical of students on today's courses, namely reasons of work, assimilation, children receiving a Welsh medium education and feelings that one should speak the language as part of one's identity.

This intensive provision – *Wlpan* and higher level courses – was located in the University of Wales and tutor/organisers were appointed to develop a network of courses in the departments of continuing education. Today, under the auspices of county consortia recently established in the wake of changes in funding methods in the field, the system is to be continued of holding the intensive provision in the departments of continuing education (as well as other institutions of higher education) and the non-intensive provision in the further education sector, WEA, local education authorities and other such bodies.[8] There is a holistic provision in the departments of continuing education with complete beginners commencing their studies on an *Wlpan* course (or a 300 hour course which is even more intensive) and continuing to higher levels over a period of time which is flexible so that they are able to reach a fairly fluent level in a comparatively short period of time. There is a structure and system of quite specific progression routes which has evolved and developed in addition to a national system of accrediting the various levels where those who reach the higher levels sit the *Defnyddio'r Gymraeg – Uwch* (Use of Welsh – Higher Level) examination – a special advanced level examination for adults accredited by the WJEC.

THE PROVISION IN THE COMMUNITIES OF THE UNIVERSITY OF WALES SWANSEA

At the moment, the Department of Adult and Continuing Education at University of Wales Swansea provides *Wlpan* courses throughout West Glamorgan and East Dyfed, as well as one 300 hour course in Swansea. There is also a full programme of follow-up courses in the community and a higher education certificate for learners – and first language speakers – who have completed *Defnyddio'r Gymraeg-Uwch*. The areas served by the Department are linguistically mixed as the following figures illustrate:[9]

	Resident population aged 3 & over	Percentage able to speak Welsh	Number able to speak Welsh
West Glamorgan			
Port Talbot	49,178	8.59%	4,222
Neath	63,051	12.97%	8,177
Swansea	174,962	10.00%	17,500
Lliw Valley	60,588	36.92%	22,369
East Dyfed			
Llanelli	72,048	46.47%	33,483
Dinefwr	37,297	66.52%	24,811

Even within the areas above, there is considerable variation, with 70 per cent or more speaking the language in several wards in Llanelli, Dinefwr and Lliw Valley. This complex linguistic situation is reflected in the demand for Welsh for adults classes in the area served by the department and in the motivation of the students who attend them.

Great emphasis is placed in the region on working together with local organisations and societies and every effort is made to hold a wide provision of *Wlpan* courses which will fulfil the varying demands of the students whatever their motives or expectations. One obvious example of this beneficial joint-working relationship is that developed over the years with the Welsh Language nursery movement – *Mudiad Ysgolion Meithrin* – and Welsh medium schools to ensure that convenient classes are held within easy access of non-Welsh speaking parents who are sending their children to receive their education through the medium of Welsh. As a result, all morning courses are either in the same centre as a Welsh medium playgroup/nursery or as near as possible to one, so that parents can learn the language whilst their children receive their education through the same language. The Welsh Office's most recent figures show that 32.4 per cent of children 3-15 years old speak Welsh but only 8.6 per cent are first language speakers.[10] It is therefore obvious that this provision has a very important role in endeavouring to ensure the reversal of language shift in the direction of English and to restore Welsh as a majority language.

During the last ten years, there has been a growth in the number of language centres and ventures in Wales. Frequently, the call for these has come from Welsh speakers in their own communities who wish to improve the situations and domains in which the language can be used: as a result of the work of countless volunteers, the Tŷ Tawe language centre was successfully established in the centre of the city of Swansea in 1987 and at the same time, the Department of Continuing Education transferred all the Welsh for adults classes in the city to that centre. Thus, through a partnership between Tŷ Tawe and the university, students in Swansea can socialise in Welsh after every class (and thereby increase their contact hours in the language), buy Welsh books in the book shop, take advantage of the Welsh medium nursery provision and meet other Welsh speakers from the city. The old complaints of learners in Swansea, namely that there was little opportunity to use the language outside of the classroom and how difficult it was to find the city's Welsh speakers (although 17,500 of them are hiding somewhere!), were therefore answered.

A more recent development in Welsh speaking areas – the areas of the Gwendraeth and Swansea/Amman Valleys – was the establishment of two *Menter Iaith* or language ventures during the 1990s. When the first one was set up – Menter Cwm Gwendraeth – an application was made by the department under the old Welsh Office Welsh for Adults funding system, with the support and co-operation of the Menter, to employ a full-time tutor-organiser in the area: the application was successful and the tutor was appointed in 1991.[11] As a result, a substantial increase in the number of Welsh for adults courses occurred in the East Dyfed area and the development of provision in new centres. In addition to that, the department's Welsh for Adults tutors and members of Menter Cwm Gwendraeth are working jointly on plans to assimilate non-Welsh speaking newcomers into the local Welsh speaking community: a positive response to the challenge of a substantial increase in the number of non-Welsh speakers who moved into the traditionally Welsh-speaking areas of the west during the 1980s and early 1990s. Success was also achieved in appointing a full-time tutor/organiser in Tŷ Tawe one year later who was responsible for the development of the first ever 300 hour course in the city (and the county), as well as developing Tŷ Tawe as an open learning centre for adults learning Welsh. Recently, the department has been working very closely with a new *menter* – Menter Aman Tawe – and once again an increase has been observed in our Welsh for adults provision in areas which are far from the University campus and have not been so evident in the course programme in the past. One of the worst implications of the most recent changes in the funding mechanism for Welsh for adults in Wales, by changing from funding posts and provision to a formula based on learning units, is that there is no means of responding as positively to calls for joint and developmental work in partnership with community organisations as was the case in the past, especially when thinking in terms of creating tutor/organiser posts – the most effective way of developing and expanding.[12]

Student Profile

Over a period of three years – 1992/93, 1993/94 and 1994/95 – a questionnaire was distributed to all prospective students on the department's *Wlpan* courses. Before the commencement of an *Wlpan* course, a preliminary meeting is held to stress the commitment needed to complete an intensive course, the teaching methods employed, the oral nature of the course and future progression routes. This opportunity was utilised during the period in question to give everybody who attended a questionnaire (including people who came to that meeting but not to the actual course itself – although this was only one per cent of the sample). In 1992–93, 165 questionnaires were distributed; in 1993–94, 270 were distributed; and in 1994–95, 173.

Gender

According to Smith, there are on average three women for every man in adult education language classes.[13] Other surveys have shown that the average is not as uneven as that in every case but one can clearly see that the general tendency on adult language courses is towards more women than men.[14] This tendency is reflected in the *Wlpan* classes:

	Men	Women
1992–93	60 (36%)	105 (64%)
1993–94	121 (45%)	149 (55%)
1994–95	76 (44%)	97 (56%)

The same tendencies have been observed in other parts of Wales.[15] A number of reasons can be offered for this but, considering the importance given in the department's provision to holding courses close to nursery groups and heavy marketing in Welsh medium schools, such a proportion as that observed above is to a certain extent to be expected. Courtney noted that adult education is more important to women from the point of view of raising self-confidence before returning to the workplace and it is possible that this is another element with some women who have a more utilitarian motivation.[16] There is also evidence that women are more likely than men to be attracted by a high status language – despite the low status of Welsh as a language in Wales, it is a high status language as the main language of education of the children of the mothers who chose to learn it;[17] although others have argued that more research is needed on this aspect of second language teaching.[18]

Age

In common with a number of studies, the largest age group observed during the three years was those aged 25 to 34:[19]

Age group	1992–93	1993–94	1994–95
15–24	17 (10%)	23 (8%)	12 (7%)
25–34	55 (33%)	95 (35%)	50 (29%)
35–44	47 (28%)	54 (20%)	36 (21%)
45–54	23 (14%)	39 (15%)	40 (23%)
55–64	19 (12%)	37 (14%)	25 (15%)
65– above	3 (2%)	20 (7%)	6 (3%)
No response	1 (1%)	2 (1%)	4 (2%)

These figures, once again, are very similar to those found in other parts of Wales.[20] From the point of view of the future of the Welsh language and language revival planning, these figures are encouraging: the language can be seen to appeal to younger age groups thus giving a young, vibrant image to it, helping to dispel the impression sometimes given of Welsh as an old-fashioned, rural language of the older generation only. This is the age range in which one finds the majority of parents with young children, who will be deciding on the medium of their education and will be able to positively influence those children's attitudes towards the language in the future by endeavouring to – and succeeding in – mastering the language themselves. There is ample evidence of parents who have succeeded in learning the language fluently and in changing the language of their home and bringing their children up to be Welsh-speaking.[21] Despite claims to the opposite, this process can be seen as a vital contribution to efforts at reversing language shift in Wales, and it is on the increase.

Places of birth and residence

It has already been seen that the population and linguistic background of the six districts contained within the department's catchment area vary enormously. This is reflected in the students' places of residence with the greatest number living in the Swansea City Council area. Secondly comes the Llanelli Borough Council area – this can be largely attributed to the tutor/organiser post there with special responsibility for developing that area (and an office in Cross Hands as well) in addition to the Dinefwr area which has increased from 8 per cent of all the *Wlpan* students in 1992–93 to 15 per cent in 1994-95. The lowest represented area is the most easterly and linguistically anglicised one, namely the Port Talbot region.

It is interesting to note the students' places of birth. On average, almost 50 per cent were born in West Glamorgan or East Dyfed i.e. within the Department's present geographical catchment area. Some 16 per cent of them were born in other parts of Wales and approximately 28 per cent in England. This last figure is significant as it is proof that a number of the people who moved into the Welsh speaking areas of the West are trying to integrate into the Welsh speaking society around them (this is also reflected in their motivation for learning the language); it would seem that a substantial number (about a third) of those born in England have spent the majority of their lives living in Wales, that is having been brought up in Wales, with parents from Wales who had returned to the country to live.[22] During the period under observation, 6 per cent of the students who came were born in

the following countries – Scotland, Ireland, Germany, the Netherlands, Italy, the Basque Country, France and from outside Europe,
USA, Canada, Hong Kong, Nigeria, India, Jamaica and Zambia.

Children and their education

Writing about the feat of reviving Hebrew in Israel, the historian and
nationalist Gwynfor Evans said:

> The easiest part of the work was giving Hebrew to the children of
> incomers. The schools made sure that the children were fluent in
> Hebrew by 15 years of age. It is the language of the vast majority of the
> children by now. This is amongst the strongest of motivations for
> parents to learn the language. It was an Israeli comedian who said that
> Israel is a country where the mother learns the mother tongue from her
> children.[23]

It could be said that this is just as true with regard to the field of
Welsh for adults in Wales. It will be seen in due course that the fact
that children receive their education through the medium of Welsh is a
strong motivation for many parents to learn the language. From the
sample being observed, 64 to 70 per cent of the students had children
with more attending Welsh medium than English medium schools. It
was decided to ask those with children in English medium schools
whether the fact that Welsh (until comparatively recently) was a
compulsory subject in the national curriculum had influenced their
decision to learn Welsh. Substantial percentages (30–47 per cent) said
that this has been an influence: an interesting point and perhaps it
would be of benefit to compare this with how many parents attend
French classes in order to help their children with their French. There
is, therefore, no doubt that the education – and the language in which it
is delivered – of the students' children is an important factor when
opting to come on an intensive course but it will also be seen that this is
only one factor among a number of others.

Passive knowledge of Welsh

It is estimated that 33.9 per cent of the population of Wales can speak
at least a little Welsh and that 16.9 per cent can speak a fair amount or
are almost fluent.[24] This is significant because there is a tendency to

view the official figure – 18.65 per cent of the Welsh population – as a black and white reflection of the actual linguistic situation of Wales in the 1990s. Of course, as the Catalans have long since realised, the picture is far more complicated with some people claiming that they are unable to speak the language but can understand it: they have a passive knowledge.[25] In consideration of this, the students were asked whether somebody else in the family could speak Welsh and it was found that a little over half of them had a relative in that category. The most frequent response was mother/father or grandmother/grandfather but a fairly high score was also given to husband/wife and a number of respondents noted every year that siblings spoke the language. There are extremely interesting sociolinguistic patterns in West Glamorgan and East Dyfed and the reasons for the decline in the language in some areas are both complex and profound.[26] As a result, it is not at all uncommon that Welsh speaking parents of one generation (or even within one generation) have not transmitted the language to the next generation – this means, on the other hand, that remembering or knowing somebody who can speak Welsh in the immediate family is a common experience to many of the students, that is, the language has disappeared as the family's main medium during their own lifetime.

Some have argued that an *Wlpan* course should not be entered upon unless the students already have some command of the language.[27] Prospective students were asked whether they had learnt Welsh as a subject at school and it was found that more than half of those who answered this question had studied the language to some degree (including a number of those who were born outside of Wales). In the light of the previous statement, it is encouraging to note that about 60 per cent had attempted to learn Welsh before. The most popular method was attending a once a week class – this is without doubt a very good preparation for an *Wlpan* course – and a number of respondents had attended the special courses run by the university during the summer for students who are considering attending an *Wlpan* course in the autumn

Motivation

The HMI (Wales) report on the teaching of Welsh as a second language to adults stated that

> it is important for class organisers and tutors to know their students and

to understand their motives so that more detailed and appropriate provision can be made for them. The continual 'beginning from the beginning' provision has now largely disappeared. Learners now expect more, and it is necessary to ask, in each case, whether the provision matches linguistic needs (personal, social, professional) and cultural and intellectual interests.[28]

In the same report, the students' motivations were broadly divided into four groups: (a) learners who were attempting to regain a language which was not transmitted to them by the older generation; (b) newcomers who wished to become integrated into the Welsh speaking communities around them; (c) those learning Welsh for work purposes or in order to improve one's chances of finding work; (ch) those having children in Welsh medium schools. Seven years on, another HMI (Wales) report was published and it suggested two main motivations: (a) a feeling of welshness coupled with a desire to acquire the native language of their country; (b) a desire to assist their children who attended the county's Welsh medium schools/units.[29]

General motivations in the field of adult education are listed by Daines, Daines & Graham, and it can be seen that language learners' motivations or motives, especially those who are learning lesser used languages in their own countries are different.[30] Gardner argues that there are two main kinds of motivation or orientation when learning a second language: an *integrative orientation* where the students learn in order to understand second language speakers better and communicate with those parts of their communities who speak the language 'for socio-emotional purposes' – and an *instrumental orientation* where the students learn in order to get a job or to improve their education, more utilitarian, practical reasons. The motivations of the Swansea sample will be analysed in the light of these two main orientation groupings.[31]

Hughes observed that integrative reasons were the most important in his survey. In the Swansea sample, the students were asked to note their reasons for learning Welsh and tick as many as they thought relevant to them. The options are listed below:

(1) I live in Wales and feel I should speak the language;
(2) I have children in a Welsh school;
(3) My family are Welsh speaking;
(4) I live in a Welsh speaking area;
(5) It will be advantageous for my work;

(6) Any other reason.[32]

They were then asked to note *one* main reason only. Reason (1) was the most popular response, with 39 to 48 per cent noting this over the three years. Second was reason (2), again an integrative motivation. The only instrumental motivation in the list is (5) and that came third, jointly with (6). A number of varied reasons were noted under (6) including some which were integrative on the whole, such as reasons of culture/patrimony, or having Welsh speaking friends; but there were also examples of instrumental motivation, for example, expanding personal knowledge/improving one's education, understanding the television and even, for one student who is a member of a choir, understanding the meaning of Welsh songs better!

The results of the University of Wales Swansea sample conform with those obtained in other surveys, namely that the integrative motivation is the most prominent one amongst Welsh for adults students in West Glamorgan and East Dyfed. This situation is a unique one in the field of second language teaching in Britain because people do not *have* to learn Welsh in a bilingual country in order to be able to communicate from day to day. As Trosset noted, 'Learners have a special significance because they represent a reverse trend in language acquisition. Unlike Welsh speakers learning English (the normal pattern), Welsh learners are not motivated by practical intensity …'.[33] There is a great need for more research to be carried out in this field and for it to be done together with our partners in other countries who are endeavouring to promote and restore their own languages.

Welsh and European perspectives

At the beginning of this chapter, it was stated that the Welsh language is one of the main differences between the continuing education provision in Wales and the rest of Britain. It has also been shown how this particular field of continuing education attracts students with very different motivations to those of other continuing education students, back into the world of education. This in itself can provide a boost for students' self-confidence and encourage them to look at new educational progression routes. As one of the pioneers of Welsh for adults, Cennard Davies, noted,'… success in learning Welsh proves [to the students] that they do have other abilities and that they can fulfil their potential'.[34] The provision is also important in the community itself, not only in assimilating non-Welsh speakers into traditionally Welsh speaking areas but in promoting the process of restoring the language in Wales. To quote Trosset once again: 'All Welsh speakers by their very existence symbolise the Welsh struggle for linguistic survival ... Welsh learners' ... voluntary acquisition of the minority language is an expression of their respect for the Welsh-speaking community and is significant of a desire to prevent the impending death of the Welsh language.'[35] Others have also noted the importance of this field of continuing education in this respect.[36] Through their Welsh for adults provision the departments of continuing education contribute to the process of reversing language shift in Wales and offer the opportunity for the inhabitants of Wales to influence the linguistic future of their country. What is needed now is to see this provision in the context of language planning and language normalisation in Wales – as is so successfully managed in other European Union countries such as Catalunya and the Basque Country – and to acknowledge its special place in the Welsh education system. The recent changes in funding methodology, in the field and the incredible decision by the Welsh Language Board to abolish the grant to CYD without any consultation or warning, have created a feeling of a lack of institutional support.[37] Such support is greatly needed in the field today after over a decade of expansion and growth. Once again, as in the case of setting up the first *Wlpan* courses twenty years ago, we will have to look beyond the borders of Wales for an answer; we will look to the tremendous successes experienced in the Basque Country and Catalunya and try to reproduce their extremely effective adult language teaching systems here in Wales.[38] The universities in Wales have a duty to continue playing a leading role, in order to ensure a continuation in the process of restoring the Welsh language as a living language in the communities they serve.

NOTES

1. R.M. Jones, 'Dysgu'r Gymraeg i Oedolion', in Jac L. Williams (ed), *Addysg i Gymru: Ysgrifau ar Addysg*, University of Wales Press, Cardiff 1966 p147.
2. I.T. Williams, *Oedolion yn dysgu Cymraeg (Astudiaeth o Gymhellion)*, Pamphlet 13: Education Faculty, University College of Wales Aberystwyth, 1965 p17.
3. See C. Rees, 'Ysgolion Iaith i Oedolion', *Yr Athro*, 24 January 1973, pp153–155; and D.L. James, 'Ulpan Cymraeg Aberystwyth (1)', 'Ulpan

Cymraeg Aberystwyth (2)' and 'Wlpan Dau, Aberystwyth (Hydref – Rhagfyr 1974)', *Yr Athro*, 26 December 1974 pp106–116, January 1975 pp172–178, March 1975 pp234–242.

4. See C. Rees, 'Wlpan', *Barn* 145, November/December 1974, pp563–565 and James, (1974), *op.cit.*

5. Rees, 1973, *op.cit.*, p153.

6. See R.M. Crowe, *Yr Wlpan yn Israel*, Canolfan Ymchwil Cymraeg i Oedolion, Aberystwyth 1988.

7. James, 1974, *op.cit.*, pp111–114.

8. Further Education/Higher Education Funding Councils for Wales, *Report of the Welsh for Adults Joint Review Group*, Cardiff 1994.

9. See J. Aitchison and H. Carter, *A Geography of the Welsh Language 1961–1991*, University of Wales Press, Cardiff 1994, pp92–93.

10. See The Welsh Office, *1992 Welsh Social Survey: Report on the Welsh Language*, Government Statistical Office, Cardiff 1995, p4.

11. See Menter Cwm Gwendraeth, *Menter Cwm Gwendraeth Strategy – Implementing the Strategy*, Llandybïe 1991, p29.

12. See WJEC, *Welsh for Adults: The Way Forward*, prepared by the Welsh for Adults Panel/WJEC, Cardiff in 1992. The members of the panel are providers in the field together with a national officer. Mention is made in the document of the 'most effective and efficient ways of teaching Welsh to adults and of assisting learners to live in a bilingual society' (p1).

13. D. Smith, 'Modern Languages and the Modern Student', in D. Sidwell (ed), *Teaching Languages to Adults*, CILT, London 1987, pp1–15.

14. See D.M. Sidwell, 'A Survey of Modern Language Classes', in *Adult Education*, Vol. 52, No. 5, January 1980.

15. See Welsh Office, *Report by H.M. Inspectors on a Survey of Teaching Welsh to Adults in Gwent – Spring Term 1991*, 1991, p4. A proportion of 18:1 is noted – which is very high – although some classes were more even from the point of view of gender. There are also similar tendencies in Basque/Irish for Adults classes in the Basque Country and Ireland: see especially J. Perales, 'Euskara – ikasleen motibazio eta jarrerak' in *Zutabe* 21, Donostia, 1989 and E.A. Hilliard, *Léirmheas ar Dhianchúrsaí Fhoras na Gaeilge/An Assessment of Dianchúrsaí Fhoras na Gaeilge*, Bord na Gaeilge, Dublin 1981.

16. S. Courtney, *Why Adults Learn: towards a theory of participation in Adult Education*, Routledge, London & New York 1992, p45.

17. See, for example, P. Trudgill, *Sociolinguistics – an Introduction to Language and Society*, Penguin, Harmondsworth 1983, pp78–99; R.C. Gardner, *Social Psychology and Second Language Learning – the Role of Attitudes and Motivation*, Edward Arnold, London 1985, p43.

18. D.R. Preston, *Sociolinguistics and Second Language Acquisition*, Blackwell, Oxford 1989, pp71–72 and p78.

19. D. Smith, *op.cit.*, p3. and S. Courtney, *op.cit.*, pp33 and 35.

20. Welsh Office, 1991, *op.cit.*, 'Some classes contain a variety of age groups, but in general the majority who attend Welsh classes are in the 25–45 age group. A considerable number of learners are over 45 years of age, but there are few under 25.' p4. See also M. Hughes, *Selecting, Adapting,*

Creating Communicative Materials for Welsh Learners, The Language Unit of the North East Wales Institute of Higher Education, 1989, pp16–17. Again, the same tendencies are noted in Basque for adults classes in J. Perales, *op.cit.*, p25.

21. See 'Families hit back over language', *Western Mail*, 12 July 1994, where families from the Rhondda area in Mid Glamorgan state their success in learning the language and speaking it with their children, i.e. making Welsh the language of the whole family. This was written in response to attacks by Tim Williams who has studied the ways in which Wales was anglicised and claimed that the language would never be revived in the East of the country.

22. See J. Aitchison and H. Carter, *op.cit.*, table 6.10, p108. Of the 508,098 who said that they could speak Welsh in the 1991 Census, 48,919 were actually born outside of Wales.

23. G. Evans, *Pe bai Cymru'n rhydd*, Y Lolfa, Talybont 1989, p184.

24. See Welsh Office 1995, *op.cit.*, p7.

25. See M. Leprêtre, 'Knowledge of the Catalan Language' in *The Catalan Language Today*, Generalitat de Catalunya, Barcelona 1992.

26. There are a number of discussions of this subject, but see in particular, H.Gruffudd, 'Iaith Gudd y Mwyafrif', in H.T. Edwards (ed), *Cwm Tawe*, Gomer 1993, pp105–142, about the Welsh language in Swansea; S.Rh. Williams, *Oes y Byd i'r Iaith Gymraeg*, University of Wales Press, Cardiff 1992, where Gwent in particular is discussed; B.B. Khleif, *Language, Ethnicity and Education in Wales*, Mouton, The Hague 1980, pp38–39.

27. See Rees, 1974, *op.cit.*, p564; James, 1974, *op.cit.*, and WJEC, *Dysgu Cymraeg? All you need to know about learning Welsh*, Cardiff 1994, p2: 'It is advisable, however, to have done a little Welsh already, as the pace is quick, especially during the first weeks, and complete beginners can sometimes feel left behind' (when talking about *Wlpan* courses).

28. HMI (Wales), *The Teaching of Welsh as a Second Language to Adults: Education Survey 12*, The Welsh Office, Cardiff 1984, p14.

29. Welsh Office, 1991, *op.cit.*, p5.

30. J. Daines, C. Daines and B. Graham, *Adult Learning, Adult Teaching*, Department of Adult Education, University of Nottingham 1993, p6; for a comparison with the situation in Ireland see D. Ó Donnchadha, 'Adult Learners of Irish', and S. Ó Longáin, 'Evening Classes for Adults in the Vocational Education Sector', both in H. Ó Murchú (ed), *Lesser Used Languages and the Communicative Needs of Adult Learners*, Irish National Committee, Dublin 1988, pp18–20 and 27–29; and E.A. Hilliard, *op.cit.*, appendix 2. For the Basque Country see J. Perales, *op.cit.*, p28.

31. R.C. Gardner, *op.cit.*, pp11–12.

32. Hughes, *op.cit.*, p16.

33. C.S. Trosset, 'The Social Identity of Welsh Learners', *Language and Society*, 15, 1986, p174.

34. Quoted in 'Diwydiant Dysgu Cymraeg', *Golwg*, Vol. 5, No. 7, 15 October 1992, pp10–11. See also R.Y. Bourhis, H. Giles and H. Tajfel, 'Language as a determinant of Welsh identity', *European Journal of Social Psychology*, Vol. 3, 1973, p457.

35. Trosset, *op.cit.*, p174.
36. See Crowe, *op.cit.*, p87; and K. Jones, 'Expanding the use of Welsh', *Planet*, 101, October–November 1993, p49; and R.M. Jones, *Language regained*, Gomer, Llandysul 1993, p10.
37. Reported in the *Western Mail*, 27 March 1995; CYD is an organisation whose aim is to bring first language Welsh speakers and learners together.
38. See 'Over 40,000 adults are studying the Basque Language in the BAC', *Euskararen Berripapera*, Vol. 2, No. 2, January 1995, Vitoria-Gasteiz.

13

SITTING PRETTY? WOMEN'S STUDIES AND THE HIGHER EDUCATION COMMUNITY

Mairead Owen and Marion Price

'GIVEN THE ODDS, A GREAT ADVANCE?'

In this paper we ask if this is an appropriate assessment of the progress made by Women's Studies within the Higher Education community in general and in our own institution in particular. How are we – both staff and students – to define and measure progress and success?

At first glance, we appear to be sitting pretty. Situated in a new university and after years of struggle, beginning with the establishment of courses in Sexual Divisions as part of our Sociology curriculum in the 1970s and watching similar developments in Literature, Politics and Media Studies throughout the 1980s, we welcomed the birth of our own full undergraduate programme in Women's Studies in the 1990s.

Listening to accounts of developments elsewhere, including the valuable results from surveys carried out by national and international Women's Studies networks, the parallels of timing and achievement are striking.[1] Over the last decade, Women's Studies has been a burgeoning field of academic study. A shared sense of monumental achievement exists alongside a sense of unease occasioned by awareness of common problems and irresolvable dilemmas. At times, the sense of unease shades over into one of dis-ease, as we reflect on the fine line between celebrating our inclusion in the academic community and worrying about our containment in alien territory. To understand this ambivalence, we constantly need to remind ourselves of the inherent contradictions between the feminist enterprise and the patriarchal academy which were inscribed in the struggle for Women's Studies from the start and which have contributed to the status of Women's Studies as outsiders within higher education.

The battle for Women's Studies was and is seen as part of the war for women's liberation. Almost three decades have now passed since a new wave of the women's movement exploded onto the scene on both sides of the Atlantic. Few fields of 'knowledge' escaped the angry and searching gaze of feminism. Time and again, established disciplines and accepted canons were investigated, found wanting and exposed. Work done from feminist perspectives challenged the theoretical frameworks, key assumptions, epistemologies, methods and findings of the patriarchal establishment. The overwhelming verdict was that what 'passed for knowledge' was in fact 'partial and patriarchal' and played a fundamental part in justifying the subordination of women.

Feminists had little difficulty uncovering the patriarchal assumptions lying at the roots of most of the established trees of knowledge. Women had either been ignored or treated as the deviant half of humanity. Such pervasive exclusions and distortions were quickly linked to the part played by 'man-made language' in upholding a gender order based on the systematic subordination and oppression of women. The means and relations of knowledge production were revealed as patriarchal. Men were identified as gate-keepers who constructed knowledge, checked with other men as to its significance and validity and built on the traditions developed by other men. As Dorothy Smith put it, men set agendas so that a tradition evolves with its own questions, solutions and standards and women have not been present in those circles, with the result that they have been 'deprived of the means to participate in creating forms of thought relevant or adequate to express their own experience or to define and raise social consciousness about their situation and concerns'.[2]

It is important to remember that the impetus for Women's Studies lay in broader struggles in wider national and international communities where questioning patriarchal knowledge led to practical interventions. For example, the process of naming and recognising the extent of violence against women led to such initiatives as Women's Aid and Rape Crisis centres, while a women's health movement sprang up to challenge the power of medical experts. There was the growth of feminist bookshops, research and resources centres, publishing houses, journals and magazines – usually existing on shoe-string budgets.

Healthily suspicious of spokespersons, formal organisation and abstract theory, women set about developing knowledge by and for women, stressing the close links between theory and practice, and acknowledging that concerns which had traditionally been defined as private and personal were in fact properly matters for political analysis.

New methods of working out and exploring the relations between experience and theory were developed, often in informal, community-based groups. At the same time, it was recognised that, if the achievements of the new wave were not to be lost once more to future generations, there was a need for them to be rooted in 'institutionalised structures of knowledge'.[3] Even the best ideas need space to develop and channels for communication, critique and dissemination. Recognising the difficulties and dangers of entering the established academy, many nevertheless felt that it had to be worth the risk. The production of knowledge was too important to be left to men. In any case, women could not afford to ignore the public world – whether of higher education or politics – since it is there that so much is legitimated and decided. Because this would be a risky business, maintaining close links with a strong women's movement was thought to be the best safeguard against the dangers of co-option and incorporation.[4]

Since feminist challenges threatened to upset not only existing findings and assumptions, but also the whole way in which knowledge was produced and valued, resistance was only to be expected. Feminist work was denounced as lacking academic respectability and rigour. While the objectivity of male knowledge was defended, feminist knowledge stood accused of being biased, subjective and political. Honest and necessary admissions of feminist 'bias' were cited 'as evidence of political indoctrination and abandonment of objectivity and reason'.[5] Moreover, while the established disciplines valued and defended their boundaries, work done by women revealed that these boundaries had systematically restricted our attention 'to the experiences and interests of men, reflecting the priorities, prejudices and power structures of male-dominated society.'[6] Feminist work implied interdisciplinary, even transdisciplinary, labour in order both to explore the mechanisms of patriarchal production and feminist alternatives across disciplines and to provide mutual support in male-dominated, discipline-based institutions.

It should be clear that given the history of feminist interventions in higher education, contradictions, dilemmas and ambiguities are likely to be with us for a very long time to come. The position of being at one and the same time, both in and against the mainstream cannot logically be otherwise since, as Aaron and Walby argue, 'we are talking of a radical oppositional culture within a mainstream/malestream institution.'[7]

Questions continually arise about how best to manage these contradictions. Discussion has long focused on the problem of ghettoisation. At first, the strategy of individual forays into specific disciplines was dictated by limited resources and the degree to which different disciplines appeared 'gender-friendly'. Discussion grew around the desirability of developing autonomous Women's Studies programmes as opposed to integrating feminist perspectives and methodologies within the other disciplines in the hope that we would ultimately transform them. The autonomy strategy had several advantages: it provided a (safe) space for women students and staff to explore common interests and to develop important support networks; it encouraged the formation of a critical mass for the further growth of feminist teaching and research; it promoted a focus on the production of knowledge across disciplines; it implied greater control over our own resources and curriculum. On the other hand, worries centred on the fear that a safe space can become a ghetto and that feminist contributions can become marginalised. It was feared that traditional courses would continue to ignore gender issues (or, at best, confine them to one section – usually the last – of the mainstream/malestream curriculum, never to be raised again in other areas). Worse still, students wanting to look at gender divisions could be told to 'go see someone in Women's Studies – they do that sort of thing there.' We have plenty of examples of this kind of response from our everyday working lives.

AT THE CHALK FACE

Of course, we could choose to muddle through, as we often do, and try both strategies: integration and autonomy. In our own case it is possible to view pragmatism in a positive way. Women's Studies is located in a School of Social Science alongside the traditional disciplines of Sociology, History, Economics, Human Geography and Politics, as well as other thematic or interdisciplinary programmes in Urban Studies, Criminal Justice and European Studies. Undergraduates can study Women's Studies as a single programme or in combination with certain other subjects some of which are located in other Schools. Modules are often shared with other programmes, for example, Women's Studies modules can also form part of a Sociology or Politics degree programme. Women's Studies students often find themselves studying alongside students on other programmes. And elective modules which introduce all kinds of students to Women's Studies are also provided. It is possible to present this situation as one which steers a middle course – offering Women's Studies students space as well as depth and breadth of coverage, promoting the cross-fertilisation of ideas and perspectives across disciplines, disseminating feminist contributions beyond the Women's Studies programme ... Yes, we have a Women's Studies degree. Yes, modularisation expands student choice and touches the parts other programmes cannot reach. *But* we could also be indicted on several counts: by traditionalists for offering a pick-and-mix system, lacking in academic coherence; and by feminists for failing to provide a truly autonomous and safe space for our students and for compromising with the malestream.

Caught between the women's movement and the demands of the academy, it may not be possible to please everyone. The tensions are evident in debates over feminist pedagogy. A feminist ethic which 'values the moral equality of those who seek education and those who teach' seems out of step with mainstream approaches to teaching and assessment.[8] Similarly, the 'subjective and experiential knowledge of women' apparently conflicts with 'the intellectual, objective expertise of mainstream knowledge'.[9] The dialectics of objectivity/subjectivity, theory/experience, teaching/learning underpin all kinds of difficulties when it comes to internal and external validation of teaching quality (including central government attempts to use quality assessment to inform funding). Questions also need to be asked about employer expectations and about the different motivations and realistic employment outcomes for both postgraduates *and* graduates.

Not enough has been written about how the positioning of Women's Studies programmes is managed in different institutional locations. Our own experience is of a great deal of hard work directed towards planning and delivering a coherent programme in Women's Studies which is interdisciplinary rather than multidisciplinary and which fits at the same time with the demands of a modular framework which in turn imposes constraints in terms of, for example, time-tabling and assessment patterns. Most importantly, we do not have control of our own resources in a system where academic leadership is separate from resource allocation – including the appointment of staff. In common with many other institutions in Britain at least, staff are rarely appointed specifically to teach Women's Studies. All but one of our staff are appointed to subject disciplines. Negotiation and persuasion at management level, which sometimes works, is not the same as arguing from well-defined rights. This leaves us worrying over what will happen if a particular woman with particular interests and expertise leaves the institution. Will the discipline replace her? How will we recover the loss? This is not a good time to be arguing for extra resources.

In the present context of introducing market principles to education, our commitment to offering Women's Studies can become yet one more example of the exploitation of women's labour. Such programmes rely heavily on the goodwill and commitment of a handful of women staff with workloads and commitments to other disciplines. These additional commitments are often not recognised when counting workloads or appraising staff. Rather like housework, the work we do for Women's Studies is seen as a 'Labour of Love'. Despite our hopes for the development of an oppositional culture, Women's Studies can become a cheap and cheerful addition to an institution's portfolio subsidised by women's political commitment. It has even been suggested that 'the move towards more courses, more students and new markets has, in some institutions, led to the welcoming of interdisciplinary courses, such as Women's Studies, previously perceived as too threatening to the disciplinary boundaries which structured education at all levels'.[10]

In our own institution, we did not experience considerable opposition to the setting up of a programme in Women's Studies. Rather, responses can be characterised as ones of vague amusement, mixed with condescension occasioned by ignorance as to what Women's Studies is really about, *and* of praise for enhancing the institution's equal opportunities' profile and expanding its portfolio of 'sexy', saleable commodities. After all, given glossy prospectuses, Women's Studies can look like 'just another course'. Moreover, because of the timing of our initiative – that is amid government promises of expanding student numbers, followed almost immediately by cuts to planned expansion and in the unit of resource – we can be forgiven for thinking that efficiency gains in our part of the institution have been achieved almost single-handedly by its distaff side!

RESEARCH: OPPORTUNITY OR CO-OPTION?

Women's Studies is also about research and here the risks of de-radicalisation and co-option are especially acute. Writing of Sociology, although her argument is of more general application , Dorothy Smith addresses the ways in which established disciplines have objectified a consciousness of society and social relations that 'knows' them from the standpoint of patriarchal and capitalist 'relations of ruling'.[11] It is here, in these multiple, extra local sites of power and the discourses which interpenetrate them, that research priorities are identified and from here that resources are controlled and allocated. It is here too that the organisational and administrative logics and exigencies of relations of ruling necessarily take for granted women's status as objects rather than subjects of the research process.

As we know, these relations of ruling have tightened their stranglehold on the research process in recent years, further reducing its already restricted autonomy, by laying down ever more stringent criteria of relevance and quality in the allocation of public money. Such developments increase the dilemmas for feminist researchers who must now decide 'how to play the research game' while maintaining a critical stance which challenges malestream knowledges and their outcomes. Should we 'turn our backs on feminist epistemologies … in an effort to gain funding and recognition?'[12]

But of course it isn't a game. Too much depends on the outcome, especially for those wanting to do research from the (sometimes overlapping) spaces of Women's Studies and the new universities. In the increasingly competitive world of league tables and performance-related funding, such groups start the race from a disadvantaged position and compete under handicap. The stakes involve not only promotion but even security of tenure; above all, they involve access to the material and social resources needed to build a tradition which will help change women's lives for the better.

The likely treatment of Women's Studies and feminist research in formal research assessment exercises may be a case in point. Given all that we have said, panels of (mostly male) assessors are particularly unlikely to reach 'objective' judgements in this case. Moreover, the interdisciplinary nature of Women's Studies and of much feminist research conflicts with the ground rules of discipline-based assessment and funding.

The relations of ruling also operate at the local institutional level via informal male networks which practise exclusionary closure against women, especially in the current highly competitive climate. 'Women are unlikely to be included in collaborative research projects because they are not part of these networks.'[13] Such capillary forms of power are extremely effective in excluding women from knowledge of how, where and when to apply for funding. Local research is also needed into the sexual division of labour as it relates to teaching, administration, research and pastoral care. The additional time devoted to caring work by women not only crowds out the time available for research and publishing, it is also discounted in appraisal exercises.[14] Here women academics are confronted with yet another choice: should we reduce the time and attention given over to caring work – thus increasing our chances of becoming insiders – or should we try to overturn mainstream priorities by increasing the visibility and value given to this kind of labour?

CLAIMING THE CREDIT?

The macro- and micropolitics of power provide a common reason for resistance to proposals to change the name of Women's Studies to the more man-friendly 'Gender Studies' – even though the change would increase our credibility in the eyes of our graduates, employers and assessors. Many feel that the term Gender Studies is too neutral and neglects the historically-based necessity of rooting analysis in the neglected standpoints and experiences of women, thus threatening 'a loss of the political edge so vital to feminism'.[15]

Because of the battles feminists have waged to create a space for ourselves and our students, it is hardly surprising that we are reluctant to include men – especially when women still make up such a derisory proportion of university lecturers and particularly at a time of backlash.[16] Surviving in a very cold climate is quite unlike worrying about the dangers of co-option in an expanding, well-resourced higher education sector.

In the present climate it is very important that we acknowledge and claim credit for the enormous contribution which *Women's* Studies has made to the opening up of path-breaking debates on 'gender and the difference it makes', especially in relation to the social production of knowledge. Over the last three decades, we have been made acutely aware of other differences – of 'race', sexuality, class, disability – which threaten/promise to challenge easy assumptions about automatic sisterhood and commonality.[17] It is these differences which may eventually pose a challenge to Women's Studies, not because it has been wrecked by self-destructive internal divisions and quarrels but because we will have come to value difference, to recognise shifting identities, divided loyalties and the need to build alliances rather than to assume commonality. There are many margins and many centres, depending on our focus. Having done so much to chart the theoretical and political territory by deconstructing identities and exploring the relationships between knowledge and power (now considered by many to be the cutting edge of 'theory'), we must claim the credit due – if, that is, we have the time, the resources, the energy and the space.

Claiming the credit and reward for work done in changing the criteria of knowledge-making and recognising the plurality of truths is likely to be a difficult task. There are already many signs that the academy is able to incorporate feminist work without advancing the position of its women workers. In this context, Kramarae and Spender write of a double-edged success story whereby 'some of the insights about the nature of knowledge, about multiple realities (of female experience), of difference, of dominance, and the politics of research, have been "appropriated" by the academy without necessarily advantaging women.'[18]

This brings us to our final and most difficult set of dilemmas raised by questions of difference when they are placed against the often unacknowledged power relations *within* Women's Studies. As teachers and assessors, we must acknowledge the specificities of our own shapings as feminists who are both white, straight, middle-class – and lots of other things besides.[19] Like many of our generation of feminists, we probably have residual, even subliminal, attachments to our commonality as women. However, given the multiple realities of female experience, we cannot assume that students share our priorities. We have to guard against the possibility that the sense of mission which motivates our teaching can become a type of recruitism to our, necessarily partial, world views. Above all, we wonder if we can ever avoid situations in which what we view as encouraging other women to explore 'the personal as political' can be seen by others as threatening and judgmental. As Maureen McNeill asks, 'the personal is political, but how personal and whose politics?'[20] Having done so much to challenge and deconstruct patriarchal claims to truth, it would be especially inappropriate if we were to set up our own dogmatic version of feminist reality. Feminism, after all, is never a final, single, fixed state but the ongoing, evolving and ever changing achievement of many different women.

WOMEN'S STUDIES AND THE STUDENT

What then of our students and their responses to these dilemmas? Where do they come from? What led them to choose Women's Studies? What do they get out of it? Do they see themselves as outsiders within higher education? Do they see Women's Studies as just another course? How do they view the dilemmas of commonality and difference? What for them are the personal, emotional, financial and employment costs and benefits of doing Women's Studies? How does what we offer measure up to their expectations? How do their definitions of women's situations and their priorities differ from our own? And what can we learn from them?

Whilst we know these are important questions, and suspect that we have some of the answers, research in this area will undoubtedly help us to understand how far we have been able to overturn the priorities of the mainstream and serve to remind us of our proper status as 'outsiders within' who must of necessity respond to and serve women in the wider community.

It is with these ends in mind that we have recently embarked on a qualitative, longitudinal research project following one cohort of our students through their programme, exploring their beliefs, feelings, hopes and ambitions. While the data collection and interpretation stages of the enquiry are still in their early days, many of the replies from open-ended, in-depth interviews address the controversies and debates already mentioned here.

From the students' responses on their thoughts about their choice of Women's Studies, it was apparent that they had rarely chosen to study the subject as an 'instrumental' decision. Many were well aware of the probable ignorance surrounding, and low status attached to, a subject labelled Women's Studies. As one woman told us, 'dodgy telling people I'm doing Women's Studies. People don't really understand or want to know about Women's Studies.' Referring to employers' attitudes, another woman felt that 'they wouldn't give it much weight'.

So would it be safer to re-name the discipline, calling it Gender Studies? Views from the classroom and interviews covered a broad spectrum. Some saw a need to educate men and felt that the label 'Gender Studies' would encourage male and female students to 'see both sides'. However, the need for a woman-friendly space was also acknowledged along with the fear of de-radicalisation implied by the new name. Arguing forcefully against any change of name, one woman put it this way:

> I think it is a ... cop-out. I think it should be like people should be aware of what they are doing and if there is anything to be afraid of doing Women's Studies then it's to do with the fear and it's not going to make it disappear by pretending it's not there.

Another point to emerge from the initial data is the crucial importance of Women's Studies to the students. We do not claim that had they chosen a more conventional subject discipline they would not have demonstrated commitment, interest and enthusiasm. However, we do suggest that overall there is a belief that Women's Studies will be salient for them in a *particular* way. For the students there was an implication that studying the subject would be an integral part of the building up of their subjectivity and identity.

Jenny described her hopes most fully:

> On one level I think it could give insights into some of the life chances that have been given or denied me and thus have both shaped and motivated my life to this point. On another level I hope to gain a more overall picture of women in society and perhaps a better understanding of why women seem unable to reach their true potential.

Carol believed that Women's Studies:

> seemed relevant to me and my experiences. Thought it would give me more understanding of what is going on in the world and how I feel about things.

Kerry wanted her studies to:

> make me more aware of 'genderism', discrimination, etc., how to deal with it and how to eradicate it within local community groups, also an insight into the struggle of women will (I feel) give me more determination to be a successful woman.

The students were aware that their position as women was a crucial shaping of their social circumstances and of their concepts of self. The students chose to study Women's Studies to explore, to put into context, one of the most crucial aspects of their identity. They wanted information about the position of women in the world and the tools to explain that position:

> It gives me a perspective of why I am where I am now, where I come from not in a historical sense but of me, why I have made the decisions that I have, does that make sense?

They wanted to site themselves and their own experience within those explanations.

At the same time they were aware that the construction of identity is as part of a community and the community they wished to find was the community of other women and the information they looked for was about that community.

It is telling that the identity of being a woman is often a surprisingly isolated one. We live in families, workplaces, schools, where this most important experience is not shared, is not made overt. It is the world taken for granted. Many of the students specifically stated that while they did not necessarily want all-women groups, they did want to discover the experience of other women both in reality, by meeting other students, and through their studies, in finding out about the experiences of women throughout history and across cultures.

Yet students knew the reality of difference as well as commonality. They wanted to contextualise both their commonality as women and their difference as black, old, lesbian, working-class, disabled etc. More than that, they wanted to work out their individual biographies, to make sense of their histories to date and they saw both commonality and difference as framing those biographies. When we interviewed the students many had disturbing stories; and the courage and strength with which they had dealt, and were dealing, with traumatic life events were sobering.

Students came to Women's Studies: to make sense of their experiences as women in a patriarchal society and to find some community with other women; to explore the differences of 'race', class, sexuality, age, disability and so on, and to value those differences; and to gain a degree in what is still the liveliest, most radical, most subversive subject in the higher education curriculum. It is vital that, given the odds, we fight to keep this space.

Acknowledgements

The authors wish to thank Karen Corteen for her invaluable help and support in preparing this chapter.

NOTES

1. J. Aaron and S. Walby (eds), *Out of the Margins*, Falmer Press, London 1991; S. Davies, C. Lubelska and J. Quinn (eds), *Changing the Subject: Women in Higher Education*, Taylor and Francis, London 1994; J. Hinds, A. Phoenix and J. Stacey (eds), *Working Out: New Directions in Women's Studies*, Falmer Press, London 1992; and C. Kramarae and D. Spender (eds), *The Knowledge Explosion*, Harvester Wheatsheaf, London 1993.
2. D. Smith, *The Everyday World as Problematic: A Feminist Sociology*, Open University Press, Milton Keynes 1987, p18.
3. J. Aaron and S. Walby, *op.cit.*, p1.
4. M. Stacey and M. Price, *Women, Power and Politics*, Tavistock, London 1981, p189.
5. V. Robinson, 'Introducing Women's Studies', in D. Richardson and V. Robertson (eds), *Introducing Women's Studies*, Macmillan, London 1993, p10.
6. M. Price, 'Still Worlds Apart? Political Sociology and the Politics of Gender', in R. Burgess (ed), *Investigating Society*, Longman, London 1989, p133.
7. J. Aaron and S. Walby, *op.cit.*, p2.
8. M. Humm, ' "Thinking of things in themselves": Theory, Experience, Women's Studies', in J. Aaron and S. Walby (eds), *op.cit.*, p49.
9. C. Lubelska, 'Teaching Methods in Women's Studies: Challenging the Mainstream', in J. Aaron and S. Walby (eds), *op.cit.*, p42. See also M. Owen, 'Commonality and Difference: Theory and Practice', in S. Davies, C. Lubelska and J. Quinn (eds), *op.cit.*
10. H. Hinds, A. Pheonix and J. Stacey, *op.cit.*, p4.
11. D. Smith, *op.cit.*, p2.
12. M. Edwards, 'Women breaking the glass ceiling : Are we prepared to count the cost?' Unpublished paper presented to Women in Higher Education Network, University of Central Lancashire, November 1994.
13. *Ibid.*
14. See B. Bagihole, 'Being different is a very difficult row to hoe: Survival strategies of women academics' in S. Davies, C. Lubelska and J. Quinn (eds), *op.cit.*
15. L.S. Robinson, 'A Good Man is Hard to Find: Reflections on Men's Studies', in C. Kramarae and D. Spender (eds), *op.cit.*, p443.
16. See for example S. Faludi, *Backlash: The Undeclared War Against Women*, Chatto and Windus, London 1992.
17. See for example C. Ramazanoglu, *Feminism and the Contradictions of Oppression*, Routledge, London 1989 and b hooks, *Feminist Theory: from*

Margin to Centre, South End Press, Boston 1984.

18. C. Kramarae and D. Spender, *op.cit.*, p2.

19. See M. McNeill, 'Pedagogical Praxis and Problems: Reflections on Teaching about Gender Relations', in H. Hinds, A. Phoenix and J. Stacey (eds), *op.cit.*

20. *Ibid.*, p21.

14

'WORKING WITH THE ENEMY?' RESPONDING TO SOCIAL CHANGE THROUGH PARTNERSHIPS IN LEARNING

Mary Stuart

Many communities in Britain have been marginalised from the core of British society. Being marginal has made them a problem. Being a problem has re-cast some of these communities as 'enemies'. This polarisation of groups in British society forces educationalists to re-think their role in the community.

This chapter argues that adult educationalists should frame their community activities in the context of wider social change by discussing the connections between social policy and education focusing on the specific context of 'communities' in Britain in the 1990s.

Education theory and policy are often divorced from other social policies in society. This is surprising in adult education where educational activities are often focused on 'the community'. Even Brookfield, an arch defendant of community education, separates the notion of community into two.[1] On the one hand he sees community as the site of learning and on the other as the focus for political, social and personal struggle. He does not draw the connections between social policies in the community and education policies and opportunities.

The notion of community is a contested idea in social theory. From Tonnies, social theory has suggested that with the advent of modern industrial capitalism we have lost a sense of community awareness and replaced this form of social identity with merely functional association between people.[2] This somewhat romantic notion of a past 'caring community' is still common, especially in some of our education discourses. We have created a dichotomy between our role as professional educators based in institutions on the one hand and the communities we work in on the other hand. Many educationalists would define their professional relationships in terms of functional association and community educationalists would contrast their professional roles in their institutions with 'the real communities out there'. Creating this dichotomy of professionalism on the one hand and community groups or partners on the other, can be a barrier to seeing how inter-related education and 'the rest' of the community are. More significantly, polarising education and community ignores the obvious, extensive re-shaping of our society that has occurred over the last fifteen years, of which both educationalists and community members have been part.

Educationalists who work 'in the community' are part of a bigger, wider social discourse about social decision making.[3] If we see both our work, as educationalists, and the people living and working in the communities of the UK, as part of a wider unfolding struggle over definitions of British ways of life, we become more aware of the constraints, changes and vagaries of planning to which we are all subject. Members of voluntary sector organisations, social services and community groups have a different place from us within the structures of our society but like education, they are negotiating and engaging with social forces. They are constrained by similar difficulties: political decision making, funding, demography and their relationship to other social institutions. Statutorily funded education institutions have greater resources than many of the partners with whom they work. Yet being part of statutory provision is also dis-empowering. Having government bodies as our direct paymasters, unlike some of our partners, we are more immediately subject to policy changes.[4] As advocates for the voluntary sector have argued, there is more 'free-play' in the voluntary sector.[5]

Community partnerships can be examined through an identification of power structures within community groups as well as power battles within educational institutions.

There has been a strong tradition of radical adult education that emphasises notions of 'community development' and 'community action'.[6] However definitions of what development and whose development should not be taken for granted. Educationalists need to be aware of the different roles their partners play and how the agendas and cultures of partners affect their interactions with educationalists. Development is often controlled by 'professionals'; such as community or social workers or community leaders who have different agendas to those expressed by community members destined to 'benefit' from 'development' or 'action'. In other words community educationalists need to be more analytical about their partnerships. There are too many taken for granted concepts in 'community education'.[7]

Recent social theory , as inspired by Foucault, has explored this notion of 'difference' within groups illuminating a number of complex interconnections and difficulties in identifying what a cultural group consists of.[8]

To illustrate this point I use the example of a partnership between the University of Sussex and our local Sudanese Refugee 'community'. Here the notion of a community leader is problematic. Although leaders who speak for 'the community' will identify themselves, it is necessary to examine which constituency these leaders represent. Members of the Sudanese women's group feel alienated by the leaders of the Coptic Church and Muslim Sudanese do not identify with the demands or beliefs of Christian Sudanese. Each 'leader' is speaking for their faction in the 'community', and each leader has her or his own local authority. The leaders who advocate for a particular group within the community are arguing for access to learning resources which the university where I work 'owns'. It is the dominant ideology that has constructed this competition. The dominant ideology only recognises 'the Sudanese'. In Sudan the different factions would be quite separate. There is a tension between the perceived ideology of 'those others' and working with a range of different groups in the community. In community education it is not enough to talk about 'the community' or 'our partners', it is necessary to engage with a broader and more radical definition of community partnerships which highlights different concerns and constraints for different groups. Recognition of individual and cultural identities require a more nuanced analysis than community education theory has often used in the past.

THE CHANGING FACE OF BRITAIN: RE-CASTING 'OTHERS' IN THE SOCIETY

British social life has radically altered in the past fifteen years and changing adult education provision is a part of this re-organisation. Community educationalists do not seem to have fully taken account of the implications of the changes when developing their provision. In this section I will highlight some of the changes in Britain since 1980 and suggest some of the effects these changes have on the notion of 'community education'.

Growing numbers of the long term unemployed are an increasingly permanent feature of British society.[9] Whole communities have seen the destruction of their major source of employment in their area as Britain's industrial base has declined.[10] The composition of the working class has altered from full-time male workers to part-time female workers, creating extensive insecurity and the loss of trade union power.[11] Access to the benefit system has become difficult for many and impossible for sixteen and seventeen year olds. Whole tiers of local government have disappeared and utilities such as water and electricity have passed from public ownership to private companies. Public provision of housing which worked to support the provisions of the welfare state has been curtailed and in some cases stopped.[12]

These structural changes have also had extensive ideological effects. Since 1990 the definition of what being British is has also changed. Our society has re-cast itself in an increasingly clear 'them' and 'us' scenario. The Thatcher years began a process that is still underway. Unlike 1985 when Mrs Thatcher first used the concept against the striking coal miners, today we have many 'enemies within'. Late capitalism has placed 'the nation state' under threat and as we move into a closer association with the European Union our sense of Britishness is under threat.

Moral panics about the state of the nation that identify such 'enemies' as: single parents and their children, teachers, travellers, homeless people, mental health sufferers, and refugees claiming asylum are common in our national and local media. All these groups in British society have been subject to legislation in the last five years. These new laws have re-cast many people living in this country as 'other' to all that 'we' call 'British'.[13] The ideological effects of this process of 'othering' people are the culmination of a process that began with the Falklands War 1982 and the miners strike in 1984-85. It is no longer possible to talk about 'others out there'. After all it is these 'enemies' that are the students of community education.

The 1970s and 1980s equal opportunities' analysis of community education that spoke of equal access to resources for all has to be seen as limited in the 1990s. To draw on social policy theory again, Fiona Williams, writing about the oppression of people with learning difficulties, expresses concern about simply arguing for equal opportunities. She says:

> By stressing the rights of an oppressed group to have access to the opportunities and life-style of mainstream society, ... could lead to an underrating of the specific needs of the group ... and perhaps their right to be different.[14]

Above all, the ideological battle of the 1990s in Britain is for the right of people and groups to be different not merely equal. Community educationalists need to find new ways of developing provision which addresses these demands of a range of different 'others' in British society.

Since 1990 the legal status of many communities has changed. For example, the Criminal Justice Act criminalises travelling as a way of life. Community education work cannot be the same as it was before 1990. It is no longer possible when devising a programme of learning opportunities with partners to believe that we are simply offering 'education'. Our professional status, which assesses learning needs, student progress and so on, is increasingly at odds when working with many of our communities. Our 'students' often do not see any future for themselves in this new Britain and are increasingly less interested in the return to work type programmes that are consistently offered because funding is available. To quote one such person:

> The best way to describe the people in our community is to liken them to the buildings we use. These buildings are redundant. So are we, we're redundant people. We're not drop-outs, we're force-outs, we're people who are not wanted anymore ... There's no future for us in Britain plc.[15]

In this climate the community education initiatives of the 1980s that simply focused on education for 'citizenship' within the state are no longer relevant to people who see themselves as force-outs from the state. Providing equal opportunities to British society is not what many of the 'force-outs' are looking for.

Changes at a national level to social policy affect the sort of adult education that should be provided. The political, social and ideological shift that I have described above will not affect all community education workers in the same way. However in choosing to work with 'force-outs' educationalists are re-defining themselves, whether they like it or not, as different from the dominant culture. Increasingly it is necessary to subvert current education discourses to meet the demands of the communities with which we work. Adult and community education has remained fixed on an education for equal access for all the community. Given the polarised society we now live in and the demands of many community groups for alternative life-styles, we need to develop a new education to enable the 'force-outs' to find their own voice and advocate for their own and often different, way of life. The second half of this chapter explores two local projects that attempt to grapple with the difficulty of offering an education appropriate to the radically polarised society I have described above.

LOCAL COMMUNITIES: PARTNERSHIPS TO ADDRESS A CHANGING POPULATION

The Sussex locale has been enormously affected by changing social policies of the 1990s. Brighton has the highest homeless population in the country after London.[16] Many of these people are young or are mental health service users who identify as 'forced-outs'. There are squats and several new age and traditional traveller sites in Sussex. These groups have been particularly affected by the (1994) Criminal Justice Act. Both East and West Sussex have extensive populations of older people. Many long stay institutions have closed down in the area as a result of community care legislation. These groups suffered institutionalisation and often find it difficult to live within the rigid structures of our society.

The geography of Sussex with its rolling downs and its picturesque little villages creates enormous isolation. Public transport has been destroyed between the villages and the towns with local councils being forced to curb spending.[17] Many older people find themselves trapped in their homes. Disabled people who are encouraged to 'live in the community' find they have no access to facilities that are still available in larger towns.

There is a growing refugee population in Sussex, some of whom have seen family members sent back to their countries of origin in fear of their lives because they did not pass their 'interview' on arrival. This complex local picture highlights the range of different communities within a locale and throws into sharp focus the difficulty of offering 'community education', in any simple sense. In my area, I am often working with groups either on the thin dividing line between legality and criminality or with fragile and often isolated minority ethnic groups and disabled people. The first project I focus on was developed to meet the educational aspirations of a group of isolated disabled people in West Sussex.

In the 1980s a sheltered housing estate was build outside Burgess Hill, a dormitory town for middle-class London commuters. The council saw the pretty countryside as ideal for the physically disabled residents who could enjoy the pleasant surroundings. As social services were cut back, many of the people living on this estate found they had no access to the town or any educational opportunities. Transport needed to be specialised and was seldom available due to insufficient funding. A local voluntary organisation working with disabled people approached the equality unit at the university, highlighting the growing isolation of disabled and older frail people in the area. Simply offering a course to people on the estate, as is often the practice in adult education centres, would not solve the problem of other housebound people in the area. The group were looking for an educational experience that alleviated their isolation and sense of being 'other' to the rest of their surrounding community. They wanted access to discussion and debate about issues.

Working in partnership with the potential 'students' and the voluntary organisation, a housebound learning scheme was devised. This scheme paired people who live on the estate, and other isolated disabled people, with students attending courses at an adult education centre. This solution was a creative attempt to engage with the different demands of this disabled community.

There were many difficult issues about offering such a course. The safety of the participants needed to be ensured. Many of the housebound participants were vulnerable and, as it was a learning opportunity, it was the responsibility of the organisers to ensure all participants could trust each other. The experimental nature of this provision made it impossible to offer the courses without partnership. A range of partnerships were developed, including the adult education centre who offered a space for the mobile students to meet and social services who could use their security system to check the participants' safety.

The participants were interested in a range of topics, most with a political edge, including: the media's role in representing 'Britishness', women's role in society, welfare rights and personal writings about their lived experience, which were compiled into a booklet.

This is an example of one response to the changing social structure of Britain in a Sussex context. The partnership with the voluntary organisation was central, as the workers were aware of the specific needs of the group and, without the link with social services, it would have been impossible to enable participants to visit each others homes.

University continuing education has had to radically remodel itself to receive funding from the higher education funding councils. The discourse of continuing education departments has altered to focus on the desire for accredited work and in some areas this discourse has emphasised vocational training. The members of the housebound learners project were not looking for vocational training or accreditation. As one student told me, 'Employers aren't interested in disabled people'. A different sort of learning experience needed to be developed and appropriate funding found. There are other funding possibilities and, depending on the nature of the work and the partnerships involved, different funding 'pots' can be tapped to meet specific community demands. Developed in 1993, the scheme has grown and is now organised entirely by the voluntary organisation, who were supported in bidding for additional funds to support the project, by the University.

Widening participation in higher education requires the institution to have a desire to engage with different demands from community groups. It requires learning to be organised and conceptualised differently. Above all it requires flexibility and an ability to relate to different community 'cultures'.[18] In the following section I will discuss an accredited programme that developed in partnership with a range of community groups who were specifically looking for a course that offered university recognition.

ADVOCATING FOR ADVOCACY

The Diploma in Advocacy and Empowerment could be seen as the perfect response to the Higher Education Funding Council's desire to see accredited continuing education. The course is a two year part-time modular university accredited programme, with vocational possibilities. Students taking the programme move from courses at first year undergraduate level to finally completing a Masters' level course at the end of their programme. The process of developing the diploma came out of a community action model of continuing education. The programme developed in response to a variety of groups expressing a desire to train as advocates for their group. These groups became partners in developing the programme.

The partners were diverse. There was a tension between those groups who were looking to support 'others' who had been excluded from society and the 'others' who were excluded. There were professionals, such as social service workers and health workers with particular agendas from their world of work, and at the same time, community members and tenants on estates wanted to use the qualification to stand up to professionals.

Some of the groups who participated in the development of the programme were overtly political, others were not. They included: an association promoting the different learning needs of people with dyslexia, a voluntary organisation working with frail older people, a women's action group for refugee support, a traveller support group and a social services department. Other organisations that were consulted included MIND, People First, workers in the local citizens advice bureau and Age Concern. As the discussions developed all the partners began to identify their interest in advocacy as a political issue. The groups wanted to use their learning to challenge systems, structures and individuals who had dis-empowered them. What united the different partners was a desire for a recognised programme of courses to enable people to respond to the difficulties they had experienced in Britain in the 1990s.

Devising an educational programme in partnership is an exciting process. People with other agendas than educationalists come to learning differently. They do not just cast a professional eye over a syllabus. Partners want to see how the learning they participate in can be applied. This difference of approach created tensions between my beliefs in a community led curriculum and the demands of the university's professional status. I wanted to ensure the development of the diploma was an empowering exercise in itself. Empowerment is defined as leading 'to greater independence, but not total independence. Paradoxically, the path to greater independence is one that reinforces the idea of interdependence and co-operation'.[19]

Offering a programme that would receive university recognition was more complex than the usual negotiation with community partners. It became essential to discuss the university's role in defining learning success. Extensive discussions focused on two areas: the sort of assessment people felt comfortable with, and who would define the measurements of success. Some groups, such as the Dyslexia Association, wanted to investigate how academic language is used as a powerful tool to exclude people. Education's role in dis/empowerment became a thread that was to run through the entire programme. The final course in the programme was devised as a critique of the role of 'research' in advocacy. Traveller groups wanted to discuss the relationship between surveillance and research. They questioned the ownership of research finding and the access to information learned. Other groups were keen to have specific skills such as counselling or computer skills built into the programme. All the partners saw practical experience of working in community groups as a central feature of the learning programme. The ideas were discussed at management committees, over coffee in family centres, with residents in housing associations and sheltered housing complexes and with travelling families in caravans. I found myself being an advocate for the university in these settings and being an advocate for the partners in the university. Sometimes the process was uncomfortable as the cultural difference between the institution and the groups was so great that it was impossible to find a solution.

Co-operation between groups and the university seemed, at times to wear thin. It seemed significant to me that no other academic visited the groups with me and that some groups found relations between themselves and other groups difficult. If academics suggested changes to the programme then these changes had to be taken back to relevant partners. Again questions of ownership were central to discussions with partners. These questions were not always resolved to the partners or my satisfaction. There remains a tension about the universities' role in community work of this nature. On the one hand we are expected in universities to question accepted knowledge and taken for granted common sense. It is this radical and critical enquiry that I emphasised in advocating for the diploma with community groups and in schools of the university. On the other hand universities are very much part of the mechanisms of social integration and the process of validation often re-enforced this aspect of our identity. The current polarised social climate in Britain exacerbated this tension. It also created the desire for the diploma in the first place as it was a response to the changes in the locale that initially encouraged the participants to make demands of the university.

The whole process of programme development and validation took over two years. Some of the partners became frustrated with the extensive negotiations and withdrew. Some groups struggling for funds and social acceptance were disbanded before the programme was validated. At the end of 1994, the Centre for Continuing Education at the University of Sussex offered for the first time a Diploma in Advocacy and Empowerment.

The team of tutors for the course come from within the university, other statutory bodies and from community groups. The people who applied to do the Diploma came from some of the partner organisations who worked on the proposal and from other groups and organisations in the area. The partners who stayed with the development of the programme are keen to continue to support the programme as it develops. An advocacy network is being established to facilitate this process. Students and tutors will also participate in partner groups' activities.

LESSONS FOR THE PARTNERSHIPS

When I was asked if the university could develop an advocacy course, it did not seem that it would be possible to develop an accredited programme in partnership with community groups and other organisations. Assessment in most universities still focused on exams and written essays. For many of the people who were interested in the programme, these forms of assessment would be like yet more surveillance in their lives. It was possible to use the current education debate around alternative forms of assessment to the programme's advantage. The diploma was validated with a range of assessment methods, including group and individual assessment but not exams. It was essential to offer assessment to which potential students and partner organisations could relate. It was also vital that learning support and study skills were built into each aspect of the programme.

Developing the programme as an accredited course also challenged my own definition of community education that had taken for granted that courses devised with partners in the community would not lead to university level credits. For the partners involved in developing the programme, a university diploma was seen as an essential requirement. Partners recognised that having a socially accepted qualification was a powerful tool when dealing with authorities. It was the partners who made the demand of accreditation not the educationalists.

My conception of community education as an education for citizenship and participation has changed to one of an education for advocacy and empowerment. In British society, in the 1990s, rather than integration, an enabling education must give people the tools to campaign for an alternative and different lifestyle against a dominant culture.

I have argued for a community education that engages with change in society and offers learning opportunities relevant to the communities universities serve. Since 1980 the communities of Britain have radically altered. The ongoing debate about the role of education, and universities in particular, in society, has highlighted some important issues for community education practice. The debate is contradictory. It has opened up the possibility for greater involvement of communities within university provision as well as greater social surveillance of our activities. Education is part of a discourse of social policy. Universities need to critically engage with these debates about the structure and purpose of our society and its members. Above all university continuing education needs to recognise that the polarisation of our society now requires us to be partial in our choice of partnerships.

This process of partnership is logistically complex, it takes time and is filled with ideological and practical tensions, and the challenge that it poses to the role of community education needs to be answered. The current social imagining of Britishness has excluded many of the constituents of community education and defined them as 'enemies within'. If universities are to respond to these communities' requests, which will include education to defend their community's way of life, universities will need to re-define their role in the wider community.

NOTES

1. S. Brookfield, *Adult Learners, Adult Education and the Community*, OUP, Milton Keynes 1983.
2. F. Tonnies, *Community and Society*, Harper and Row 1957.
3. C. Griffin, *Adult Education as Social Policy*, Croom Helm, Beckenham 1987.
4. *Ibid*.

5. Report on the Wolfenden Committee, *The Future of Voluntary Organisations*, Croom Helm, London 1978.
6. A. Rogers, *Adults Learning for Development*, Cassel, London 1992; T. Lovett, *et al*, *Adult Education and Community Action*, Croom Helm, London 1983; T. Lovett, *Adult Education, Community Development, and the Working Class*, Wardlock Education, London 1975; K. Ward and D. Taylor, *Education for the Missing Millions, Education for the Working Class*, Croom Helm, London 1986.
7. P. Jarvis, *The Sociology of Adult and Continuing Education*, Croom Helm, Beckenham 1985.
8. N. Yuval-Davis, 'Fundamentalism, Multiculturalism and Women in Britain', and S. Hall, 'New Ethnicities', in J. Donald and A. Rattansi (eds), *Race, Culture and Difference*, Sage, London 1992.
9. C. Leadbeater, 'In the Land of the Dispossessed', in L. McDowell, P. Sarre and C. Hamnett (eds), *Divided Nation: Social and Cultural Change in Britain*, Hodder and Stoughton, London 1989.
10. J. Allen, 'Towards a Post-Industrial Economy?', in J. Allen and D. Massey (eds), *The Economy in Question*, Sage, London 1988.
11. L. McDowell, 'Gender Divisions', in C. Hamnett, L. McDowell and P. Sarre (eds), *The Changing Social Structure*, Sage, London 1989; Allen, *op.cit.*
12. M. Harloe and C. Paris, 'The Decollectivization of Consumption: Housing and Local Government Finance in England and Wales 1979-81', in L. McDowell, P. Sarre and C. Hamnett (eds), *Divided Nation: Social and Cultural Change in Britain*, Hodder and Stoughton, London 1989.
13. M. Stuart, and A. Thompson (eds), *Engaging with Difference: The 'Other' in Adult Education*, NIACE, Leicester 1995.
14. F. Williams, 'Mental Handicap and Oppression', in A. Brechin and J. Walmsley, *Making Connections*, Hodder and Stoughton, London 1989, p258.
15. T. Malyon, 'The New Exodus', in *The Big Issue*, No. 98, 1994.
16. Brighton Homeless Acceptance List, 1994, Brighton Borough Council.
17. A. Thomson and J. Lowerson (eds), *Out of Sight, Out of Mind? Barriers to Participation in Rural Adult Education*, Centre for Continuing Education, University of Sussex 1995.
18. Stuart and Thomson, *op.cit.*
19. Williams, *op.cit.*, p257.

15

DEVELOPING HIGHER EDUCATION WITH A SIKH COMMUNITY

Alan Parton, Jeff Braham, and Davinder Panesar

The notion of a 'community' within English higher education has traditionally been associated with occupational sectors, the manufacturing community, the financial community and so on, so that the traditional student base of most universities has continued to be national rather than local, and educational need has been served through the requirements of those nationally relevant sectors. Only very recently for some institutions, and not yet for others, have local geographical and culturally diverse concepts of community been relevant. These concepts require a paradigm shift in the notion of defining provision, so that institutions serve the needs of communities, in all their cultural, economic and educational diversity, rather than of institutions themselves, as was suggested by Fulton and Ellwood, and more strongly by Parry and Ball.[1] In 1988, the Universities Council for Adult and Continuing Education (UCACE) established a working party on continuing education provision for the minority ethnic communities. The report of this working party confirms inertia to be widespread within universities.[2] The working party examined course provision across the country and identified a few programmes in Afro-Caribbean and South Asian Studies. However, for some time it has been possible to read American Studies, Welsh literature and history, and European Studies. The context of the discussion which follows is very clearly that of a local community, and is specifically related to the development of provision with and for the Sikh population of Coventry, most of which is resident within two miles of the Coventry University campus.

The developments which are discussed, however, are not exclusive to this particular community – that would be entirely wasteful of the considerable resource which has been and will be involved. What has emerged instead is a coherent plan for developing previously rather *ad hoc* community provision into a community-based continuing education programme of considerable importance within the university's overall strategic mission.

What follows therefore is a description of the community in question, its historical and geographical development, and current cultural definition and requirements, and an identification of the themes and issues which the university has addressed in both strategic and operational terms, in order to become responsive to the needs of that community. Questions still remain about the future – most particularly since we are still at the developmental stage, and therefore operational difficulties are yet to be faced in practice.

THE COMMUNITY DEFINED

The Sikh settlement in Britain began in the early years of this century, the first Gurdwara being established in Southall in 1908. By 1987 there were approximately 175,000 Sikhs and 150 Gurdwaras in Britain, and by 1992 the corresponding figures were 500,000 and 170, respectively.[3] The Gurdwaras include a temple, but also cater for the cultural, social welfare and educational needs of the local Sikh community. The numbers of Sikhs given above must be treated with caution. Prior to 1971, the census of population only recorded the ethnic background of people born outside the United Kingdom; in 1971 country of origin was given but no twentieth-century census has been able to identify people specifically of the Sikh religion.

Coventry's ethnic minority communities principally comprise Muslims, largely from Bangladesh, Hindus from the Indian sub-continent, and Sikhs who have moved directly from the Punjab, or via Kenya or Uganda in East Africa. The major influx of both Indian and East-African Asians began in the 1960s, and increased dramatically in the 1970s and then again in the 1980s, in line with government policy in respect of immigration.[4] Since the 1980s, the population has largely stabilised and grown in line with the indigenous population's growth. This means that the ethnic population of Coventry now includes second and even third generation (i.e. UK born and educated) individuals. These communities provide a valuable addition to the city in respect of increased cultural diversity, and a significant contribution to commercial activities, in line with the disproportionate contribution made by the Asian population generally to the UK Gross National Product.

An examination of the age structure of the Indian households in Coventry, based on the 1981 census, confirms that at that time the vast majority were born outside the UK. However, almost all of the Indian population aged fifteen or under had been born in the UK, emphasising the 1960s as an important period of change. With a greater number of UK-born individuals in the population, there was pressure to preserve the culture of groups such as the Sikhs. This pressure has continued to mount with the further shift in the balance of population born in the UK.[5]

The Sikh community in Coventry, which numbers approximately 20,000 people and represents a fifty-four per cent majority within the total Asian community, is distinctive in culture and location. The 1991 census provides quantitative evidence of the geography of Indian settlement.[6] As is common amongst immigrant groups there is a tendency for settlement to be within a particular sector of a city; other examples of this are the Jewish immigrants in Leeds, the African Caribbean community in Moss Side, Manchester, and internationally the Europeans in Nairobi and the Chinese in San Francisco. The Asian community is located almost entirely within the 'railway triangle' of Coventry, in the inner north-east sector of the city. This district is largely one containing housing constructed between 1850 and 1900. It has had a sequence of occupancy; originally a working class English area, it became a focus for Irish settlement in the 1930s and 1940s, and more recently has become a large Sikh district. In 1981, twenty-five per cent of Punjabi speakers were located in one ward within this area of the city.[7] The physical evidence for the ethnic nature of this area is everywhere apparent, in the specialist food and clothing shops, and the temples which are the focal points for the community.

The Sikhs are often very successful in business. Coventry was an important textile centre in the nineteenth century; the advent of Sikh settlement has seen a rebirth of this industry, and today there is a lively clothing industry in which ninety-five per cent of the workforce is

Asian. As the Sikh community has grown, so too has this industry; between 1974 and 1987, employment in clothing grew from 147 to 1392; in 1989 there were ninety-three clothing firms in the city. This community has brought a wealth of business skill to Coventry, and plays an important role in the retail trade.[8]

SIKHISM

The founder of Sikhism was Guru Nanak Dev, a fifteenth-century mystic who challenged the political and caste systems in India. Guru Nanak was followed by nine other Gurus, each playing an essential role in the development of the Sikh culture and religion. The tenth Guru, Guru Gobind Singh Ji, bestowed the uniform and way of life of the Sikhs. After Guru Gobind Singh Ji, the Sikh consider the *Guru Granth Sahib* as their Guru today. The *Guru Granth Sahib* is the sacred text of the Sikhs, and embodies the spirit of the Ten Sikh Gurus and the Saints, whose Word is included within it. The *Guru Granth Sahib* presents a balanced combination of action, devotion and knowledge. The *Guru Granth Sahib* receives, and shall receive, veneration like the 'living Guru'. No living Guru can take its place. Its Word directs the devotee in all his functions, secular as well as spiritual. The *Guru Granth Sahib* is compiled in thirty-one *Raags* (male musical modes) and *Raaginis* (female musical modes).

The main tenet of Sikhism is the belief in the one Creator, which is both transcendental and immanent. The Sikh must meditate (*Nam Japna*), must work for a living, (*Kirt Karni*) and must share earnings with the needy and deserving (*Wand Chhakna*). The Sikhs are Saint-soldiers (*Sant-Sapie*).

The work 'Sikh' means to learn. Guru Nanak Dev Ji laid great emphasis on the education of individuals and was instrumental in challenging the monopoly of education held by the Brahman at that time. Education features very highly within the Sikh community, and has been incorporated within the Gurdwaras today.

The Gurdwara is the Sikh place of worship. There are seven Gurdwaras in Coventry and several hundred in Britain. They are places of worship, of learning and of socialising. All Sikh Gurdwaras are open to everyone and provide *Gur Ka Langer*, a free kitchen. The *sangat*, or congregation, all sit together and partake in the *Langer*. This gives the opportunity for socialising, serving the community through the provision of food, and ensures that, irrespective of class, creed, gender or race, all must eat together. The Gurdwaras are slowly becoming community resource centres in a much wider sense, with libraries, childcare facilities, teaching and music rooms, as well as the kitchen and worship facilities which are common to all.

The Sikh community has made significant progress in Britain but is faced with several issues which require urgent action from the community. The second and third generation Sikhs who were educated or/and born in Britain and who communicate in English, face increasing difficulties due to the language barrier which exists between them and their parents and grandparents, who use Punjabi. This has resulted in a lack of awareness of their cultural and religious history. However, with the increased interest in the East by the West, e.g. in acupuncture, homeopathy, yoga, meditation and Eastern mysticism, this 'disadvantaged' section of the Sikh community has started to respond to these difficulties itself. With part-funding from the Sikh community and Gurdwaras, and with the potential infrastructure available, the Sikh community is ready and able to have its needs and the needs of its future generations fulfilled. Many Gurdwaras are now teaching *Keetan*, *Raag Sangit*, GCSE and A level Punjabi, and Sikhism. Additionally there is growing interest in Sikh theology from the younger Sikh generations and non-Sikhs. Currently this need is partly satisfied by visiting *Gianis* (those with professional training in theology and divinity) and *Raagis* (those with professional training in *Raag Sangit*) from India. There is however a genuine opportunity for the development of a locally-based degree platform for the theology and *Raag Sangit* (the musical presentation of the *Raags* and *Raaginis*).

THE COMMUNITY AND THE UNIVERSITY

Coventry University declares in its Strategic Plan that it is committed to maximising access and participation, particularly in the local and sub-regional context, providing flexibility in entry and in modes of study across all areas of work.[9] In order to put some practical potential into that statement, four objectives inform the continuing education work of the university in general, and, in this context, its work with the Sikh community in particular. Those objectives are:

> to build on the university's long-standing commitment to serving its community;
> to build upon established contacts and to create new ones, forming

a comprehensive network for community-based provision;
to focus initially upon those identified as target populations and areas, but to continue to identify need and to respond positively to it;
to fulfil the university's commitment to providing support for increased participation in higher education.

The capacity of the university to support the development of a community-based continuing education programme with the Sikh community in Coventry, and indeed with other target communities within the local and sub-regional context, relies essentially on two strategic moves. The first is the development of a community-based network; the second is the further development of a responsive university-based infrastructure. The university is committed to a four-year development period, with the intention that the network and the infrastructure will be fully operational by the year 1999.

The network puts the university at the centre of a web of provision which may range from short non-accredited, non-vocational programmes, to full degree programmes. The critical feature of all programmes, however, is that they are developed and delivered in response to the needs of the community, identified in collaborative discussions with the community. Meeting those needs is crucial to the success of the initiative. The structure of the web combines four different sorts of resource: people, places, materials and technology. Using this combination, we will be creating a series of locally based opportunities for delivering relevant programmes across a wide range of identified need.

The people are community leaders, Gurdwara leaders, university staff, adult education staff, school and college teachers, and other members of the local communities as appropriate. The university has recognised the need to coordinate activity by this disparate group of individuals, and has created a unit with that specific remit. The Educational Development Unit came into existence in September 1994, and combines the functions associated with accreditation of prior learning (APL), credit accumulation and transfer (CATS), open and distance learning, computer-aided learning, work-based learning, compacts, and community education, amongst other things! In addition, locally recruited field officers operate within the community, identifying need, and coordinating the resources which make up the fabric of the network at a local level.

The places, that is the sites where provision will be available, include the Asian Community Centre, Gurdwaras, schools and colleges. The university already has links with many potential centres within the community, and is keen to develop its large Compact scheme so as to involve schools more in local HE level provision, both for school leavers and adults within their catchment areas. The aim is that by 1997, every local secondary school will be included in the compact scheme. Also, the *Dharamic* Institute, a charitable trust within the Sikh community itself, has pledged to support the development of educational provision. This Institute has substantial support from across the British and international Sikh populations, and has the potential to develop a community-specific centre for the delivery of a wide range of programmes at HE level and below. Gurdwaras, both in Coventry and nationally, are continually improving their educational provision. In Coventry, this has resulted in one of the Gurdwaras opening its own substantial 'college' in 1995, with provision already available at further education level through a local FE College, and with planned expansion into a wide range of accredited and non-accredited vocational and non-vocational higher education programmes, offered in collaboration with the university. Another Gurdwara is seeking to develop the same sort of range of activity during 1996. There is active discussion about the extent to which the university may contribute also in 1996 to the development of a Sikh National Cultural Centre in the city.

Materials will be adapted or adopted from existing programmes, such as those available through the OLF, the university's own Return to Learn (HE) programme, and the Higher Education Lead-in Programme (HELP), to form a foundation programme for those needing pre-HE provision, but aiming to gain access to the wider university prospectus. In addition, a series of short courses in Punjabi studies, covering the history, culture, religion and language of the Punjab, and of the Punjabi groups in Britain, was developed during 1995, and is available not only to second and third generation Punjabis, but also to the indigenous population. Liaison with the community has identified several other needs. Those at FE level, such as food hygiene programmes for catering outlets, have resulted in contacts being developed to service those needs and, eventually, towards the year 1999, the development of the human elements of the network will allow all such provision also to be brought within the network. At HE level, identified need will build primarily on the existing educational and training opportunities within the community itself, many of which are directly related to the business educational needs of the community. The university response to the area of most significant need has led us to investigate with the community the development of a degree in Sikh Theology and *Raag Sangit* (see below).

Technology is increasingly available to support the delivery of university programmes in the community. Linking centres both with each other, and with the university, through audio and video technology, will provide the opportunity for cost-effective programmes where small numbers are involved, and, together with stand-alone technology, will enable the use of open and computer-aided learning formats. The Department for Education announcement of the widespread development of the internet adds potentially a significant further dimension to the technological strands of the network, and sources of funding are continually being explored which will specifically support the expansion of technological linkages within the network.[10] The university intends that by 1996, the installation of video conferencing stations will support the development of community-based facilities.

One of the prime roles of the Educational Development Unit is to develop the infrastructure within the university which supports the strategic objectives of the network. This infrastructure builds on the existing modular framework within which all current university provision is delivered. An APL procedural framework was approved by the university's Academic Board in 1994, and a CATS-based route to the General BA was approved in 1995. This enhances the ability of the university to respond to a more diverse range of individual study needs than can be accommodated within the named degree programmes which have traditionally made up its prospectus. In addition, work with the Adult Education Division of Coventry City Council developed a credit-based access programme, into which individuals are able to transfer credit from other programmes. The final piece of this part of the jigsaw is the facility by which the university can offer accreditation of appropriate existing programmes within the Sikh community. The existence of a coherent APL strategy makes this process straightforward.

In line with the Higher Education Quality Council and Universities Association for Continuing Education (UACE) guidelines on quality in continuing education, an additional quality assurance structure specific to the community-based initiatives has been developed, which is linked into the existing Coventry University procedures.[11] A Local Management Committee (LMC) will monitor provision as it becomes available, taking feedback from the community via individual participants, programme leaders, and the coordinating Field Officer. This LMC will in turn provide feedback to a Continuing Education Steering Group within the university, chaired by the Director of the Educational Development Unit, with specific responsibility for monitoring the progress of the university towards its four strategic objectives for community-based continuing education (listed above), and the resulting operational objectives, defined within an Annual Operating Plan. The development of the LMC, and the inclusion within it of the local field worker, provides a clear feedback loop between the network and the university.

By the end of 1995, this management structure will be in place. What will it actually produce in terms of visible provision? Discussions with the Sikh community began in mid-1994, and a number of specific programmes have been, or are being, developed. The community itself, through the instrument of an experienced teacher and community leader, has developed a series of short courses in Punjabi studies, which the university has accredited. These short, taster programmes are of interest to the second generation Sikhs, and will eventually be so more particularly to third generation Sikhs, but will also be of considerable use to the public sector services within the city. It is intended that they be made available to the Police, to the Education Authority, the Regional Health Authority, and to the City Council, as staff development programmes from 1996 onwards. A programme of Stress Management Through Meditation has been created by another community leader, and Coventry City Council is already committed to using the material for staff development. The university is in discussion about the possibilities for accrediting this programme, and for creating Open Learning material to support its wider application. Several of the existing modules within the School of International Studies and Law relate specifically to the culture, history and economics of the Asian sub-continent, and are available as elective modules to supplement the development of the degree, which has been the main thrust of our discussions so far.

The degree in Sikh Theology and *Raag Sangit* has created much excitement, both within the Sikh community (locally, nationally and internationally) and within the university. The community has responded to the positive approach of the university by setting up a charitable trust called the *Dharamic* Institute, as mentioned above. This Institute has the support of the international Sikh community, to negotiate with the university over the curriculum, method of delivery, ownership and so on. The university, for its part, has committed itself to providing academic staff time to assist the community in identifying appropriate curriculum content, in creating an appropriate structure, and preparing for University Approval, which will take place during 1996.

The two elements of the proposed degree (Sikh Theology and *Raag Sangit*) are inextricably intertwined within the religious practices of the Sikhs, and need to be linked within the programme that is developed. Having discussed within the community and inside the university the requirements for supporting such a degree, it has become clear that the expertise for delivering such a programme is largely (if not entirely) within the Sikh population itself. Itinerant peripatetic *Raagis* travel from across the world to lead worship through music in Gurdwaras throughout the British Sikh communities, supplemented by cultural and theological visits from academics and *Gianis*. It is therefore clear that the community must be centrally involved in creating the curriculum for the programme, and almost certainly that community-based staff will ultimately be involved in its delivery, since, like the non-accredited short programmes, the most appropriate place for the delivery of at least the practical parts of such a programme is within the community, if not within the Gurdwaras themselves. The Sikh community has made clear that it sees the quality issue as central, and that the programme must be owned by the university, and delivered by its academic staff. This effectively pre-empted the university's own stance, and removed what we had originally seen as a source of potential conflict. The community has also demonstrated its commitment to the support of study at a high level by discovering and offering a library of some 60,000 volumes, which is dedicated to Sikhism and comparative religious study. Such a resource is naturally of great interest since we are keen to develop the possibility of supporting research in this area before the year 2000.

CONCLUSION

Coventry University is committed to working with its local community. This is partly because its historical base has always been relatively locally focused, and its current mission commits it to continue to contribute to the social, cultural and economic regeneration of the region. It is also partly because the shifts in the demographic and economic profile of the higher education populations together with the fluctuation in government funding policy mean that the most significant area for potential growth within most institutions is likely to be in locally-based, part-time students. However, rather like employer-funded Employee Development Schemes, which have begun to convert those employers who were only interested in bottom-line profits to the holistic benefits of a learning culture, serious conversations with specific local communities become enthusiastic very quickly. A city-centre university responding to its city's various needs in a community-focused way is a powerful tool in the promotion of lifelong learning. As an emerging Continuing Education Unit, that must be a major fillip to our morale, as well as to that of the communities we seek to serve.

There are clearly issues emerging during the continued development of these programmes. The funding of development work will be greatly supplemented by the award of a grant from the Higher Education Funding Council for England (HEFCE), under its call for bids to support widened provision, which it was always intended would include work with minority ethnic populations in Coventry. This funding is for a four year period (1995–1999) which coincides with the University's four year development cycle. The issue of funding individual participation is potentially more problematic. It seems likely that a mixture of full-cost programmes, subsidised places, bursary support from the community, and grant funding from such sources as the European Union and Single Regeneration Budget, will be employed. The Sikh community in Coventry is not a poor one, and has demonstrated its financial commitment to its own educational development through the investment in new and emerging facilities. However, the university will work with the community to ensure that individuals who have need of the provision are not disadvantaged for financial reasons.

The issue of ownership, which the university had seen as perhaps problematic, has in fact been addressed by the community, which requires the programmes to be as closely allied to the mainstream of university provision as possible. The university will own the programmes, validate the curricula through its normal procedures, and appoint the staff who will teach them. The Sikh community is quite happy with this approach; indeed the Council of Sikh Gurdwaras in

Coventry, which is the body through which the university has taken forward the development work, is anxious that delivery of the degree programme takes place largely within the university, rather than within the community. It has also suggested that there will be the opportunity to offer exchanges to visiting professors from the Punjab, and to look at supporting research fellowships, all within the context of a Coventry University programme.

The university's relationship with the Council of Sikh Gurdwaras is crucial, in that it allows the university to liaise with all the different sections of the Sikh community within a common forum. It also demonstrates the commitment of the community to work with the university. In 1995 the setting up of Sikh Week, attended by the leaders of both the Sikh community and the host community, including the Chief Education Officer for the city, two Members of Parliament, the Leader of the City Council, and the Lord Mayor, provided a highly visible boost to the emerging relationship. The university's commitment was demonstrated to a wide section of the community by having two of our three Pro-Vice Chancellors, two Deans of School, lecturers from two other schools, and three of the Educational Development Unit's staff present.

Quality assurance, particularly in relation to off-campus provision, will be the responsibility of the university. There will continue to be a need for close scrutiny of the development and delivery of provision for and within the community, especially where peripatetic staff are involved. The extension of the university's existing quality procedures to embrace all continuing education work is an important step in maintaining control of quality issues.

As the relationship develops towards 1999, and subsequently beyond, the most important single issue will undoubtedly remain one of communication. It will always be central to the initiative to be able to communicate the commitment of the university to responding to the needs of the community. Having a positive relationship with the Council of Sikh Gurdwaras, a major voice in the community, is therefore a central plank upon which to build.

NOTES

1. O. Fulton, and S. Ellwood, *Admissions to Higher Education: Policy and Practice*, Training Agency, Sheffield 1989; G. Parry, 'Access Courses in Post-school Education' in G. Parry (ed), *Engineering Futures, New Audiences and Arrangements for Engineering Higher Education*, London

1990; Sir Christopher Ball, *More Means Different – Widening Access to Higher Education*, Royal Society of Arts, 1990.

2. UCACE, *UCACE Occasional Paper No. 2: Report of the Working Party on CE provision for the Minority Ethnic Communities*, April, 1990.

3. HMSO, *Britain: An Official Handbook*, Central Office of Information, London 1987 and 1992.

4. Coventry City Council, *Ethnic Minority Statistical Digest: City of Coventry*, 1989.

5. *Ibid.*

6. OPCS, *Census Data*, 1991.

7. Coventry City Council, *op.cit.*

8. Coventry City Council, *Coventry Economic Monitor – Quarterly review of trends in the local economy*, June 1989.

9. Coventry University, *Strategic Plan, 1992/93–1995/96*, 1991.

10. Department for Education, *Information Technology Provision in Schools in England, Government Objectives*, DFE, London, June 1995.

11. UACE, *UACE Working Paper No. 6: Handbook for Quality Assurance in University Continuing Education*, UACE, 1995.

16

COMMUNITY REGENERATION AND SOCIAL EXCLUSION: SOME CURRENT POLICY ISSUES FOR HIGHER EDUCATION

Kevin Ward

Rhetoric about community regeneration and social exclusion, and underlying concerns about long-term unemployment and widening inequality are commonplace, and increasingly evident in the European Union, and amongst political parties, central and local government, training agencies (Training and Enterprise Councils [TECs]), and educational institutions (both Further and Higher Education). Elements of this rhetoric have been utilised by large numbers of higher education institutions in mission statements which refer often to universities and 'their' communities.

Within this context, this chapter provides an overview of recent institutional responses to these issues. This includes central government, local authorities and TECs. The overview highlights the need to translate the rhetoric and the emerging policy consensus about community regeneration and social exclusion into practical action.

This is followed by reference to recent developments in university continuing education, and their implications for the role of universities in community regeneration and social exclusion. This section includes a brief critique of the 1994 Committee for Vice-Chancellors and Principals Report, *Universities and Commu-*

nities.[1] The final section outlines a current major TEC partnership initiative in Leeds which is focused on community regeneration and social exclusion. Some important policy questions emerge from this case study and these are outlined in the final section, together with critical questions about the role of universities, and university continuing education in particular.

FROM RHETORIC TO REALITY – DEBATE AND INSTITUTIONAL RESPONSES

> Come 1995, and community is now the 'banner word' at the front end of political rhetoric and major policy rethinks. From 'Revitalising Local Democracy' and the Social Justice Commission to the Single Regeneration Budget (SRB); from the new European Union programmes to individual local authorities developing 'Community Development Strategies', the idea of harnessing community initiatives and energies is seen as a keystone for building sustainable and cohesive societies for the future in the eyes of all the 'powers that be'.[2]

This apparent policy consensus, however, is based on conflicting assumptions, aims and objectives. Voluntarism and self help, for example, have been promoted by the government in Britain throughout the 1980s and 1990s in the context of an emphasis on the free market and individualism, in place of public ownership, planning and collectivism in social welfare. Community participation, self-help and community development strategies, however, have been supported and promoted for alternative aims and objectives. These include a focus on active citizenship, decentralisation and democratisation, with a radical potential for developing a post-bureaucratic welfare state.

A cursory overview of recent reports, think-tank publications and academic publications, indicate the extent to which the term 'community' and discourse around issues such as social exclusion and increased levels of inequality have (once again) become fashionable. The recent media publicity surrounding Amitai Etzioni, the American sociologist, and his book *The Spirit of Community* is symptomatic of this. Also, the recent Rowntree Foundation Inquiry into Income and Wealth received extensive publicity when it reported that the numbers living on less than half of average income had tripled since 1978.[3] Up to 30 per cent of the population had not shared in the gains in economic growth since 1979. Reports from the independent Commission on

Social Justice, the National Commission on Education, and think-tanks such as Demos and the Institute for Public Policy Research (IPPR) all highlight increasing inequality and the need to counteract increasing divisions or 'social exclusion' in society.[4] Notions of partnership with economically disenfranchised communities have been re-emphasised, and there has been increasing debate about the need to revitalise local democracy via new approaches to community participation.[5]

For the purposes of this chapter, it is not relevant to restate the debates about the concept and definitions of community.[6] These debates, as any student of social and public policy is well aware, are not new. They are reminiscent of the reports, and subsequent central and local state initiatives in North America and Britain in the late 1960s and 1970s; for example, the United States' 'War On Poverty' and Model Cities Programmes; in the UK, the Educational Priority Areas and the Community Development Projects.[7]

In practice, however, in the mid 1990s in Britain, with the government relying primarily on a *laissez-faire* approach to inward investment, there have only been tokenistic gestures towards community regeneration and the direct involvement of local communities as key partners in any initiatives.[8] The City Challenge programmes from the Department of the Environment, for example, and most recently the bidding process for the Single Regeneration Budget have included the rhetoric of community participation for regeneration.[9] In many areas, however, the bidding process and the principles supposedly underpinning them seem to have bypassed most community organisations in economically disenfranchised areas.[10] Some government initiatives have encouraged community participation; for example, Section 16 of the 1986 Housing and Planning Act provides opportunities for tenants to control their own housing services through a Tenant Management Co-operative or an Estate Management Board. This housing initiative, however, has to be seen in the context of a wide range of central government strategies designed to minimise the role of the local state, and is not indicative of a central government framework designed to empower local 'disadvantaged' communities.

For local government, faced with decreasing budgets, and pre-occupied with implementing the 'contract culture' imposed on them through Compulsory Competitive Tendering (CCT), it has been difficult to develop extensive developmental and partnership arrangements for community regeneration with 'socially excluded' groups. Many local authorities have, however, recognised the need for community development strategies and support for the community sector. The Association of Metropolitan Authorities (AMA) has held national conferences about these issues in conjunction with community work practitioners, and their recent publication was discussed by many local authorities.[11]

The TECs, as is made clear later in this chapter, have been concerned primarily with contracting and overseeing government training programmes. They have also, however, developed extensive relationships with the commercial and industrial sectors in their areas; in the context of the debates about community regeneration and social exclusion referred to above, and given the scale of social exclusion and long-term unemployment in many areas, it is not surprising that some TECs have recognised the need to develop similar relationships and partnerships with the community sector.

Overall, then, during the 1990s, there is evidence of increasing concern about social exclusion, widening inequality and long-term unemployment; there is also growing recognition that any attempted solutions must involve local communities from economically disenfranchised areas as key partners. One of the key challenges facing organisations such as local authorities and TECs is the extent to which these emerging policy needs are translated into practical action.

It is relevant, at this stage, to consider briefly the role of universities in this context.

UNIVERSITIES AND COMMUNITIES

> Most universities honour that item in their statutes ... that obliges them to be active in their local community. But all too few have much commitment to people around them who cannot come up with course fees or consultancy charges that are the real reason for much recent academic enthusiasm with dealings with the outside world.[12]

A recent report commissioned by the Committee of Vice-Chancellors and Principals (CVCP) provides the most recent evidence on university-community relations, and enables one to assess to some extent the validity, or otherwise, of the apparently cynical editorial from the *Times Higher Education Supplement* quoted above.[13]

For the purposes of this chapter, concerned with university links to economically disenfranchised areas, three models of university-community relations can be utilised when examining the evidence from the CVCP report. These are the economic benefit model, the community service model, and the community empowerment model.

The economic benefit model – whereby universities contribute to local economies as major employers, land owners, investors and purchasers of local commodities – is highlighted in the CVCP report. For example, universities are often amongst the major employers in the ten largest cities; third and fifth in Newcastle and eighth in Nottingham.

The community service model, in which universities encourage students to support local community and voluntary organisations, is well established in the USA, with nation-wide organisations such as the Campus Outreach Opportunity League, and regular debates about the role of universities in decaying inner cities. In the UK, there are some 125 student community action groups from HE providing volunteers who work with existing voluntary and statutory organisations. Most recently, the Community Enterprise in Higher Education project has adopted the US model of utilising voluntary contributions from students to their local communities as part of a process of 'service learning' which provides students with transferable skills such as problem solving and negotiation through involvement in the community as part of their curriculum.

Both the economic benefit model and the community service model, however, do not have a systematic focus on engaging the university in the long term with individuals and groups from economically disenfranchised areas.

A community empowerment or community development model – which, in spite of the use of the term 'community development', is conspicuously absent from the CVCP report – would engage the university in collective, participatory research, and innovative educational development work as part of a long-term commitment to community organisations in economically disenfranchised areas. The community empowerment or community development model raises fundamental questions about the nature and role of universities. It means the development of ongoing democratic and strategic partnerships which will result in universities becoming more of an integral part of local communities. The CVCP report is misleading in this context because it omits examples of both old and new universities which have been developing elements of this model in recent years. In

Swansea, for example, the Community University of the Valleys, has had a primary focus on economically disenfranchised areas; in Leeds, a wide range of action research projects and educational partnerships have been developed systematically over the past fifteen years with community organisations from council estates and inner city areas.

Overall, however, there does not appear to be extensive evidence which can refute the assertions of the *THES* editorial which is quoted above. Even universities such as Swansea and Leeds which have utilised continuing education departments to initiate and maintain links with economically disenfranchised areas, will have to examine the extent to which new funding regulations for Continuing Education hinder or facilitate community linkages.

In 1992-93, the Higher Education Funding Council for England (HEFCE) conducted a review of the funding of university continuing education (CE). Prior to this, non-accredited work with 'disadvantaged' adults had guaranteed funding if institutions bid for, and met specific targets. HEFCE decided, inter alia, that it would provide support for 'widened provision'; it is relevant to note the change in language from 'work with disadvantaged adults' to 'widened provision'. Specific funding was made available and this was allocated on a bidding process.[14] For example, ninety-one institutions from both the 'old' and 'new' universities bid for 'widened provision' funding. Does this mean that those which did not bid have no interest in such work? Or, does it imply that they have already embedded such developments into their provision and priorities, and are funding it in other ways?

From the ninety-one bids, fifteen received 75 per cent of what they requested, and a further thirty-two institutions received 50 per cent of what they had applied for. What impact will this reduced level of funding have for the successful 'bidders'? Also, what policies will now be adopted by the forty-four institutions who received no funding? For those institutions which received funding, will the dominant model be access development for non-traditional students at the expense of previous (and sometimes extensive) direct non-accredited provision with 'disadvantaged' groups? Or, is it possible to combine these elements?

These and other issues will need to be systematically monitored and evaluated, as the new funding regulations and the 'widened provision' projects come into operation from 1995–96.

The following section, and the conclusion to this chapter, outlines a major community development initiative sponsored by a local TEC in partnership with a University Continuing Education Department which has had a long-standing interest and involvement in 'social exclusion' issues and work with 'disadvantaged' communities.

LEEDS TEC – THE COMMUNITY SPRINGBOARD INITIATIVE: AN EXPLICIT FOCUS ON COMMUNITY REGENERATION AND SOCIAL EXCLUSION

An analysis of the expenditure plans for the Training and Enterprise Councils (TECs) following the 1994 Budget and Public Expenditure Statement indicates that their primary role will continue to be that of contractors for Training for Work and particularly Youth Training Programmes. In 1995-96, TECs' expenditure on these programmes will be £1267 million from a total expenditure of £1434 million.[15] In recent years, however, TECs have been allowed to build up substantial cash reserves. By the end of 1992-93 for example, the TECs in London had cash reserves of £17.6 million (equal to almost 10 per cent of their annual income).[16] These funds have provided an opportunity for TECs to move beyond their primary role of training contractors and, in the context of the increasing rhetoric and concern with social exclusion and widening inequality outlined at the beginning of this chapter, it is hardly surprising that some TECs are beginning to grapple more explicitly with this issue.

The following case study outlines an initiative currently being developed by Leeds TEC.

Leeds TEC have recently established a major initiative (Community Springboard) costing £1.8 million which aims to reverse the cost of social exclusion by supporting community groups and long-term unemployed people in economically disenfranchised areas. Nine local projects have been developed in partnership with community groups and practitioners from the voluntary sector and local government in inner-city areas and council estates. Representatives from these local projects are joining an autonomous but accountable think-tank and action team that will analyse the emerging lessons and common issues from projects, and also work with key resource agencies in Leeds to inform and influence policy development. The two universities in Leeds are responsible for evaluating the initiative.

There are several key elements and issues about the Community

Springboard initiative. It is concerned explicitly with structural inequality and the dangers this creates.

> Leeds thrives, (but) as the city has succeeded as a regional financial sector ... its traditional manufacturing industry has declined, leaving a legacy of structural unemployment. The overall picture of prosperity masks the communities who feel left out of the city's economic opportunities. Unemployment in Leeds is 9 per cent but there are communities where it is much higher than 30 per cent ... there is a danger that the isolation felt by communities will turn to alienation and exclusion. If Leeds is to continue to prosper, we must tackle this situation which threatens our business and its communities, the life quality of our citizens, and the sustained competitiveness of our city.[17]

The TEC Board, perhaps even encouraged by the Government Regional Office for Yorkshire and Humberside, recognised both the need for a more proactive response to long-term unemployment and social exclusion, and the need to move beyond traditional Government training programmes. Recent interviews with the TEC Board indicate clearly that the TEC directors supported the social as well as the possible economic objectives of the initiative.[18]

By March 1995, the TEC had agreed to fund nine community-based projects that have 'close working links with those individuals and their communities facing the problems of structural inequality and social exclusion'.[19] The projects include a music and media project, youth projects, and a range of local community development and enterprise initiatives. After an initial development phase, the TEC encouraged community groups and local workers to propose projects according to local needs and priorities. The TEC, then, is investing in a community development process, and Community Springboard is an acceptance by the TEC, of the importance of community involvement and community partnership in practice.

Local project representatives are enthusiastic about the need to share lessons from local experience and relate these to particular policy and strategic contexts, via the think-tank which is referred to above. In recent meetings, they have been vociferous about their long-term exclusion from policy debate, and they feel that the think-tank provides a unique opportunity for their involvement.

Overall, the early stages of the TEC's first systematic partnership with 'socially disadvantaged' areas and community groups, has been a constructive learning process on both sides. Other aspects of the partnership are more problematic. Not unsurprisingly, the local authority had some reservations about the TEC (an unelected quango) funding a high profile 'flagship' community and policy initiative. Also, since Leeds has never embraced a systematic community development strategy, there may be some worries on the part of the local authority about the funding of independent local projects. The success of some of the projects, and the potential value of the think-tank, may be jeopardised unless these issues are resolved.

CONCLUSION: FURTHER ISSUES FROM THE TEC CASE-STUDY AND THE ROLE OF UNIVERSITIES

It was stated earlier that the University of Leeds Department of Adult and Continuing Education has developed a wide range of action-research projects and educational partnerships over the past fifteen years with community groups from council estates and inner-city areas. In this context, it was not surprising that some local community groups, local workers, and the TEC itself approached the department for assistance with Community Springboard. From the outset, then, on the basis of its previous work, the university was a fully involved partner. Subsequently, it was contracted to monitor and evaluate the initiative, and invited the Policy Research Unit of Leeds Metropolitan University to join in this task.

The research obviously includes an analysis of quantifiable outcomes from local projects, as well as a process-led qualitative examination of local 'successes' and 'problems'. It also includes an examination of the workings of the think-tank, and the extent to which partnerships between local projects, the private sector and the local authority can influence policy debates and practices which impact on disadvantaged areas.

As stated earlier, this type of action-research is not new, and was indeed extensive in North America and the UK in late 1960s and 1970s, but the re-invented rhetoric of community regeneration, social exclusion, and partnership, provides opportunities for universities to engage with community groups.

The Rowntree Inquiry into Income and Wealth stressed that improvements in economically disenfranchised areas 'are not possible without resident involvement, but residents need strong and consistent long-term support'.[20] This support should include an educational underpinning for local residents' involvement in community issues. In economically disenfranchised areas, compared to better-off areas, there is the increasing complexity of issues involved in local housing management, social and economic regeneration, policing, and education. In this context, there is a strong argument for priority funding across the FE/HE divide, which focuses on responsive community education partnerships with community groups. There is a danger, however, that the Further Education Funding Council's regulations, and the recent HEFCE funding changes for continuing education, which were briefly referred to earlier in this paper, may minimise the opportunities both for FE and HE to engage in flexible and responsive community education programmes. 'The free enterprise culture of higher education does not readily reward the kind of collective, participatory, or collaborative activity associated with a long-term commitment to community organisations or to community-based research.'[21] In addition, meetings between senior university personnel and senior figures from the public and private sector, and university membership of new partnership bodies and *ad hoc* taskforces may simply become symbolic gestures. They should be judged by the extent to which they enhance or initiate long-term university partnership with community groups in economically disenfranchised areas.

Many of the new universities and a smaller number of old ones have been attempting to broaden their student base and extend opportunities for non-standard students in recent years. Whatever the varied motivations for these developments (although the 'economic imperative' – the pressure to increase students numbers and thereby funding – may have been paramount), and valuable as they have been in opening up institutions to new types of students, they are essentially individual, vertical progression models. These should be an essential part of, but not the total focus, of university community partnerships which involve long-term educational and research commitments to, and with, community organisations from economically disenfranchised areas.

The TEC case-study outlined earlier is an attempt to match the rhetoric of concern with practical action in local communities. Whether the local projects, and the proposed policy developments through the think-tank are seen as successful or not, the TEC has at least shown some direct commitment. It remains to be seen whether universities will move beyond rhetorical mission statements, and develop partnerships in practice which truly reflect a concern with community regeneration, social exclusion, long-term unemployment and widening inequality.

NOTES

1. *Universities and Communities*, Committee for Vice-Chancellors and Principals (CVCP), London 1994.
2. *Standing Conference for Community Development*, Issue No. 12, Summer 1995, Sheffield.
3. *Joseph Rowntree Foundation Inquiry into Income and Wealth*, Vols. 1 and 2, Joseph Rowntree Foundation, York 1995.
4. See, for example, *The Justice Gap, The Commission on Social Justice*, IPPR, London 1993; and, Social Justice in a Changing World, IPPR 1993. Also, *Learning to Succeed*, Report of the National Commission on Education, Heinemann, London 1993.
5. Recent examples of these debates include D. Donnison, *Social Justice from the Bottom*, IPPR, 1994; D. Burns, R. Hambleton, and P. Hoggett, *The Politics of Decentralisation – Revitalising Local Democracy*, Macmillan, London 1995; also, the BBC Reith Lecture by Sir Richard Rogers, February, 1995.
6. For recent reviews of these debates and the contrasting ways in which the term has been used, both historically and more recently, and for analysis of related policy developments, see: H. Butcher *et al, Community and Public Policy*, Pluto Press, London 1993; also M. Mayo, *Communities and Caring: The Mixed Economy of Welfare*, Macmillan, London 1994.
7. For more details about these developments, see: M. Loney, *Community Against Government*, Heinemann, London 1983. R. Kramer, *Participation of the Poor*, Prentice-Hall, New Jersey 1969.
8. See K. Cowling, 'Moving Away from Monopoly Capitalism – a New Focus for Industrial Strategy', in 'UK Economic Underperformance', Centre for Industrial Policy and Performance, University of Leeds 1994.
9. See *Single Regeneration Budget – Department of Environment*. Note on principles, London, November 1993.
10. For a review of recent developments, see *Community Development and the Single Regeneration Budget*, Standing Conference on Community Development, *op.cit.*
11. *Local Authorities and Community Development: A Strategic Opportunity for the 1990s*, Association of Metropolitan Authorities, London 1993.
12. Editorial, *Times Higher Education Supplement* (*THES*), London, 29 January 1995.
13. CVCP Report, *op.cit.*
14. For details of the funding changes, see *Continuing Education Circular 18/93*, HEFCE, London 1993; also, Circulars 3/94 (1994) and 4/95 (1995).
15. See Employment Department Briefing Note. November 1994/040, 22 November 1994.

16. See D. Finn, *A New Partnership? TECs and the London Voluntary Sector*, Unemployment Unit, London 1994.
17. *Community Springboard*, Leeds TEC, Leeds 1994.
18. *Community Springboard Research and Evaluation Project*, Leeds TEC, Department of Adult Continuing Education, University of Leeds, 1995.
19. *Community Springboard*, Leeds TEC, *op.cit.*
20. See Rowntree Inquiry, *op.cit.*, Vol. 1, p63.
21. J. Mohan, *Universities as Civic Institutions*, Appendix 3, in CVCP Report, *op.cit.*

17

READING THE WORD AND THE WORLD: THE CENTER FOR LITERACY STUDIES

Brenda Bell

In this chapter I wish to present the work of a university-based Center which works exclusively with community-based efforts. By looking at the ways the Center for Literacy Studies at the University of Tennessee links literacy and community development, supports communities of learners, and uses new technologies to foster community across distance, I hope to bring a useful perspective to the discussions of communities and their universities. Briefly I describe three of our projects: Community in the Classroom, Participatory Staff Development, and the Tennessee Reporting and Improvement Management System. The second part of the chapter is devoted to an exploration of our work with online communications in adult literacy programmes. I have chosen this focus because I think it gives us the opportunity to think together about the role of adult education in an information society, and ways universities can support communities seeking access to new technologies.

The over-arching theme for these reflections, reading the word and the world, comes from well-known thoughts of Paulo Freire about literacy for critical thinking and active participation. At the Center for Literacy Studies (CLS), our definition of literacy is shaped by Paulo's insistence that literacy is the reading of the world, not just the word, just as our actions are guided by Myles Horton's (and others') insistence that learning starts where people are, not where we think they should be.[1] We define literacy as the reading, writing, speaking, listening, and critical thinking skills and practices essential for full participation in our democratic society. We link the skill and practice of reading and writing (reading the word) and the speaking, listening and critical thinking skills and practices (reading the world) with the action of full participation in a democratic society. Our challenges come with trying to be true to these educational principles in all settings, whether we are working with members of rural grassroots community organisations or Adult Basic Education teachers or directors of state agencies.

The Center was founded in 1988 at the University of Tennessee to bridge theory and practice in adult education, and to build the capacities of communities to foster life-long learning.[2] We work on specific projects, funded by a variety of sources, with moral and philosophical support and limited financial support from the College of Education within the University. In choosing our work, we try to be led by the contribution of the work to the field and to the communities for which it is intended or out of which it has grown – and by the degree to which we can remain true to our principles. During the past year, the staff of the Center for Literacy Studies have thought hard about who we are and what we do, about our place in the community and in the university. While our graphic presentation of how we see literacy is not perfect, it does begin to show the interlocking relationships among literacy and the significant corner-stones which interact in our daily lives: our economy, democracy, culture and communities.

By seeing literacy as more than discrete practices, by looking at literacy as the foundation on which we build democratic institutions, a sustainable economic system, and strong, culturally responsive communities, we could say that we broadly define literacy as the reading of the world in which we live and the building of the one to which we aspire.

Several of the Center's current projects reflect the variety of ways in which the word community is used in our work: a distinct place with specific geographical boundaries; a group of people with common work or interests who live in widely scattered locations; a context of shared ideas and goals. We try to incorporate an even broader definition given by educational philosopher Parker Palmer, who defines community as the 'capacity for relatedness within individuals – relatedness not only to people but to events in history, to nature, to the world of ideas, and yes, to things of the spirit.'[3]

Writing in a 1987 article in *Change* magazine, Palmer is wrestling with the community-university link from within the field of higher education, suggesting that the very nature of the academy and its dominant mode of knowing, objectivism (with its 'us-them' split, which allows us to analyse and experiment with things and people, and 'reshape the world in an image more pleasing to us') works against community; and further, that this objectivism must be countered if we are to 'make a contribution to the reweaving of community.' Though situated within the world of higher education, our work at CLS tries hard to steer away from this objectivist stance. Instead, we see ourselves as part of communities with which we interact, not control; communities with which we seek to build the capacity for relatedness.

Let me briefly describe three parts of our current work before moving into a look at ways online computer communications may or may not contribute to Parker's 'reweaving of community.'

COMMUNITY IN THE CLASSROOM

In the Center's Community in the Classroom project, community means both geographical location: the ten, rural isolated mountain communities whose grassroots organizations participate in this project; and the ideal, as described by Palmer: the efforts to build our capacity for interrelatedness to each other, to history, to nature, to things of the spirit. For the past three years, we have explored the ways in which literacy education can help build communities. Through a series of workshops and on-site work, teachers, paraprofessionals, and volunteers from the participating groups have used community issues to develop curricula for literacy education classes, to try out new approaches, and to reflect on the role of the teacher in creating a learner-centred, participatory education programme. Rather than separate adult basic education and literacy into a 'programme over there' with a curriculum of high school diploma preparation workbooks and standardised testing, participants in this project bring the community into the classroom as the curriculum for learning. In turn the classroom becomes the community of shared goals and interests. The focus is on contributing to the well-being of the larger community and building grass-roots organisations while strengthening individual skills, not solely on individual achievement and advancement out of the community.

In rural Appalachian communities, education is inextricably linked to jobs and the economy.[4] To talk about adult education is to talk about job skills, and all too often, unskilled adults are blamed for the lack of jobs. 'If only people had better skills, our communities would attract better jobs, everyone could work, and we wouldn't need welfare.' In this view, attracting the right new industry becomes the end and the means to community prosperity. Failure to attract new business and industry is laid at the feet of undereducated adults. Adult education is seen as remedial and skill-based, and responsible for 'fixing' the workforce so that communities can grow and be healthy. Community in the Classroom experiences reinforce our belief that a strengths model rather than a deficit model is needed for meaningful progress in building sustainable communities. When neighbours organise together to force the clean up of a toxic dump, when adult students write letters to lobby legislators for more resources for the ABE programme, when citizens come together across race and class lines to work for safe and healthy communities for their children, that's education for sustainable communities.

Educators have not been concerned about the ways in which education has taken people away from the community, how education has been the one-way ticket out, as high skilled jobs requiring more education have been developed in urban areas.

> Our assumptions have been that education is an intrinsic good, always valuable. In these changing times we need to reassess the value of education and re-focus on building communities, not just individuals. We need to create education programmes in which people gain the skills and the sense of efficacy to become involved in their community's development ... If we want education to be the 'ticket in' rather than the 'ticket out' for rural communities, then we must make education an integral part of community development rather than simply preparing people for their place in 'business as usual.[5]

'Business as usual' for impoverished rural communities has meant reliance on welfare or exodus to the big city. By supporting adult learners as active contributors rather than passive participants in the community-building process, we in the university may begin to contribute to the reweaving of community.

TEACHERS AS LEARNERS – PARTICIPATORY STAFF DEVELOPMENT

A major part of the Center for Literacy Studies' work is around participatory staff development for literacy practitioners. Working with Tennessee teachers in institutes and workshops, we have identified key characteristics of effective staff development: it recognises the roles of reflection, analysis and questioning, based on one's experiences; there is shared responsibility and accountability among facilitator and participants for the outcomes of the experience; it sets an atmosphere which respects the dignity and diversity of all involved. Participatory staff development seeks to expand the knowledge base of the field of adult education; together participants create new knowledge. Above all, participatory, process-oriented learning opportunities for teachers breaks isolation and builds a community of learners.[6]

One example of staff development which builds a community of learners is a recent year-long action research group on learning disabilities. Eight practitioners from literacy and adult basic education programmes came together to explore strategies for working with adults who find learning difficult. They reviewed material from elementary school education sources, learned from a resource person who has extensive experience in working with children with learning disabilities, and discussed their own teaching styles. In between each group meeting, they tried out new strategies, documenting the results and the ways in which they adapted the strategy to fit the needs of adult students. The behind-the-scenes view of what went on during this year shows the building of a community of teachers as learners, with a focus on relatedness to each other, to their students, to their history of past failures and frustrations, and to the renewed spirit that comes from energetic and thoughtful experiences together. Looking back, members of the action research group reflected:

> Most of us started out believing that we didn't know much about the topic, that somebody out there had all the answers if we could just find that person or approach and use it. At the beginning we didn't much believe in our own ability to produce knowledge about teaching people who struggle with a learning disability. But through trying things out and documenting them and talking with each other and our resource person, we began to trust our own capacity to make good judgements.

We found ourselves being less tentative, more confident in our willingness to talk about our own approaches and methods with other teachers. We became more flexible, quicker to take a risk and try something new.[7]

Though separated by distance and programme differences, these teachers found the support and courage to trust their own experiences in a learning group, and built a community for themselves.

TENNESSEE REPORTING AND IMPROVEMENT MANAGEMENT SYSTEM (TRIMS)

Another major project at CLS is one which directly pulls together the literacy cornerstones described earlier. TRIMS, The Tennessee Reporting and Improvement Management System, a two year demonstration project funded by the National Institute for Literacy, is attempting to create the framework for a seamless system of service delivery, with common assessment, placement and referral procedures among all of the government agencies which work with undereducated adults. This project has tried to keep the best interests of the individual learner at the centre of the system, while being responsive to the needs of the patchwork of different agencies which provide basic skills education. Mid-way through the second year, four local county task-forces and a state-wide policy team have analysed the current system and envisioned a new one, and have drafted policy outcomes and performance measures for adult basic skills education. The challenge now is to create a user-friendly, multi-system-compatible computer database, which will allow all agencies, and adult students, to report and retrieve data related both to the individual student and to the state-wide performance measures.

Now, one might wonder how all this relates to community: the forty-plus members of the local task-forces will be quick to tell us that it has everything to do, not just with serving specific communities in the geographical sense, but in building interrelatedness, co-operation, and understanding among service providers at the grassroots level. TRIMS has engaged practitioners in the process of changing the focus of thinking from the 'services we provide' to the 'outcomes for students'. The project has provided neutral space for agency representatives to come together to describe the barriers and opportunities for basic skills education, and to create a vision of healthy, economically sound communities. As the technology part of the project enters the picture with the designing of a database which will allow the major agency mainframe computers to share information, the challenge is to keep the responsiveness to local needs and the focus on the outcomes for adult students. While the project may design a sophisticated computer system which will serve the needs of the state for reports and statistics, if it does not give students and local programmes more access to useful information about the quality of their work and its impact on their communities, it will not have succeeded.

Working with technology in this way is new to us, and it has not been undertaken without the assistance and technical expertise of others both within and outside of the university. More familiar to us, however, is using the Internet with students and practitioners to build skills and foster shared communication in a variety of adult education programmes across the state.

ABE ON AOL: ADULT BASIC EDUCATION USING AMERICA ONLINE

We became interested in the possibilities of online computer uses in 1993, when CLS was designated the State Literacy Resource Center for Tennessee. Part of the National Literacy Act of 1991, which was intended to build a stable literacy and lifelong learning infrastructure in the US (and whose funding was rescinded by Congress in July, 1995), State Literacy Resource Centers were mandated to stimulate innovation and capacity building, disseminate information and resources, and promote collaboration among the many literacy and basic skills providers. Looking closely at that term innovation, we focused on bringing to bear some of the latest advances in technology. We were intrigued by the growth of the Internet, by the possibilities of using computers as open systems, for creating and sharing information, rather than closed systems, as in computer-assisted instruction.

The growing use of computers and other information technology in literacy programmes offers an opportunity to help students become knowledge producers, to access information that can have immediate impact on their lives, and to build relationships with other adult learners in other towns and states, even other countries. In our experience, however, computers in adult basic education are used

222

mainly for drill, as ever-patient tutors who never get upset when students don't 'get it'. Although computer-aided instruction may claim to be student-centred, students have very little control over their education, only over pace and selection among a finite number of lesson plans. We suggest that these systems address 'literacy as skills' in the framework developed by Hanna Fingeret.[8] For those who see literacy as something more than a mechanical skill, who hope that acquiring literacy becomes learning to 'read the word and the world,' narrow computer-aided instruction is not very exciting. It further separates learners rather than bringing them together. It does not help us address 'literacy as social and cultural practices,' or 'literacy as critical reflection and action,' as Fingeret's framework describes literacy. If this is all we use computer technology for, neither practitioners themselves, nor students, are learning the new skills and knowledge needed to participate fully in the ever-growing high tech world of information.[9]

In today's world, we know that knowledge and information is power, and that the production and application of information has been largely controlled by the 'knowledge elite'.[10] Even in the burgeoning new world of the World Wide Web, where anyone (with the know-how and the access) can post a homepage, and the ethic is equal access, these knowledge producers are not found in the ranks of local adult education programmes, and not very often in the ranks of professional adult educators. Those of us whose literacy skills and/or computer skills are limited are quickly becoming the 'have-nots' of the information society, or as we say in East Tennessee, up the dirt road of the information highway. What is the role of a university-based Literacy Resource Center in bridging the gap between these haves and have-nots? We wondered, as adult educator Tom Heaney put it way back in 1982:

> Can these media (computers and telephone technology) be convivial tools for reconstructing the social order in the hands of common, unsophisticated, and unprofessionalized people? ... Can microcomputers mediate communications within and among community-based groups and further their efforts to know the world and to use that knowledge to bring about social change?[11]

On a more practical level, we wondered what would happen if teachers and students in adult literacy programmes had access to the wealth of resources available online; would they use this new communications tool to develop and share projects, to create, to explore; would it strengthen the links between teachers, students, and administrators across the state, as well as build skills? While there was growing documentation of the uses of electronic communication in K-12 education, little was known about how adult basic education students, staff, and administrators would respond to the wide array of possibilities opened by electronic communications. How would adult students respond to and use the online encyclopaedia, current news, stock market reports, shareware, or academic assistance center? How would teachers, students, and administrators use e-mail, bulletin boards and on-line conferencing to problem-solve, build their skills and knowledge, and strengthen ties across the state? What types of staff development were needed to help teachers and administrators make full use of these new capabilities?

Lessons learned

These were the more realistic questions we had when we decided to use a portion of the TLRC grant to place modems and ten hours per month of online time in over 30 adult basic education programmes. At the end of two years, we have some observations which may be useful to others considering using online communications to build skills and community.

Introducing a new communications and programme resource tool is a lengthy process which cannot be hurried, even with a simple, easy to install and easy to use service like America Online. Many adult basic education programmes have had long and frustrating delays getting 'hooked up' due to antiquated computers, lack of telephone lines in classrooms, and inadequate technical expertise on staff. ABE and literacy programmes are very unequal in their access to computer hardware: many have old computers, many have none. Serious development of technology requires serious investment or leveraging of other resources. Our experiences underline the findings of a 1993 report by the Office of Technology Assessment of the US Congress which says that adult education is woefully underfunded and underequipped to take full advantage of new technologies.[12]

For teachers to incorporate electronic networking into their classrooms, they themselves must acquire a level of comfort with the technology that few now have. Teachers experience the same fears and frustrations that their literacy students feel in learning to read.

Practitioners and students each need time to explore, play, experiment and to find their own areas of interest. So 'forming the habit' becomes an important step in implementing online communications with both practitioners and students. We have tried to help practitioners form the habit of getting on line and developing a comfortable use by using e-mail as much as possible; by developing partnerships or penpals between programmes; and by beginning to hold online conferences on different topics. Interestingly enough, it is the sense of personal connection and shared interests that pushes reluctant users forward, not the ease of sending e-mail or the novelty of exploring online databases.

Using a computer as an open system to create, find, and/or communicate anything with anybody, rather than as a closed computer assisted instruction system, can contribute to a truly learner-centred classroom environment. For example, students in the local adult basic education programme now use the computer in a variety of ways, and the computer lab is a self-directed learning environment where a student may work with a word processing programme to write an article for the student newsletter or use the Internet service to send out the newsletter to all of the Tennessee programmes; use a graphics programme to create a calendar of events or go online to search for background information to use for classroom discussion. Students often lead the way in making the most creative uses of a system like America Online. For over a year, students have had a weekly online chat, on topics ranging from favourite pastimes to politics, from religion to child discipline. The computer screen shows only part of the interaction which takes place during an online chat. By typing in questions and responses, several students are exchanging ideas and questions, while at each local site a group of fellow students is clustered around the computer, talking among themselves about the topic under discussion and contributing to the online text. Only a small part of the conversation actually reaches the screen in a typed form. Teachers tell us that this use of the computer has brought a new dimension to classroom discussions, that the sense of relatedness and sharing among students and teachers has been enhanced by participating in these online discussions.

Transcripts of chats can be used as the 'text' for other student work. Using the transcript of a discussion on health care and health problems, students can look up new words; using a word processing programme, they can select out the portions of the chat which came from their programme, and arrange the comments in a logical order; they can revise for spelling and grammar; they can write follow up essays, adding new information and resources; they can post additional questions to other students; the possibilities are many.

Far from being an anonymous, impersonal medium, the computer terminal becomes the link with new friends, the bridge to more resources, the free space needed to express oneself. For example, James, a shy, quiet young man in an East Tennessee programme, surprised his fellow students and teacher by revealing during an online discussion that he writes poetry; he shared some of his poems with students in a programme in West Tennessee by sending them online. Now he writes for the student-led newspaper in his programme. And while teachers and administrators appreciate the benefits of e-mail as a replacement for playing telephone tag, they also are using the medium to share information and build networks. As the national adult education community has responded to the budget cuts proposed by the current Congress, online communications has meant rapid response to action alerts, sharing of information across the state and from state to state, and networking for shared goals.

We continue to explore the potential of the Internet for adult education. Through the Tennessee Division of Adult and Community Education, we have helped all state-funded adult basic education programmes get on TecNet, the Tennessee Education Network, and learn how to use the Internet gateway. We have a WWW homepage and are seeking funding to provide Web access to low-income community groups and adult basic education programmes. With colleagues in Texas, we are coordinating the development of an Internet infrastructure (expanding the National Institute for Literacy's LINCS system) and technology training for the fourteen literacy resource centers in the southeastern US, with the emphasis on helping practitioners and students develop their own meaningful uses for the Internet.

We are far from answering the questions posed by Heaney, and still learning, in partnership with teachers and students, about the uses for the Internet in adult education. What happens when the 'glamour' of online communications wears off? What are our responsibilities to monitor the overload of stimuli which come from too many e-mail messages, subscribing to too many listservs, access to too much information? Can grassroots activist community groups and adult education programmes use the Web for their own interests or will the

Web become the overtaken by advertisers and commercial interests? Is the world of cyberspace another techno-hype that will drain people's energies away from the issues of community and literacy we raised earlier?

To this last question we answer, it is up to us. Just as other technologies such as audio and video recorders, radio and TV have been used by and for the undereducated and powerless to gain a voice and for ordinary citizens to participate in public life, online communications can be a tool used by literacy students and practitioners for participatory, learner-centred education. How far it will go will depend, in part, upon those of us within universities and other institutions with power: the partnerships we build with communities and their organisations to ensure low-cost public access; the space we carve out in the academy, for involvement by communities in the production, not just the consumption, of knowledge; and our willingness to act on our theories and principles about progressive education for social change.

As simple and modest as it is, an online conversation among adult students in a welfare to work programme about their experiences with the health care system is one way students can express their view of reality, i.e. read the world, while strengthening reading, writing and communications abilities. As electronic communications become more accepted and used, our role as university-based 'community-builders' is to continue to encourage the creative and empowering uses of computers for reading the world, for nurturing relationships, for supporting action, as well as giving adult students the opportunity to learn the reading, writing and computer skills that are needed as we enter the twenty-first century.

LINKING COMMUNITY AND UNIVERSITY

While service to the community is a common denominator among public universities in the United States, the definition of community most often translates into serving the needs and interests of business, industry and institutions of power. However, there are signs of a revitalisation of the service mission to meet the changing frontiers of society, frontiers described by one observer as 'the challenges of inequality, injustice, ignorance and unconcern'.[13] Recent grants from the US Department of Housing and Urban Development to fourteen universities, including the University of Tennessee, will tackle these frontiers and others. University-community partnership centers will involve faculty and students in joint efforts with low-income community organisations to solve their own problems. US universities are beginning to learn from the university network of 'science shops' in the Netherlands, where faculty and students coordinate research on social and technological issues raised by community groups, public-interest organisations and workers. We may begin to see true involvement of universities in the re-creating of communities in place, the re-weaving of community in spirit, a task to which the Center for Literacy Studies is committed.

NOTES

1. See Bell *et al*, (eds), *We make the Road by Walking: Conversations on Education and Social Change by Myles Horton and Paulo Freire*, Temple University Press 1990.
2. The Center for Literacy Studies, University of Tennessee, 600 Henley Street, Suite 312, Knoxville, TN 37996-4351. Director: Juliet Merrifield.
3. P. Palmer, 'Community, Conflict, and Ways of Knowing: Ways to Deepen Our Educational Agenda', *Change*, Vol. 19, No. 5, pp20–5, 1987.
4. From unpublished remarks by C. White to the Education Working Group of the President's Council on Sustainable Development, 1995.
5. Merrifield, White, and Bingman, 'Community in the Classroom: Literacy and Development in a Rural Industrialized Region', in Hautecoeur, (ed), *Alpha 94: Literacy and Cultural Development Strategies in Rural Areas*, Culture Concepts, Toronto 1994.
6. B. Bingman and B. Bell, 'Teachers As Learners: A Sourcebook for Participatory Staff Development', *Seeds of Innovation*, Vol. 2, Spring 1995. Center for Literacy Studies, University of Tennessee.
7. C. White (ed), 'If Only I Could Read, Write, Spell ... Identifying and Helping Adults Who Find Learning Difficult', *Seeds of Innovation*, Vol. 1, Fall 1994, Center for Literacy Studies.
8. H. Fingeret, *Adult Literacy Education: Current and Future Directions – An Update*, ERIC, 1992.
9. J. Merrifield, and B. Bell, 'Don't Give Us The Grand Canyon to Cross: Participatory Literacy in the Information Society', *Adult Learning*, Vol. 6, No. 2, 1994.
10. See J. Gaventa, 'The Powerful, the Powerless, and the Experts: Knowledge Struggles in an Information Age', in P. Park, *et al* (eds), *Voices of Change: Participatory Research in the United States and Canada*, Bergin and Garvey, Place 1993.
11. T. Heany, 'Power, Learning, and "Communication" ', in Gueulette (ed), *Microcomputers and Adult Learning*, Follette Press, New York 1982.
12. US Congress, Office of Technology Assessment, *Adult Literacy and New Technologies: Tools for a Lifetime*, OTA-SET-550, US Government Printing Office, Washington, DC 1993.

13. P. Marden, 'Higher Education Must Chart New Frontiers', *Knoxville News-Sentinel*, 12 March 1995. For more on community partnerships, see R. Scolve, 'Putting Science to Work in Communities', *Chronicle of Higher Education*, 31 March 1995; and J. Snyder, 'HUD Enlists Universities in Attempt to Revitalize Neighborhoods', *Chronicle of Higher Education*, 14 April 1995.

18

COMMUNITIES, VALLEYS AND UNIVERSITIES

Hywel Francis and Rob Humphreys

INTRODUCTION: CONTINUITY AND CHANGE

The South Wales coalfield is perhaps the only area in Britain for which adult education has become an established part of popular images of its culture and politics. The travel writer H.V. Morton, in his 1932 best-seller, *In Search of Wales*, tells of his encounter, on a street corner of the Rhondda town of Tonypandy, with two young miners engaged in a discussion about Einstein's Theory of Relativity.[1] John Ormond's elegiac 1961 film, *Once There Was a Time*, focuses solely on two elderly Rhondda men counter-posing respectively the explanatory powers of Christianity and Marxian social analysis.[2] The film achieves its effect in part because it does not have to be explicit about adult education being a part of the men's cultural heritage; it makes the assumption that the audience is already aware of this. Some of the leading political and trade union figures of twentieth-century Britain, such as Aneurin Bevan, James Griffiths, Arthur Horner and Will Paynter, were (and remain) identified in the public imagination as being products of a working-class culture of learning in South Wales. And miners' libraries and institutes are rightly seen as an integral part of the history of coalfield culture and politics in the region.[3]

These popular images, albeit romanticised at times, have their roots in a real history, which saw the rapid industrialisation of the coalfield giving birth to a cosmopolitan – yet still self-consciously Welsh – society and culture, in which autodidactism, trade union education, and political education were central.[4] Much of this grew out of local communities themselves and was a result of the activities of such bodies as trades unions and co-operative societies, as much as it was the result of outside organisations. The relationship of the University of Wales and its constituent Colleges to the coalfield was (as we argue below) always an ambivalent one, though at the same time not insignificant. In the case of adult education as a whole, however, it is not possible to understand the history of politics and political leadership of the coalfield without also having a grasp of the role of adult education, which was both an agent, and a site of, political argument and action.[5] That history, especially so in the case of the inter-war period, has been described in terms of an 'inheritance', and a 'series of legacies',[6] and it is still sufficiently part of a popular memory that it can be invoked in latter day debates and discussions about policy making in adult education and in areas of wider social policy.[7]

An emphasis on the continuity or tradition of adult education can, however, mask discontinuities and new developments, which have arisen in the context of social, cultural and institutional change since 1945, and since the mid-1980s in particular. In this chapter, we discuss a new initiative in university adult education in South Wales, which in one sense might be seen as part of the tradition of adult education in the coalfield, but which at the same time represents a sharp break with that tradition. The initiative is the Community University of the Valleys (CUV), which is a programme developed and run by the University of Wales Swansea (UWS), and which is currently based at Banwen, a former mining community in the north-west of the coalfield. As well as outlining the development and nature of the provision of the CUV, we seek to contextualise its development in social, cultural and institutional change in South Wales and in higher education more generally. As Scott has argued, recent fundamental changes in higher education 'must be interpreted in the context of the restless synergy between plural modernisations – of the academy, polity, economy, society and culture.'[8] Following this kind of approach in the case of the CUV, however, requires an analysis which also takes into account the specificities of South Wales, and of higher education and its governance and funding in Wales.

The debates around the slippery nature of the concept of community will not be rehearsed here (though we do have things to say later about the changing nature of ideas of community in South Wales), but Martin's comment about *community education* is very pertinent to this discussion: 'The inherent ambiguity of the term provides a convenient cover for all manner of expedient reinterpretation.'[9] Our intention in what follows is to avoid ambiguities by grounding our analysis of the CUV in wider developments and in an historical context. By undertaking this kind of analysis, and by using the CUV as a case study, we are able to discuss the wider relationship of the University of Wales – and its College in Swansea in particular – with the communities of the coalfield.

In the 1980s and 1990s, those communities – defined in a geographical or territorial sense – have undergone, and continue to experience, a fundamental and very rapid transformation, most obviously in that following the rapid run-down and near closure of the deep mining industry in South Wales during the 1980s, communities whose very existence was originally owed to the coal industry, are now part of a post-coal society. But, dislocating and disruptive though this has been, it is far from the only change which has taken place. Since 1945, women have become active in the labour market in South Wales to a far greater extent than previously, when patterns of female participation in paid employment were far lower than the British average.

Taken as a whole, these changes have led to opportunities for a re-making of the relationship of the University of Wales Swansea to that part of the coalfield which, though responsible in part for the historic growth of Swansea, is now generally considered to be Swansea's hinterland. It will be argued that the CUV, and a more regionally orientated mission for UWS, have begun to contribute – along with British-wide changes in higher education – to a re-making of the institution itself. It should be emphasised at this point that the analysis presented here is not one which is deterministic or teleological. An initiative such as the CUV was not somehow 'inevitable'; there were many contingent factors, not least impetus for change within the institution and within local communities. But its development must be understood in historical terms, especially in the context of social change through time and across space in South Wales.

THE CUV: HIGHER EDUCATION IN THE COMMUNITY

Banwen and its locality

The CUV offers community-based part-time undergraduate provision. In its most developed form, it is located at Banwen, a former mining community in the north-west of the South Wales coalfield. Banwen and its adjacent communities of Dyffryn Cellwen and Onllwyn, are at the head of the Dulais Valley, on the northern rim of the west of the coalfield, where anthracite was mined, rather than the steam coal of the central and eastern valleys. The population of the Onllwyn ward (in which the three communities are situated) is 1,318, and the population of the Dulais Valley as a whole is 5,676.[10] Both figures show an overall decline since 1951. The settlement pattern of this part of the coalfield has been somewhat different to the densely-populated central valleys, such as the Rhondda, which have become identified in the public imagination as the quintessential image of South Wales. Banwen, and other anthracite communities, are semi-rural in character, with little of the civic and economic infrastructure which marks out areas like the Rhondda.[11] This has left such communities particularly vulnerable and isolated in the 'post-coal' era. Whilst sharing with the rest of the coalfield a political culture in which the Labour Party was dominant, in which the Communist Party also gained support, and in which the South Wales Miners' Federation was the single most important institution in civil society, there were – and are – also cultural differences, most notably, perhaps, the fact that Welsh is still widely spoken in the area.[12]

Provision and student support

The CUV provision is delivered at the Banwen Community Centre by the Department of Adult Continuing Education (DACE) of UWS, in partnership with the DOVE Workshop, a locally based training organisation, and with Onllwyn Community Council.[13] This partnership has been central to the origins and continued development of the project. The CUV is designed to attract adult students who, for whatever reason, would not be able to take up educational opportunities on the main Swansea Campus. It therefore specifically targets those who are unemployed, those who have caring commitments (for older or younger relatives), lone parents, and those who are on low incomes or without transport. As this is an area in which historically there has been a male-orientated labour market (most obviously in the mining industry), women returners are especially targeted. This is an aspect of the provision which requires very careful strategic planning, and will be influenced by a number of different – at times contradictory – factors. Opportunities for women in an area like Banwen have historically been limited, because of prevailing labour market conditions and cultural patterns. Further-more, women's employment in Wales as a whole is marked by part-time – often low-skilled – work, and low pay, so education and training opportunities for women are a necessity.[14] But recent research has suggested that in a general Welsh context of high numbers of school leavers with few or no qualifications, particularly in South Wales valley areas (in contradiction to another myth of the Welsh 'educational tradition'), long-term unemployed and economically inactive men face especially difficult problems in the labour market.[15] Thus far, the CUV has been very successful in attracting female students, less so in attracting men. Research is needed into the reasons for unemployed men appearing to be less likely than women to take up education and training opportunities.

Modules from the BA Degree in Humanities (which is offered on the main Swansea Campus) are made available at the CUV at Banwen, and students there have access to library and other facilities on site. It is possible to complete a degree, including the sitting of examinations, within this community setting. In 1995–96, the scheme was in its third year of operation, and there were fifty-two students enrolled on the BA scheme at Banwen, with a further fourteen enrolled on the one year pre-degree Foundation programme. These students are over-whelmingly female, with an average age in the mid-30s. Many are women returners, a number are lone parents, and a number have caring responsibilities for older relatives. Around twenty per cent of the students are working part-time, including six who work in the nearby Lucas SEI electrical components factory (situated in the upper Swansea Valley town of Ystradgynlais), which has been very supportive of those of its employees who have enrolled on the CUV. The students overwhelmingly come from the Dulais Valley, the upper Swansea Valley, and the Neath Valley, although the day-time provision and creche has attracted some students from as far afield as the outskirts of Swansea. There is a small number of retired students, but most have enrolled on the scheme with the specific aim of improving their employment prospects – though there are few illusions about local job opportunities in the short-to-medium term. Systematic research into the motivations and previous educational experiences of the CUV students is currently at an early stage, but it is interesting to note, in the context of debates about the desirability of accreditation of continuing education, that the CUV has been successful in attracting students who are active (or potentially active) in the labour market, and who have enrolled for an undergraduate programme, with all the commitments, in terms of time and intellectual effort, which that involves.

Teaching on the undergraduate and Foundation programmes takes place during the day, on weekdays, and the timetable is organised around school times. There is always a half term, in line with local school half terms, in order that parents (and particularly lone parents) are not deterred from enrolling and attending. Modules on the BA programme often include an additional day school, which is usually on a special theme, and can involve guest tutors from other higher education institutions. These day schools are held on a Saturday, and are always open to the wider general public, and advertised locally. This aspect of the provision is intended to increase local 'ownership' of the CUV as a whole, and, of course, serves to create a potential starting point in an educational progression route.

A number of UWS staff are permanently or partly located at the Banwen Centre. These include a Tutor in Community Education, the Co-ordinator of the CUV scheme, a secretarial assistant, and a library assistant. The holders of the two latter posts are themselves products of short courses held at the Banwen Centre. At present, teaching on the CUV is undertaken on a 'face-to-face' basis, but plans are in place to develop a plurality of modes of provision, by the utilisation of video-conferencing and other distance learning technologies. This will create opportunities to widen the curriculum.

It is often the undergraduate level provision at the CUV which has aroused most interest from others working in the field of continuing education, as it is this, perhaps, that is the most innovative feature of the scheme in terms of actual course delivery. But the plurality of levels of provision, which is designed to create a plurality of potential progression routes, plus the fact that UWS is not the only provider at the Banwen Centre, are also vitally important parts of the scheme. The range of provision offered by DACE at the Banwen Centre includes short accredited and non-accredited courses in a variety of subjects – from art to information technology. In addition, an innovative Return to Learn class has been developed which runs all year round, and which students can attend on a 'drop-in' basis. Whilst students can gain direct entry to the BA scheme of the CUV, these different levels of potential starting points have been very important. In addition to those who have opted for the direct entry route, the undergraduate modules have also attracted students who first came to the Centre to follow non-accredited art or language classes, and IT courses.

Given that the CUV provision is targeted, student support mechanisms are vital. Educational guidance is embedded in the provision, and a DACE Guidance Worker is present at Banwen one day per week, and at other times by appointment. In addition, one of the DOVE employees is also a qualified educational guidance worker. UWS counselling and careers services are also made available to CUV students by appointment. Students enrolled on the undergraduate scheme attend Study Skills sessions, which are designed to assist with the processes of studying. A bursary system is in operation, which gives students on the BA scheme the opportunity to apply for some remission of course fees (in 1996, the fee levels were £125 per module). At least as important in terms of student support, however, is that free creche facilities are made available to CUV students. The creche is run by qualified staff of the DOVE Workshop, and has proved to be a vital resource for students.

Working in partnership

The actual provision at the CUV is undoubtedly innovative, particularly as the BA scheme is offered in a community setting, but the nature of the local partnerships is equally – perhaps more – innovative, and it is the nature of these partnerships which mark out the CUV from the work of UWS in the coalfield in the past. The recent work of UWS at Banwen arose in the specific context of the aftermath of the 1984-85 Miners' Strike, and the creation of the DOVE Workshop out of the local Women's Support Group for the miners and mining communities (this is discussed in a later section). Set up in order to provide training opportunities for women, the DOVE Workshop also works with the local branch of the Workers' Educational Association, and with Neath College (the local further education College) in creating a varied portfolio of education and training opportunities. In 1994–95 (the most recent figures available), there were over 200 students per week using the Centre for educational purposes.[16] The Centre is also the local Community Centre, and is owned by Onllwyn Community Council. UWS, through DACE, works with both these organisations in seeking to widen educational opportunities locally. A Community Development Strategy Group consisting of representatives of the various providers and agencies which use the Centre, meets once per term in order to plan future provision, and to respond to student or public demand for courses.

The Banwen provision is not the only form of community-based education provided by UWS. In addition, again through DACE, UWS provides community-based provision elsewhere in south-west Wales at Foundation level, and a wide range of short courses, of both an accredited and non-accredited nature, in many centres in the region. Here, too, partnership with community-based groups is a key component of the work. It is anticipated that in time, modules of the BA programme will be offered in the other locations which are currently running the Foundation programme.

UWS works with other providers in the wider region, through the Valleys' Initiative for Adult Education (VIAE), a 'network of statutory and voluntary organisations concerned with the role of Adult Education in the survival and development of valley communities'.[17] The membership of VIAE includes Local Educational Authorities, the University continuing education departments of UWS, the University of Glamorgan and University of Wales Cardiff, the Open University, the WEA, and community-based and national voluntary organisations.

THE HISTORICAL CONTEXT

The provision of educational opportunities within the coalfield is not a new development for the University of Wales and UWS. From its creation in the late nineteenth century, the University of Wales placed an emphasis on extramural and extension provision for the education of adults. It is important to recognise that the creation of the university took place in the distinct political and cultural circumstances of the time, in which a radical and nonconformist Liberal Party had become dominant at the expense of landed Conservative interests.[18] The creation of the university has been described as 'the crown and summit of the Liberal ascendancy in Wales in the late Victorian era',[19] and it has since become known by its unofficial motto of 'Prifysgol y Werin' (this can be loosely translated as the 'people's university'). This motto owes its origins to a Liberal ideology of classlessness, which was later undercut by the rise of trades unionism and Labour politics in the early twentieth-century, but it also has been used as a rallying call and benchmark in latter day debates about the future of higher education in late twentieth-century Wales.[20]

The Colleges of the University contributed to the adult education movement in the coalfield in the inter-war period. By 1937, there were nine university educational 'settlements' in the east of the coalfield, with the largest being at Maes-yr-haf in the Rhondda. Various tutorial and extramural classes, and 'one-off' lectures were held in communities throughout the region, often being held in association with such organisations as non-conformist chapels and co-operative societies. The University College of Swansea (UCS)[21] was not established until 1920, but with the seminal *1919 Report* on adult education[22] having appeared just one year earlier, it is perhaps not surprising that there was a strong commitment to extramural and extension work from the earliest days of the College. Viscount Haldane, who had a strong interest in adult education, had chaired the Royal Commission on University Education in Wales,[23] which led directly to the creation of UCS. Like much of the university extension work elsewhere, however, the College's work in this field was not free from political considerations and influences. The threat to the existing order posed by organised labour in the coalfield, led to education for adults often being provided in an attempt to lead the working class and its rank and file leaders away from socialist and revolutionary ideas, and in opposition to educational provision organised by the explicitly left-wing National Council of Labour Colleges (NCLC). As the periodical *Welsh Outlook* put it in 1916, 'what is needed is a University with as missionary spirit that will spread its teaching to the Valleys of the coalfield and will equip minds, now immature, to deal with the great problems that vitally affect the social life of the nation.'[24] The early days of extension work at UCS fitted into this pattern. The Joint Tutorial Classes Committee of the College was set up in 1921 with an annual grant of £200 from the local Coalowners' Association.[25]

Some commentators, such as Alfred Zimmern, Professor of International Politics at the University College of Wales Aberystwyth, bemoaned the fact (in 1921) that 'the University should mean so little to the coalfield, that it should display, on occasion, a deliberate preference for the unlettered, if titled, capitalist over the zealous and lettered proletarian'.[26] However, as Richard Lewis has argued in his definitive study of adult education in South Wales in the inter-war period, whatever the motives of leading figures and institutions, the reality on the ground was altogether more fluid.[27] The educational provision of rival bodies such as the NCLC and the WEA often involved the participation of the same activists and students. It would appear that adult education provision, whatever its formal institutional links, provided what might be described as an intellectual and practical space, in which both teachers and taught were able to shape the content and purpose of the curricula to a greater or lesser extent. By 1931, the Tutor in charge of Extramural Studies at UCS was able to celebrate the fact that by this time his work was radical in content, and was carried out in partnership with local trades unions.[28]

In the postwar period, UCS followed a pattern exhibited by many of the 'red brick' universities in terms of student recruitment. There was less focus on home-based students than on the annual cohort of school leavers across Wales (and Britain more generally). Adult education was from 1960 established as a separate department within the college, and the provision of liberal adult education classes across the region was considerable expanded. In the 1970s close links were developed with the South Wales Area of the National Union of Mine Workers (NUM). DACE provided a substantial number of day release courses for NUM activists.

The purpose of the preceding historical sketch (and it is no more than a very skeletal outline) is merely to illustrate the fact that adult education provision within the coalfield is nothing new to UCS, and nor are links with community organisations and trades unions. However, the provision and links were of a *particular kind*, and were heavily shaped by the circumstances of the inter-war period, and by the institutional priorities which led to adult education being to some extent marginalised within a single Department. The provision itself had become focused in the main on liberal adult education classes which, while undoubtedly having great strengths, had less and less relevance to communities in the coalfield in the 1980s, which were experiencing rapid and dislocating change.

The coal industry was by now in terminal decline in South Wales, which led directly to increases in already high levels of unemployment and social deprivation in those communities which depended on employment in mining. In addition, longer-term social changes, especially in the area of gender relations, were beginning to have real influence. There was also a different institutional context in the making, in the form of a moves towards a mass higher education system, a changed set of funding mechanisms (or potential funding mechanisms) in Wales for further and higher education in general, and for continuing education in particular. There was also pressure – from within and outside the institution – to give practical form to the regional role as part of the overall mission of UWS. It is within this context that the CUV was created, and it is to these developments that we now turn.

THE CONTEMPORARY CONTEXT: ECONOMIC AND SOCIAL CHANGE

South Wales had undergone considerable change since 1945. Although the coal and steel industries remained dominant, in the 1950s and 1960s there was an increase in the proportion of employees in manufacturing work, and in the 1970s, in services.[29] Both of these developments, but particularly the latter, created considerable opportunities for women to enter paid employment, which, though the effects were incremental and gradual, rather than sudden, began to alter the prevailing political and cultural landscape of the area.[30] To some extent, there were grounds for optimism about the South Wales economy after the slump of the inter-war period. Two further developments are important here: first, the diversification of employment and increased prosperity was unevenly distributed in spatial terms. New industries and services tended to be concentrated on the southern coastal strip of the region, and in towns and cities such as Bridgend, Swansea, and Cardiff. The valleys continued to exhibit high levels of unemployment, and social deprivation, and were (and continue to be) considered as a 'problem region'. Secondly, the South Wales region as a whole remained heavily dependent on the state for employment. This was to make it particularly vulnerable in the circumstances of cuts in state expenditure and regional aid from the late 1970s.[31]

The UK-wide miners' strike in 1984-85 was a pivotal moment in the history of the coalfield in South Wales.[32] The defeat of the strike, which had been in opposition to the closure of pits, led to the rapid run down of the deep mining industry in South Wales. In 1996, there is just one remaining deep mine in the region, the co-operatively owned Tower Colliery. Although by this stage mining was not the dominant industry in the region as a whole, it remained of fundamental importance to valley communities in which there was little locally based alternative employment. Communities such as Banwen and its neighbouring communities were particularly vulnerable, as they had few alternative sources of employment, and were relatively isolated, with very poor public transport links to larger centres of population such as Swansea and Neath. Recent research has revealed new spatial patterns of social inequality emerging, even *within* the coalfield area, with communities at the head of the valleys faring most poorly.[33] These communities had to a large extent been in decline since the early 1960s, and, by 1991, the Onllwyn ward was placed twenty-fourth of 908 wards in Wales ranked in order of relative deprivation.[34]

The rapid social changes in the region are the context in which all adult education providers are having to fundamentally re-assess their provision and curricula.[35] It was in the specific contexts of the disappearance of the coal industry, and a recognition that existing provision was inappropriate or inadequate, that DACE, and hence UWS, began to reformulate its relationship with the coalfield. One of the features of the strike was that women were active in support of the miners and their own communities – and at the same time contested some of the pre-existing notions of the nature of these communities. As Rees has argued, the active participation of women in support of the miners' strike can be explained in part by reference to their growing role in the labour market in the post-1945 period.[36]

In the Dulais Valley, the women's Miners' Support Group had continued to exist after the strike, and sought to play a role in the future of the valley. This led to the setting set up of the DOVE Workshop, a small voluntary training organisation for women, which was funded initially by the Urban Aid scheme. After gaining a premises for its activities in the form of the Community Centre at Banwen (a former National Coal Board building), DOVE began to seek out educational providers, such as the WEA, Neath College, and DACE, in order to enhance its portfolio of provision.[37]

After initially providing short liberal adult education classes and IT classes (the latter funded through the European Social Fund), DACE set up a community-based Access course at the Banwen Centre in 1989, the first of its kind in Wales. Once the case had been made for community-based Access provision, on the grounds that it targeted students who could not otherwise avail themselves of similar provision on the main Swansea Campus, a key and pressing question was inevitably posed: access to what? The barriers which had prevented potential Access students from taking up opportunities on the Swansea Campus would still exist after the completion of an Access course. The need for continued educational progression routes became clear, and consultation with existing and former Access students at the Banwen Centre began, as part of a one year project funded by the Universities Funding Council (UFC). Local organisations such as the DOVE workshop and Onllwyn Community Council were also involved in this process. The result of the consultation exercise was the identification of a need for a *community-based* undergraduate curriculum. The eventual development of such a curriculum, in the form of the CUV, took place in the context of a new set of institutional and funding relationships for higher education in Wales which pertained in the 1990s.

THE CONTEMPORARY CONTEXT: FUNDING AND GOVERNANCE OF HIGHER EDUCATION IN WALES

The CUV has in part been the product of a changing system of governance of higher education in Wales, and of a plurality of funding regimes for infrastructural developments. The creation of a separate Higher Education Funding Council for Wales (HEFCW) in 1993 meant that there was a potential degree of flexibility in the funding of higher education in Wales which did not exist previously. A concern of HEFCW since its creation, is that continuing education opportunities should be provided in all parts of Wales. This criterion applies to the funding of some continuing education provision, and would appear to mark out the Welsh Funding Council from its counterpart in England.[38] In addition, strategic goals of further and higher education funding in Wales are shaped by, and increasingly linked to, Welsh Office policy on economic development.[39] The fact that an area like the Dulais Valley was an area which was targeted by a number of Welsh office initiatives – most notably the *Valleys Initiative*, launched by the then Secretary of State for Wales Peter Walker in 1988 – meant that the proposal for the CUV fitted into wider strategies for economic regeneration. The proposal was approved by HEFCW on a recurrent funding basis, calculated on an orthodox full-time student equivalent (FTE) basis. The first cohort of students enrolled in October 1993.

The CUV benefited also, however, from European funding. UWS was successful in bidding for money from the European Regional Development Fund (ERDF), in order to substantially enlarge the Centre at Banwen. Other funds at the 'start-up' stage were forthcoming from Neath Borough Council, British Coal, the Coal Industry Social Welfare Organisation (CISWO), and Onllwyn Community Council. Together with the DOVE Workshop and the other educational providers which utilise the Centre at Banwen, these various agencies might be seen as a kind of coalition which temporarily came together under the overarching theme of economic and social regeneration. Of course, there were differing nuances and emphases within this coalition, not least tensions between community development and individual student achievement, and between those outcomes measured in terms of employment for students, and those measured – more intangibly – in terms of individual and social well-being. There are, of course, occasions when these issues are not in any way oppositional, but there are also occasions when they can appear to be contradictory, and, as is to be expected, the various providers and funders have differing views as to the priorities of this kind of provision, in terms of outcomes. There is no doubt, however, that this new set of institutional and funding relationships was critical in the creation of the CUV.

In the specific case of UWS, the inclusion of an enhanced regional role as a part of its developing mission statement, meant that the CUV became both a real and symbolic feature of an institution undergoing real change. The nature of the provision at the CUV is, to some extent, inevitably constrained and influenced by the existing internal organisation and culture of UWS. Providing modules from the part-time degree in Humanities has been relatively straightforward, for example (though certainly not problem-free), as these require little technical support or special equipment, and are relatively low cost; moving the curriculum into applied science will clearly be a more difficult task. But at the same time that the provision is to some extent constrained in this way, its very existence is acting in subtle ways to re-shape the institution as a whole. Formal meetings of the College, library provision, staffing, and indeed the Students' Union, have each been affected by the fact that there is now a not insignificant body of students who are registered members of the College, but who may well never have to visit the main Campus. Most of all, in this context, the creation of partnerships at local level has influenced university policy, and the processes by which policy is made.

The focus in this chapter is on the development, partnerships with local organisations, and current provision at Banwen, but it should be noted that the CUV has a wider meaning than community-based HE at any one physical location. It also serves as a metaphor for a rolling strategy of building community-based educational provision throughout the South Wales coalfield, in collaboration with other educational providers and locally based groups.[40] Other HE institutions involved include the Open University in Wales and the University of Glamorgan, and the overarching role of VIAE will be central in developing strategy. In the future, there is likely to be a plurality of locally based educational opportunities available for adults in the coalfield, delivered in a variety of ways, by a network of educational providers, rather than by single institutions.

RE-MAKING COMMUNITIES

Throughout this chapter, we have – knowingly – used the concept of community to signify territorially defined social formations. In the case of the mining communities of South Wales, which historically were once single industry communities, it might be argued that this is relatively unproblematic. But even at the high point of employment in mining, communities did, of course, contain divisions. In recent years, with the decline of the mining industry, territorially defined communities have become more diverse, in line with the diversification of employment, and, in particular, with the growth of employment opportunities for women. Cultural and leisure patterns have also become more diverse than had been the case in the past. As in other parts of Britain (and elsewhere), communities need not be defined solely in a geographical sense.

But the idea of 'community' in that geographical sense has remained a very powerful, and highly normative, social construct. In the 1984-85 miners' strike, it became an important concept around which support for the miners' case was mobilised, and drew on aspects of the wider modern Welsh political culture in which territorially defined concepts of community have been central.[41] Mobilisation in support of the miners' strike was of an essentially defensive nature, but it contained elements within it, notably the active participation of women, which were suggestive of new concepts of community. The DOVE workshop and the CUV are in many ways products of the miners' strike and of its aftermath, but they are serving to re-define notions of community in two distinct ways. First, the role of women in DOVE workshop has in itself opened up new, gender-based, definitions of community which signify something wider than Banwen itself. DOVE, for example, has links with women's groups elsewhere in Wales, Britain, and Europe.

Secondly, geographical definitions of locality and community are themselves being re-made. Banwen is within a very few miles of the boundaries of seven local government districts or counties, and three travel to work areas. It is also on the boundary of rural and industrial Wales. Though local constructions of community in a territorial sense are very strong, the fact that the residents of Banwen and its locality are familiar with crossing boundaries (including linguistic ones), means that there are also ambiguities and a sense of fluidity present. (This invites caution in the aggregation of statistical data for any one of these areas in respect of Banwen.[42]) In recent years, particularly after the closure of local pits, the inhabitants of Banwen have invariably journeyed down the Dulais Valley for such things as shopping and leisure activities, and, of course, for employment. But the DOVE Workshop attracts students to Banwen from lower down in the valley, and from towns and villages in nearby valleys, thereby contributing to a re-shaping of the recent cultural geography of the area. A key component in the making of conceptions of community and locality are local institutions, as Day and Murdoch have suggested.[43] The DOVE Workshop, and the CUV, are local institutions of this kind, and are therefore contributing a re-making of the very idea of locality in the case of Banwen. It is important to note, however, that these new imaginings of locality and community are overlain on older ones, and on older patterns of culture and mobility. Pre-existing ideas of community defined in a territorial sense remain very strong, as anyone who has gone to work in the area will testify! The key point here, however, is that whilst the miners' strike, as we noted above, was a defensive form of political mobilisation, the DOVE Workshop and the CUV are actively promoting change and – both consciously and otherwise – a re-making of ideas of community in a number of ways.

CONCLUSION

This chapter has focused on the CUV programme, which, in the overall scheme of British higher education, is a relatively small initiative if measured in terms of student numbers. We have attempted to show that only by understanding the specific historical and contemporary contexts of South Wales, seen in economic, social and institutional terms, can the CUV be properly understood. The CUV has been developed in a context of rapid social change, and is being shaped by – and to some extent is a product of – national, regional and local factors in the realms of the economy, social and institutional change, and matters of public policy. At the same time, the CUV is acting upon these areas, and is beginning to influence the shape of its parent institution.

But there are wider themes and issues which emerge, which are linked to themes which run through other contributions to this book. Whatever the rhetoric about the relationship of communities to institutions of higher education, the contribution of a university to the economic and social well-being of its surrounding region requires long-term investment of resources, both human and financial, and careful, strategic planning which is alert to social change and the needs of the wider community. In the case of opening-up educational opportunities for communities in so-called economically and socially 'disadvantaged' areas, it also requires patience and – crucially – partnership. Once local partnerships are made, and in particular if community-based provision is offered, then change will become a two-way process. Communities – however defined – will be re-made, but the institution will not be unaffected. It too will be altered, and its culture will be re-shaped to some extent. Both of these processes are incremental and at times imperceptible, but they will certainly take place. These are the inevitable consequences of communities having a more meaningful relationship with 'their' university.

It is a sign of the speed with which social and institutional change is taking place in Britain in the late twentieth century that the words 'university' and 'community' can convey competing meanings. But nor is the term 'the valleys' fixed or unproblematic. The leading historian of twentieth century South Wales has pointed out that the valleys were, and continue to be, a 'mindscape' as much as they are a landscape, and that the term itself 'floats free from its moorings'.[44] The CUV is a collective agent and symbol not only of an active re-shaping of the relationship between communities and their university; it is also both agent and symbol of a re-shaping of the 'mindscape' of the valleys of South Wales.

NOTES

1. H.V. Morton, *In Search of Wales*, Methuen, London 1932, p247.
2. John Ormond, *Once There Was a Time*, BBC, 1961. For a brief discussion on the film, see D. Berry, *Wales and Cinema: the First Hundred Years*, University of Wales Press, Cardiff 1994, pp290–294.
3. See H. Francis, 'The Origins of the South Wales Miners' Library', *History Workshop Journal*, 2, 1976.
4. See H. Francis and D. Smith, *The Fed: a History of the South Wales Miners*

in the Twentieth Century, Lawrence & Wishart, London 1980; and D. Smith, *Aneurin Bevan and the World of South Wales*, University of Wales Press, Cardiff 1993.

5. R. Lewis, *Leaders and Teachers: Adult Education and the Challenge of Labour in South Wales 1906–1940*, University of Wales Press, Cardiff 1993.

6. R. Lewis, 'The Inheritance: Adult Education in the Valleys between the wars', in H. Francis (ed), *Adult Education in the Valleys: the Last Fifty Years*, Llafur, Cardiff 1986, pp7–14.

7. See, for example, the contributions in S. Reynolds and H. Francis (eds), *Learning From Experience: The Future of Adult Education in the Valleys*, VIAE, Tairgwaith 1988.

8. P. Scott, *The Meanings of Mass Higher Education*, Open University Press, Milton Keynes 1995, p10.

9. I. Martin, 'Community Education: Towards a theoretical analysis', in R. Edwards *et al* (eds), *Adult Learners, Education, and Training*, Routledge, London 1993, p189.

10. OPCS, *Census Data*, 1991.

11. For the history of Banwen and the Dulais Valley, see, respectively: C. Evans, *Blaencwmdulais: A Short History of the Social and Industrial Development of Onllwyn and Banwen-Pyrddin*, CFP 1977, and J. Sewell, *Colliery Closure and Social Change*, University of Wales Press, Cardiff 1975, pp3–10. For a general survey of the anthracite coalfield, see I. Matthews, 'Maes y Glo Carreg ac Undeb y Glowyr, 1872 – 1925', yn G.H. Jenkins (gol), *Cof Cenedl VIII*, Gomer, Llandysul 1993, pp133–164.

12. Figures from the 1991 census show that in the Onllwyn ward, 25.8 per cent of the population aged three and over were able to speak Welsh. The equivalent figure for the Dulais Valley was 29.5 per cent. OPCS, *Census Data*, 1991.

13. The acronym stands for 'Dulais Opportunities for Voluntary Enterprise', but the full title is rarely used.

14. See D. Istance and T. Rees, *Women in Post-compulsory Education and Training in Wales*, Equal Opportunities Commission, Manchester 1994.

15. D. Istance and G. Rees, *Lifelong Learning in Wales: A Programme for Prosperity*, NIACE, Leicester, 1995. See also, D. Evans, 'A Community Development College', *Adults Learning*, November 1994, pp92–93.

16. Figures supplied by DOVE Workshop.

17. VIAE, *Next Step for the Valleys: regenerating Valley communities through Adult Education*, VIAE 1990, p2.

18. The standard history is K.O. Morgan, *Rebirth of a Nation: Wales 1880–1980*, Clarendon Press, Oxford 1981. See also, G. Day and R. Suggett, 'Aspects of Nationalism in Nineteenth-century Wales', in G. Rees *et al*, *Political Action and Social Identity*, Macmillan, London 1985, pp91–115.

19. G.H. Jenkins, *The University of Wales: An Illustrated History*, University of Wales Press, Cardiff 1993, p1.

20. For example, H. Francis, *'Do Miners Read Dickens?' Communities, Universities and a new Beginning*, Inaugural Lecture, University of Wales

Swansea, 1994; and K.O. Morgan, *Solo Voice* broadcast, BBC Radio Wales 1994.

21. The College was re-named 'University of Wales Swansea' in 1994. The standard history of the College is D. Dykes, *The University College of Swansea: An Illustrated History*, Alan Sutton, Stroud 1992.

22. *Report of the Adult Education Committee of the Ministry of Reconstruction*, London 1919.

23. *Royal Commission on University Education in Wales: Final Report*, London 1916.

24. *Welsh Outlook*, August 1916.

25. Minutes of the Joint Tutorial Committee of the College Council, 1920–28, UWS Archives.

26. A. Zimmern, *My Impressions of Wales*, Mills & Boon, London 1921, p38.

27. R. Lewis, Leaders and Teachers, *op.cit.*

28. P.S. Thomas, 'Adult Education in Swansea', *Cambria*, 4, Spring 1931, pp33–35.

29. See G. Humphrys, *Industrial Britain: South Wales*, David & Charles, Newton Abbot 1972.

30. See V. Winckler, 'Women and Work in Post-war Wales', *Llafur*, 4,4, 1987, pp69–77; and T. Rees, 'Women and paid work in Wales', in J. Aaron *et al* (eds), *Our Sisters' Land: The Changing Identities of Women in Wales*, University of Wales Press, Cardiff 1994, pp89–106.

31. See K. George and L. Mainwaring, 'The Welsh Economy in the 1980s', in G. Day and G. Rees (eds), *Contemporary Wales* I, *op.cit.*, pp7–37; and T. Rutherford, 'Industrial Restructuring, Local Labour Markets and Social Change: the Transformation of South Wales', in G. Rees and G. Day (eds), *Contemporary Wales* 4, University of Wales Press, Cardiff 1991, pp9–44.

32. H. Francis and G. Rees, ' "No Surrender in the Valleys": The 1984–5 Miners' Strike in South Wales', *Llafur*, 5, 2, 1989, pp41–71.

33. See J. Morris, 'McJobbing a Region: Industrial Restructuring and the Widening Socio-economic Divide in Wales', in R. Turner (ed), *The British Economy in Transition: From the Old to the New?*, Routledge, London 1995, pp46–66.

34. *Index of Socio-economic Conditions*, Welsh Office, 1991. The tables are calculated from data on unemployment, low economic activity, low socio-economic groups, population loss, numbers of permanently sick, overcrowding in housing, lack of housing amenities, and standard mortality rate.

35. See C. Trotman and S. Morris, *Communities in Transition: The Role of Adult Continuing Education*, DACE Research Papers in Continuing Education, University of Wales Swansea, forthcoming, 1996.

36. G. Rees, 'Regional Restructuring, Class Change and Political Action: Preliminary Comments on the 1984-1985 Miners' Strike in South Wales', *Society and Space* 3, 1985.

37. For discussions of the formation of the DOVE Workshop, see: M. Francis, 'Dulais Opportunity for Voluntary Enterprise – (West Glamorgan)', in S. Reynolds and H. Francis (eds), *Learning From*

Experience, op.cit.; and M. Francis, *Women and the Aftermath of the 1984–85 Miners' Strike: A South Wales Analysis*, unpublished MSc Thesis, University of Wales Swansea, 1995.

38. The new arrangements for the funding of higher education in Britain and Northern Ireland are discussed in John Field, *National Overview – Pickin' the Blues*, unpublished paper, 1995.

39. See *People and Prosperity: an Agenda for Action in Wales*, Welsh Office, 1995.

40. For a discussion of community provision elsewhere to which DACE has contributed, see S. Reynolds, 'Amman Valley Enterprise: a Case Study of Adult Education and Community Revival', in M. Mayo and J. Thompson (eds), *Adult Learning, Critical Intelligence and Social Change*, NIACE, Leicester 1995, pp242–252.

41. See H. Francis and G. Rees, ' "No Surrender in the Valleys" ', *op.cit.*; R. Williams, 'Mining the Meaning: Key Words in the Miners' Strike', *New Socialist*, 25, March 1985; D. Adamson, *Community, Ideology and Political Discourse in Welsh Nationalist Politics*, unpublished paper, 1988, and D. Gilbert, *Class, Community and Collective Action*, Clarendon Press, Oxford 1992.

42. For a general discussion of these issues, see J. A. Peck, 'Reconceptualizing the Local Labour Market: Space, Segmentation and the State', *Progress in Human Geography*, 13, 1, 1989.

43. G. Day and J. Murdoch, 'Locality and community: coming to terms with place', *The Sociological Review*, 1993, pp82–111.

44. D. Smith, *Aneurin Bevan and the World of South Wales, op.cit.*, p92.